Book of Saints

"SUPER-HEROES OF GOD"

By REV. LAWRENCE G. LOVASIK, S.V.D.
Divine Word Missionary

PART 2

CONTENTS

St. Agnes 3	St. Rose of Lima................21
St. Bernadette 5	St. Therese of the Child
St. Dominic Savio.............. 6	Jesus 22
St. Dymphna....................... 9	St. Gerard Majella.............25
St. Joan of Arc 10	St. Stanislaus Kostka 27
St. Aloysius Gonzaga...........13	St. Lucy 29
St. Maria Goretti 14	Blessed Kateri
St. John Berchmans 16	Tekakwitha....................31
St. Tarcisius 19	Prayer..............................32

NIHIL OBSTAT: Daniel V. Flynn, J.C.D., *Censor Librorum*

IMPRIMATUR ....se of New York

© . ... RP., N.J.

MW00769716

Saint Agnes

January 21

A GNES was only twelve years old when she was led to the altar of the pagan goddess Minerva in Rome to offer incense to her. But she raised her hands to Jesus Christ and made the Sign of the Cross.

The soldiers bound her hands and feet. Her young hands were so thin that the chains slipped from her wrists. When the judge saw that she was not afraid of pain, he had her clothes stripped off, and she had to stand in the street before a pagan crowd. She cried out: "Christ will guard His own."

Agnes was offered the hand of a rich young man in marriage, but she answered: "Christ is my Spouse. He chose me first and His I will be. He made my soul beautiful with the jewels of grace and virtue. I belong to Him Whom the angels serve."

She bowed her head to the sword. At one stroke her head was cut off. The name Agnes means "lamb." She was gentle and pure.

Saint Bernadette

February 18

BERNADETTE'S parents were very poor. They lived in Lourdes, France.

One day, in 1854, while Bernadette was gathering firewood, a beautiful Lady stood in a cave before her. She was dressed in blue and white, and there was a rose on each of her feet. She smiled at Bernadette and asked her to say the rosary with her.

Bernadette saw the Lady eighteen times. The Lady asked Bernadette to tell the world that people must do penance for their sins and pray. She once told Bernadette: "I do not promise to make you happy in this world, but in heaven."

Large crowds followed Bernadette to the grotto to say the rosary with her. They could not see the Lady. The Lady asked Bernadette to scrape the earth. The miraculous spring of Lourdes started to flow. Many sick people have been cured.

When Bernadette asked the Lady her name, the Lady looked up to heaven and said: "I am the Immaculate Conception." She asked that a chapel be built near the grotto.

Later, Bernadette became a nun and suffered very much, She died at the age of thirty-six.

Saint Dominic Savio

May 6

DOMINIC was born in Riva, Italy, in 1842. When he was five years old, he learned to serve Mass. At twelve he visited St. John Bosco and told him that he wanted to be a priest. They became good friends. Dominic entered the Oratory school, which John Bosco started.

Dominic's schoolmates liked him because he was very kind and cheerful. He studied hard and loved to pray. But his health was poor, and after two years he had to return home.

Dominic always kept these rules, which he had written in a notebook on his First Communion Day: (1) I will go to Confession and to Communion often. (2) I will keep holy the Feastdays. (3) Jesus and Mary will be my best friends. (4) I will rather die than commit a sin.

When Dominic was dying, he said: "What beautiful things I see!" He was only fifteen years old. St. John Bosco wrote the story of his life.

Dominic Savio was made a saint of the Catholic Church and is honored as the patron of teenagers.

8

Saint Dymphna

May 15

DYMPHNA was born in Ireland in the seventh century. Her father, Damon, a chieftain of great wealth and power, was a pagan. Her mother was a very beautiful and devout Christian.

Dymphna was fourteen when her mother died. Her father was so sad that he sent messengers everywhere to find some women of noble birth like his wife, who would be willing to marry him. When none could be found, his evil advisers told him to marry his own daughter. Dymphna fled from her castle together with a priest, St. Gerebran, and two other friends.

Damon found them in Belgium. He gave orders that the priest's head be cut off. Then he tried to make his daughter return to Ireland with him and to marry him. When she refused, he drew his sword and struck off her head. She was then only fifteen years of age.

St. Dymphna is the patron of those who suffer with mental illness, because her father acted as a man out of his mind when he killed his own daughter.

Saint Joan of Arc
May 30

JOAN was born in France in 1412. She helped her brothers on the farm and often went to a nearby chapel to pray to Jesus.

When she was seventeen, Joan heard the voice of God calling her to drive the enemies of France from the land. Going to the king, whose army was defeated, she asked for a small army. The king believing that God had sent her to save France, gave her a band of brave soldiers.

Joan went before the soldiers carrying her banner with the words: "Jesus, Mary." The soldiers became filled with courage and drove the British army away.

Joan fell into the hands of the British and remained in prison for nine months. She was asked why she had gone to confession almost every day. She said: "My soul can never be made too clean. I firmly believe that I shall surely be saved."

She was taken to the marketplace of Rouen and burned to death. With her eyes on a crucifix, she cried out, "Jesus, Jesus," through the flames.

Saint Aloysius Gonzaga

June 21

ALOYSIUS lived in the castle of the Gonzaga family in Italy. As a little boy he spent some time with his father in the army. There he picked up rough language. His mother scolded him and taught him what a terrible thing it is to offend God. He began to love prayer and to think about his soul and God.

Aloysius was sent to Madrid, in Spain, to become a page to a prince, and to receive an education. But his motto was: "I was born for greater things." At twenty he signed away forever his right to the lands of the Gonzaga family and became a Jesuit novice.

Aloysius' fellow students loved him because he was kind and willing to help them. They respected him because of his great love for purity.

In Rome Aloysius took care of sick people in a hospital, and before long he himself was ill. The sores caused by the disease were very painful. Aloysius never reached the priesthood; he passed away quietly as he gazed at a crucifix where he found strength to suffer. He was only twenty-three years old. He is a patron of young people.

Saint Maria Goretti

M ARIA was a beautiful Italian girl of twelve who lived on a farm. One day Alessandro, a nineteen-year-old boy, who was working on the farm, stopped at Maria's house and wanted to do wrong with her.

"No! No!" Maria cried out. "Do not touch me, Alessandro! It is a sin. You will go to hell!"

When Maria began to fight him, he took a knife and stabbed her fourteen times. Maria fell to the floor with a cry of pain: "O God, I am dying! Mamma!" Alessandro ran out of the room.

Maria was taken to the hospital and suffered there for two days. When the priest asked her if she would forgive her murderer, she said: "Yes, I forgive him for the love of Jesus, and I want him to be with me in heaven. May God forgive him!"

Maria died kissing the crucifix and holding a medal of the Blessed Virgin Mary. This happened in 1902.

Maria Goretti was canonized by Pope Pius XII in 1950. She was chosen to be the patron of boys and girls, that she might help them to be pure.

Saint John Berchmans

August 13

JOHN was born in a small town in Belgium in 1599. As a boy John had a very great devotion to Holy Mass and the rosary.

When John was but nine years of age, his mother became ill. As many hours of each day as he could after school he gave to the care of his suffering mother. For three years he was a pupil of a pastor of a parish who prepared boys for the priesthood.

John entered the Jesuit seminary in Rome. There he became ill. He pressed to his heart his crucifix, his rosary, and the book of rules, and said: "These are my three treasures; with these I shall gladly die." He died with his eyes on the crucifix.

In 1888 Pope Leo XIII made him a saint. He is the patron of altar boys, and all boys and girls who want to love Jesus in the Blessed Sacrament and his Mother Mary.

We should pray to St. John for vocations to the Holy Priesthood and the religious life.

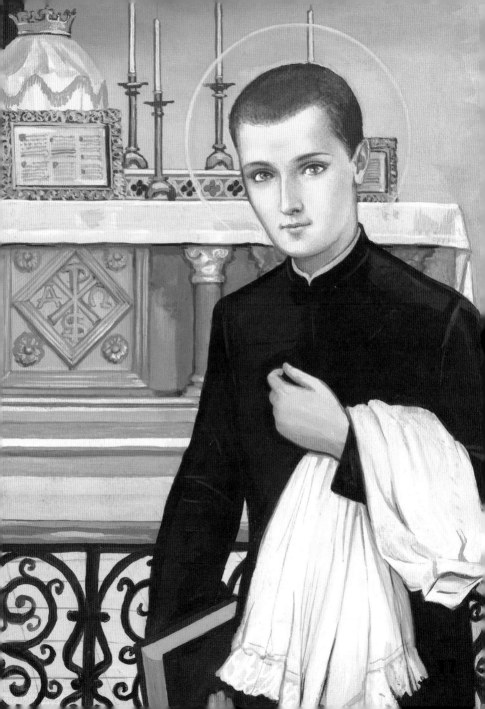

Saint Tarcisius

August 15

TARCISIUS lived in Rome. He served Holy Mass in the catacombs, where the Christians worshiped God because they were persecuted by the pagans.

One day Tarcisius was carrying the Blessed Sacrament to the martyrs in prison when he was caught and beaten. But he did not give up the Eucharist. He died as a boy martyr of the Holy Eucharist. The Christians buried his body with honor in the catacombs. This happened in the third century.

The story of Tarcisius reminds us how much the Christians loved the Blessed Sacrament. Holy Mass and Holy Communion gave them strength to die for their Faith.

Tarcisius teaches children to love Jesus in the Eucharist as their best Friend. He will help them to be good and to make sacrifices for their Holy Faith as Tarcisius did, for he gave his life for the love of Jesus.

We should ask St. Tarcisius for a greater love of Jesus in Holy Communion.

Saint Rose of Lima

August 23

ROSE was born in Peru, South America. She was very obedient to her parents. She did all she was told to do with a happy smile for the love of Jesus. She always tried to help people.

Rose was very beautiful. Her mother wanted her to wear beautiful clothes, but Rose would say: "Mother, only beauty of the soul is important."

A rich young man wanted to marry Rose. He offered her a beautiful home and many servants, but she refused. She loved Jesus with all her heart and wanted to serve God.

When her parents became poor, Rose went out every day to work, and at night did sewing, to help her parents.

Rose visited the homes of the poor and brought them food. She offered all her sufferings and good works to God for sinners. Our Lord often appeared to her as a little child to tell her how pleased he was with her kind deeds.

Rose died when she was only thirty-one years of age. She is the first saint of the Americas.

Saint Therese
of the Child Jesus

October 1

WHEN Therese was eight years old she was cured because of the intercession of our Lady.

When Therese was still very young she did kind little deeds for everyone. She prepared for her First Holy Communion by making many little sacrifices. She became a very special friend of Jesus. She once said, "From the age of three, I never refused our good God anything. I have never given him anything but love."

Therese entered the Carmelite convent at the age of fifteen. She wanted to save souls, and to help priests save souls, by prayer, sacrifice, and suffering. Her "Little Way" means loving and trusting in God as a child.

When she was dying, Therese pressed her crucifix to her heart and, looking up to heaven she said: "I love Him! My God, I love You!" She was only twenty-four years old when she died in 1897.

St. Therese is the patroness of the foreign missions.

Saint Gerard Majella

G ERARD was born in Muro, Italy, in 1726. His father, a tailor, died when the boy was twelve, leaving the family very poor.

Gerard was accepted by the Redemptorists as a lay brother. He served as sacristan, gardener, porter, infirmarian, and tailor.

Even during his life Gerard was called "the wonder-worker" because so many miraculous things happened through his prayers. God gave him special knowledge. He suffered quietly when he was accused of immoral conduct by an evil woman who later confessed her lie. Because he helped a woman who was about to have a child, he is invoked as patron of mothers who are expecting a child.

Gerard died of tuberculosis in 1755 at the age of twenty-nine. He had a small note tacked to his door: "Here the will of God is done, as God wills, and as long as God wills." Brother Gerard was canonized by Pope St. Pius X on December 11, 1904.

Saint Stanislaus Kostka

STANISLAUS was born in 1550 of a noble Polish family. At fourteen he studied at the college of the Jesuits in Vienna with his brother Paul. Though Stanislaus was always bright and kind, he was treated badly by his brother for two years. He always forgave his brother.

Stanislaus became very ill. He prayed to St. Barbara to help him. Then he had a vision in which two angels brought Communion to him. The Blessed Virgin Mary cured him and asked him to become a priest in the Society of Jesus. Stanislaus had to leave Vienna because his father did not want him to become a priest.

At Rome Stanislaus lived for ten months as a novice. A priest said to him: "Stanislaus, you love Our Lady very much." "Yes," he replied. "She is my Mother!" And then he said: "The Mother of God is my Mother."

Stanislaus died on the feast of the Assumption of the Blessed Virgin Mary in 1568, at the age of seventeen. His example teaches young people to love Jesus and Mary.

28

Saint Lucy

December 13

LUCY lived in pagan Sicily about the year 300. At an early age she offered herself to God. The rich young man who wanted to marry her was so angry when she refused that he accused her of being a Christian.

Lucy was led to the governor of her city for trial. Unable to make her give up her Faith, he asked: "Is this Holy Spirit in you, this God you speak about?" Lucy answered: "They whose hearts are pure are the temples of the Holy Spirit."

The governor spoke angrily: "But I will make you fall into sin, so that the Holy Spirit will leave you." She replied:"I will never sin, so that the Holy Spirit will give me a greater reward."

Nothing could make her commit sin. She said: "You see now that I am the temple of the Holy Spirit, and that He protects me."

The governor ordered a fire to be lighted around her, but Lucy was not harmed. At last, a sword was buried in her heart. She did not die until a priest came to her with Holy Communion.

Blessed Kateri Tekakwitha

KATERI was born near the town of Auriesville, New York, in the year 1656, the daughter of a fierce, pagan Mohawk warrior. Jesuit missionaries brought the Catholic Faith to the Mohawk Valley. Kateri was only four years old when her mother died of the disease called small-pox. Her two aunts and uncle adopted her. The disease also disfigured her face.

Kateri was baptized when she was twenty years old. She said she would rather die than give up her Christian Faith. She had much to suffer to be true to her promise.

Kateri went to the new Christian colony of Indians in Canada. Every morning, even in bitterest winter, she stood before the chapel door until it opened at four and remained there until after the last Mass. The Eucharist became her one desire. She was also devoted to Jesus Crucified. She died of a disease on April 17, 1680. Her last words were: "Jesus! Mary! I love you!" when she was twenty four years old. She was known as Kateri of the Mohawks.

Prayer

JESUS, the Church honors the saints
who are already with You in heaven
because they give us a good example
of the way we should live,
and because they pray to God for us.

Help me to try to love God
with all my heart as the saints did,
and for the love of God to love my neighbor.
But they could not live a holy life
without Your grace.

I ask You to give me the grace
to be more like the saints.

Book of Saints

"SUPER-HEROES OF GOD"

By REV. LAWRENCE G. LOVASIK, S.V.D.
Divine Word Missionary

PART 5

CONTENTS

St. Basil the Great	3	St. Ignatius of Loyola 19
St. Anthony the Abbot	4	St. John Eudes 20
St. Isidore of Seville	7	St. Gregory the Great 23
St. Vincent Ferrer	8	St. Robert Bellarmine 24
St. Gemma Galgani	11	St. Paul of the Cross.........28
St. Phili Neri	12	St. Leo the Great 28
St. Camillus of Lellis	15	St. Peter Canisius 31
St. Christopher	16	Prayer 32

NIHIL OBSTAT: Daniel V. Flynn, J.C.D., *Censor Librorum*

IMPRIMATUR: ✠ Joseph T. O'Keefe, D.D.,
Vicar General, Archdiocese of New York

The Nihil Obstat and Imprimatur are official declarations that a book or pamphlet is free of doctrinal or moral error. No implication is contained therein that those who have granted the Nihil Obstat and Imprimatur agree with the contents, opinions or statements expressed.

© 1985 by CATHOLIC BOOK PUBLISHING CORP., N.J.

Printed in Hong Kong   ISBN 978-0-89942-393-7

2

Saint Basil the Great

January 2

BASIL was born at Caesarea, in Asia Minor, in the year 329. His mother and father were nobles and also Saints. There were ten children in the family, four of whom became Saints.

Basil went to school in Constantinople and then in Athens, and later became an eloquent lawyer in Caesarea. But he felt that God called him to become a monk. He sold all his goods, gave the money to the poor, and became a monk.

Basil visited the monks who lived in the desert and founded several monasteries. He drew up rules for the monks to lead them to holiness. Although he was in poor health, Basil lived a life of penance and prayer.

Basil became the Archbishop of Caesarea and defended this people against the Roman Emperor.

Basil wrote many books and defended the Church against the Arian heretics. He was given the titles "Doctor of the Church," and "Father of the Church." Basil died in the year 379.

Saint Anthony the Abbot
January 17

ANTHONY was born in Egypt in the year 251. While still a young man, he gave away all his goods and begged an old hermit to teach him how to live a holy life. He lived the life of a hermit in the desert for many years, devoting himself to prayer and penance.

Many people came to Anthony for advice. He taught them the way to holiness. He founded a monastery and was the first Abbot to form a rule for his family of monks dedicated to Divine Service. For this reason he is called the "Patriarch of Monks."

His miracles drew so many people to him that he fled again into the desert where he lived by hard work and prayer.

In the year 305, Anthony founded a religious community of hermits who lived in separate cells.

He died in 356, at 105 years of age.

Anthony is called the Father of monastic life.

5

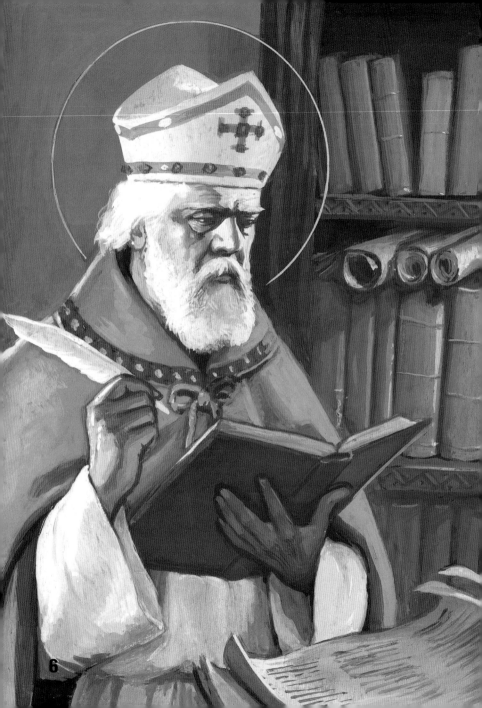

6

Saint Isidore of Seville

April 4

ISIDORE was born at Cartagena in Spain. His two brothers and sisters are Saints. As a boy Isidore was discouraged because he failed in his studies, but with the help of God he became one of the most learned men of his time.

Isidore helped to free Spain from the Arian heresy. Following a call from God, he became a hermit. But after his brother's death he became the Archbishop of Seville. Both of his brothers were bishops.

Isidore was admired for his preaching, his miracles, his work for the liturgy and the laws of the Church. He brought many Catholics in Spain back to the Church. He was the head of the Fourth Council of the Church in Toledo in 633.

Isidore wrote many books. He governed his diocese about thirty-seven years. He died in Seville on April 4, 636. He is honored as a Doctor of the Church.

Saint Vincent Ferrer

April 5

VINCENT was born in Valencia, Spain, January 23, 1350. He was educated at the Dominican school in Barcelona and later entered the Order. He became a doctor of sacred theology.

Vincent devoted himself to missionary work and preached in nearly every province of Spain. He also preached in France, Italy, Germany, Holland, England, Scotland, and Ireland. Many conversions followed his preaching. He is one of the most famous missionaries of the fourteenth century.

Vincent's main virtues were humility and the spirit of prayer, which made his work successful. His motto was: "Whatever you do, think not of yourself, but of God."

His wonderful missionary work lasted twenty-one years. He died in France on April 5, 1419.

10

Saint Gemma Galgani

April 11

GEMMA was born near Lucca, Italy, in 1878. At the age of twenty she had an incurable tuberculosis of the spine. Through her prayers to St. Gabriel of the Sorrowful Mother, she was cured.

Gemma tried to become a Passionist nun, but was rejected. She was again stricken with an illness. She lived a very prayerful life and suffered patiently. She said: "Jesus, I can bear no more. If it be your holy will, take me."

Gemma died on April 11, 1903, as she lifted her eyes to a picture of the Blessed Virgin Mary and said: "Mother, I give my soul into your hands. Ask Jesus to be merciful to me." She was only twenty-five years of age.

Gemma's remains are in the chapel of the Passionist Sisters in Lucca. A table at her tomb states that she was more consumed by the fire of divine love than by her wasting disease.

Saint Philip Neri

May 26

PHILIP was born in Florence in 1515. His family was poor. He went to Rome to act as a teacher for two boys. He began to visit the hospitals of the city, taking a great interest in the sick and the poor.

Philip was ordained a priest and founded the Congregation of the Priests of the Oratory. With his priests he helped the boys of Rome when they were in trouble. He found places for them to study and to play. He showed great zeal in helping sinners through the Sacrament of Penance.

Philip encouraged frequent Confession and Communion. Young and old, attracted by his cheerful holiness, came in large numbers to hear his words of wisdom.

For sixty-two years Philip gave advice and a good example to all classes of people in Rome and tried to fill their hearts with the love of God.

Philip died at the age of 80 in 1595.

13

14

Saint Camillus of Lellis

July 14

CAMILLUS was born in Italy in 1550. As a young man he became a soldier and led a wayward life. He lost so much in gambling that he was forced to work on a building which belonged to the Capuchins.

He was converted and tried three times to enter the Capuchin order, but each time a wound in his leg forced him to leave. He went to Rome for medical treatment, and there took St. Philip Neri as his confessor.

Camillus entered the hospital for incurables. Later he had charge of it. At the age of thirty-two, he began to study grammar with children.

Of the noble family of Lellis, Camillus, when still a young priest, consecrated his life to the service of the sick. He founded the Order of Hospitallers, or the Congregation of the Servants of the Sick. The Brothers served the sick not only in hospitals but also in their homes.

Camillus died a victim of his charity in 1614.

Saint Christopher

July 25

THERE is a legend that in the land of Canaan in Palestine there lived a very strong man called Offero. He is said to have left his native land looking for adventure. He said: "I will roam through the whole world in search of the greatest of kings, and I will be his servant."

Offero met a hermit who guarded a dangerous passage across a stream, and guided travelers to a place where they could cross safely. The hermit instructed him about our Lord, the greatest King. Offero settled down near the stream and carried travelers across on his shoulders to serve the great King.

One day he carried a little boy on his shoulders. Offero cried out: "Child, I feel as if I were carrying the whole world upon my shoulders."

The little boy answered smiling: "You are carrying more than the world; you are carrying Him Who created heaven and earth." It is said that the boy Jesus baptized Offero. Since then he is called Christopher or Christ-bearer.

17

18

Saint Ignatius Loyola

July 31

IGNATIUS, born in 1491 at the royal Castle of Loyola, Spain, became a knight in the court of King Ferdinand V. Wounded in the siege of Pampeluna, he lay ill in a castle, where he picked up a book of the Lives of the Saints and started to read.

When he left the castle, he went to confession. For almost a year he lived in a cave on the banks of a river. He fasted, prayed, and took care of the poor and the sick.

A man of thirty-five years of age, he entered a school in Barcelona, Spain. After being ordained a priest, he founded the Society of Jesus at Paris. Schools, preaching, retreats, missionary work— any work was to be their work, especially at a time when many were falling away from the Church. Many of his men became missionaries, and some taught the Indians in America.

For fifteen years Ignatius directed the work of the Society. Almost blind, he died at the age of sixty-five on July 31, 1556.

Saint John Eudes

August 19

JOHN Eudes was born in France, November 14, 1601. As a priest he was full of zeal for the salvation of souls. During a plague he spent two months ministering to the sick and dying.

John preached as a missionary among the people in France for ten years.

His great work was in starting seminaries for the education of priests. He founded the Congregation of Priests of Jesus and Mary to form virtuous priests in seminaries. They wore a badge on which were inscribed the hearts of Jesus and Mary. They were also called Eudists.

John also founded the Congregation of the Sisters of Our Lady of Charity to work for penitent women.

John spread devotion to the Sacred Hearts of Jesus and Mary. He died in 1680.

Saint Gregory the Great

September 3

GREGORY was born in the year 540. He was the son of a wealthy Roman senator, who sent him to the best teachers. His mother was St. Silvia.

Gregory sold his property and built six monasteries in Sicily and one in Rome, where he went to live as a monk. But he continued his kind deeds to help the needy.

Gregory was sent as a missionary to England by the Pope. Later he was elected Pope and sent St. Augustine and a company of monks to England in 597. He also sent missionaries to France, Spain, and Africa.

Gregory is called "Great" above all because of the many books he wrote on the liturgy. He is also honored as Doctor of the Church because of his great learning. He made wise laws to govern the Church.

Gregory was a Benedictine. He died in the year 604.

Saint Robert Bellarmine

September 3

ROBERT was born in Italy in 1542. He joined the Society of Jesus. Although ill health was his cross all during his life, he became the great defender of the Church against the followers of the Protestant Reformation.

Robert wrote many books that were read by Catholics and Protestants. He wrote two famous catechisms which were much used in the Church.

Having become a cardinal, he laid aside his books and began preaching to the people, teaching catechism to the children, visiting the sick, and helping the poor.

But three years later Pope Paul V always had Cardinal Bellarmine at his side. As a member of almost every Congregation at the Vatican, he took an important part in the affairs of the Holy See.

He died at the age of seventy-nine in 1621. He is honored as a Doctor of the Church because of his great learning.

Saint Paul of the Cross

October 19

PAUL was born in Genoa, Italy, on January 3, 1694. After his ordination he was inspired in a vision to found a congregaion in honor of the Passion of Jesus Christ. He was invested by the bishop with the habit that had been shown to him in the vision.

Paul chose as the badge of his congregation a heart with three nails, in memory of the sufferings of Jesus. The Rule he wrote was approved by Benedict XIV. A large community of the Passionists lived at the Church of Saints John and Paul in Rome.

The work of the Passionists was preaching to the people in parishes. For fifty years Paul remained the untiring missionary of Italy. He believed himself to be a useless servant and a great sinner, though God granted him many wonderful gifts of soul.

Paul died at Rome in the year 1775, at the age of eighty-one.

Saint Leo the Great

November 10

LEO was born in Tuscany in Italy. He reigned as Pope from 440 to 461. At this time Attila, called the Scourge of God, with his hordes of Huns invaded Italy and marched toward Rome.

Moved with pity for his suffering people, Leo went out to meet him. His pleading persuaded the invader to leave Rome.

Later, when Genseric, another invader, entered Rome, Leo's holiness and eloquence again saved the city.

Heresies attacked the Church. Leo called the Council of Chalcedon and condemned them.

The holy Pope built many churches. He left many letters and writings of great historical value. For this reason, but especially for his holiness, he is called "the Great." He is honored as a Doctor of the Church.

Leo died on April 11, 461.

Saint Peter Canisius

December 21

PETER was born in Holland on May 8, 1521. He became a Jesuit. St. Ignatius kept him by his side for five months. On the day of his final vows, as he knelt in St. Peter's Basilica in Rome, he was favored with a vision of the Sacred Heart. From that time he never failed to make an offering of all his work to the Sacred Heart of Jesus.

Peter became known for his preaching and writing. He was sent to Germany where he attacked heretical teaching. He wrote a catechism which was translated into many languages. He founded a number of colleges.

Peter was the second great Apostle of Germany, the first being St. Boniface. He was one of the greatest opponents of the Reformation through his preaching and writing of books in defense of the Faith.

Peter died in Switzerland in 1597. Pope Pius XI canonized him in 1925 and proclaimed him a Doctor of the Church.

A Prayer of the Church

FATHER, all powerful and ever-living God, we do well and always and everywhere to give You thanks.
Around your throne the Saints,
our brothers and sisters,
sing Your praise for ever.
Their glory fills us with joy,
and their union with us in Your Church
gives us inspiration and strength,
as we hasten on our pilgrimage of faith,
eager to meet them.
With their great company and all the angels
we praise Your glory.

32

(Preface for the Feast
of All Saints, November 1.)

Book of Saints

"SUPER-HEROES OF GOD"

By REV. LAWRENCE G. LOVASIK, S.V.D.

Divine Word Missionary

PART 6

CONTENTS

St. Edward	2	St. Gabriel the Archangel	16
St. John Neumann	5	St. Jerome	19
St. Benedict Labré	7	St. Francis of Assisi	20
St. Catherine of Siena	8	St. Ignatius of Antioch	22
St. Madeleine Sophie Barat	11	St. Anthony Mary Claret	25
St. Bonaventure	12	St. Pius V	26
St. Maximilian Kolbe	15	St. Martin of Tours	29
		St. Ambrose	30

Nihil Obstat: Daniel V. Flynn, J.C.D., *Censor Librorum*

Imprimatur: ✝ Joseph T. O'Keefe, D.D., *Vicar General, Archdiocese of New York*

© 1985 *by Catholic Book Publishing Corp.*, *N.Y.* — Printed in Hong Kong

ISBN 978-0-89924-394-4

Saint Edward

January 5

EDWARD was raised to the throne of England at the age of forty years, twenty-seven of which he had passed in exile. He and his wife, Edith, lived a saintly life.

Edward was generous to the poor. He used to stand at his palace gate, speaking kindly to the poor beggars and the sick who crowded about him.

No matter how busy he was, he would be present at Mass daily. He built and enriched churches. Westminster Abbey was his last work.

One of the noblemen at his palace wrote: "Edward was a man by choice devoted to God, living the life of an angel in ruling his kingdom, and therefore was directed by God. He was so gentle that he would not say an unkind word even to the meanest person."

Edward died on January 5, 1065. In 1611 he was canonized. His incorrupt body was taken to the shrine of the Abbey by St. Thomas Becket.

Saint John Neumann

BORN in what is now Czechoslovakia, John Nepomucene Neumann came to the United States, became a priest, and joined the Redemptorists.

In 1852 he was consecrated bishop of Philadelphia and labored zealously to begin parishes and schools.

John did missionary work in Maryland, Virginia, Pennsylvania, and Ohio. He knew eight Slavic dialects and modern languages, and traveled through his vast diocese by canal boat, stagecoach, railway, or horseback and on foot.

He drew into the diocese of Philadelphia many teaching Orders of Sisters and Christian Brothers. He was the first bishop to organize the parochial school system, and he wrote a catechism.

He died in 1860 performing his duties, and he was canonized on July 19, 1977.

Saint Benedict Labré

April 16

BENEDICT Joseph Labré was born in France in 1748. He received a good education under the care of his pious parents and his uncle, a priest in the town of his birth.

At the age of sixteen he tried to join the Trappists, but was rejected. Then he was with the Carthusians for six weeks. He took to the life of a pilgrim, living on alms and practicing poverty.

Benedict made pilgrimages to many of the great shrines of Europe. He spent the last years of his life in Rome, visiting various churches.

Benedict loved the Bible and always carried a copy with him. In all his travels he tried to keep before him the sufferings of Jesus and Mary.

He died in 1783 in his favorite church of Our Lady of the Mountains in Rome, while those attending him said the invocation of the litany of the dying: "Holy Mary, pray for him."

Saint Catherine of Siena
April 29

CATHERINE was the youngest of a very large family. In 1353, at the age of six she had a vision in St. Dominic's church in which our Lord appeared to her and blessed her.

She knew that he wanted her to do some special work, so she prepared for it by penance and prayer. She became a Dominican tertiary and devoted herself to the care of the poor.

The Popes had been living in Avignon, France, instead of in Rome for many years because of the unsettled times. Catherine made a visit to Pope Gregory XI and asked him to return to Rome. He did so, and once again Rome became the home of the Popes.

Catherine's last days were full of suffering. Jesus imprinted His five wounds on her body because of her love for Him on the Cross.

Catherine died at the age of thirty-three. Pope Paul VI proclaimed her a Doctor of the Church in 1970.

Saint Madeleine Sophie Barat

May 25

MADELEINE was born in France in 1779. In Paris, she met Father Joseph Varin, who wanted to found a congregation of women devoted to the Sacred Heart of Jesus and dedicated to the education of girls.

On November 21, 1800, she and three other postulants began their religious life. The following year she was sent to Amiens to teach in a school. Although she was only twenty-three, Madeleine Sophie was appointed superior and held that office for sixty-three years as Superior General of the Society of the Sacred Heart.

Madeleine Sophie built one hundred and five houses in the principal countries of the world, including the United States. She admonished her Sisters to seek the glory of the Heart of Jesus in laboring for the saving of souls. Her motto was: "To suffer myself and not to make others suffer."

She died at Paris on May 25, 1865. She was canonized May 24, 1925.

Saint Bonaventure

July 15

BONAVENTURE was born in Tuscany, Italy, in 1221. He entered the Franciscan Order and lectured at the University of Paris, where he was acquainted with St. Thomas Aquinas and enjoyed the friendship of King St. Louis.

Bonaventure is known as the Seraphic Doctor, because of the warmth of love found in his writings. He became General of the Franciscan Order and Cardinal of Albano.

St. Thomas asked Bonaventure one day where he acquired his great learning. His friend answered by pointing to his crucifix.

Bonaventure wrote the life of St. Francis of Assisi and spoke at the Council of Lyons.

Bonaventure is considered one of the greatest writers of spiritual theology in the Middle Ages.

He died in 1274.

Saint Maximilian Kolbe

MAXIMILIAN was born on January 7, 1894, in Poland and became a Franciscan. He had tuberculosis and, though he got well, remained frail all his life.

He founded a Movement dedicated to Mary Immaculate and spread it through a magazine called "The Knight of the Immaculate." It helped to form a community of 800 Franciscan men who dedicated themselves to the service of Our Lady.

Maximilian went to Japan and India spreading the Movement. Because of ill health he returned home in 1939. After the Nazi invasion of Poland, he was imprisoned and released for a time. But he was arrested again in 1941 and sent to the concentration camp at Auschwitz.

On July 31, 1941, for one prisoner's escape, ten men were chosen to die. One was a young husband and father. Father Kolbe offered himself in his place. He died after two weeks of starvation. He was canonized by Pope John Paul II in 1982.

Saint Gabriel the Archangel

September 29

THE Prophet Daniel wrote that it was Gabriel the Archangel who announced to him the time of the coming of Messiah.

Gabriel also appeared to Zechariah "standing on the right side of the altar of incense," as St. Luke writes, to make known the future birth of John the Baptist.

But Gabriel's greatest honor was to be sent to Mary at Nazareth and to announce to her that she was to be the Mother of God. When she consented, Mary became the Mother of the Son of God.

Gabriel's name means "the strength of God." God sent him as a messenger in the work that shows the power and glory of God.

Through many centuries Gabriel has been honored by Christians as the Angel of the Incarnation, of consolation, and of mercy. He left us the first words of the "Hail Mary."

Saint Jerome
September 30

JEROME, born in Dalmatia, was sent to school at Rome. He visited foreign countries, devoted himself to the sciences and finally became a lawyer.

For a time Jerome lived a worldly life, but later he was baptized at Rome.

Jerome became a priest at Antioch. He went to Palestine and joined a monastery at Bethlehem. He translated the Bible into Latin, which was to be his noblest work.

For thirty years Jerome wrote many books, especially about Holy Scripture. He spent the last 34 years of his life in the Holy Land.

Jerome is called a Father and Doctor of the Latin Church and "the man of the Bible."

When he died in the year 420, his body was buried at Bethlehem and later removed to Rome.

Saint Francis of Assisi

October 4

KNOWN as the Seraphic Saint, Francis was born at Assisi, Italy, in 1182. In his youth he loved pleasure and fine clothes. but he renounced his wealth and lived in poverty because he heard our Lord calling him to leave the world and follow Him.

Francis put on the clothes of a poor shepherd and began to preach to the people about peace with God, peace with one's neighbor, and peace with one's self. He looked on all people and things as his brothers and sisters because they were all created by the same God.

Francis took twelve young men to Rome with him, and the Pope gave him permission to start a new religious order, the Franciscans. He also helped St. Clare to start the order known as the Poor Clares.

Francis had a vision in which he saw Jesus hanging on the Cross. The marks of the five wounds of Jesus were left in his hands, his side, and his feet. Francis died on October 4, 1226.

Saint Ignatius of Antioch

October 17

BORN in Syria, Ignatius converted to Christianity and later became Bishop of Antioch, following St. Peter.

In the year 107 the Emperor Trajan forced Christians in Antioch to choose between death and the denial of Christ. Ignatius was condemned to be put to death in Rome.

On the long journey to Rome, he wrote seven letters, five of these were to Churches in Asia Minor. The sixth was to Polycarp, Bishop of Smyrna, who was later martyred for the faith. The final letter begs the Christians in Rome not to try to stop his martyrdom.

"The only thing I ask of you is to allow me to offer the sacrifice of my blood to God. I am the wheat of the Lord; may I be ground by the teeth of the beasts to become the pure bread of Christ."

He was later thrown to the beasts in Rome and died a martyr. Strengthened by the love of God, Ignatius showed great concern for the unity of the Church and faithfulness to Christ.

Saint Anthony Mary Claret
October 24

BORN in Sallent, Spain, Anthony worked as a missionary in Catalonia and the Canary Islands for ten years. In 1849 he started the Congregation of Missionary Sons of the Immaculate Heart of Mary. The institute is known as "the Claretians."

Father Claret was appointed Archbishop of Santiago in Cuba. He founded the Teaching Sisters of Mary Immaculate.

At the request of Pope Pius XI, he returned to Spain and devoted himself to missionary work and the spreading of good literature.

Anthony also spread devotion to the Blessed Sacrament and the Immaculate Heart of Mary by preaching and writings.

Anthony died in a Cistercian monastery in France on October 24, 1870. He was canonized by Pope Pius XII in 1950.

Saint Pius V

April 30

PIUS V, of the Dominican Order, was a Pope of great holiness. The family of God had been shaken by the Reformation, by corruption, and by the threat of Turkish invasion.

He carried out many reforms and called for the Council of Trent, which lasted 18 years. He ordered the founding of seminaries for the training of priests, published a new Missal, Breviary, and Catechism, and started the Confraternity of Christian Doctrine (CCD) classes for the young.

Only at the last minute was Pius able to organize a fleet which won a victory against the Turks in the Gulf of Lepanto, off Greece, on October 7, 1571.

This saintly Pope also served the sick and the poor by building hospitals and providing food.

His pontificate (1566-1572) was one of great renewal in the Church. He died in 1572.

Saint Martin of Tours

November 11

MARTIN was born of pagan parents in what is now Hungary around the year 316 and was raised in Italy. The son of a Roman officer, he was forced to serve in the army at the age of 15. He was baptized at 18.

On a cold day, the legend goes, Martin met a poor man, almost naked, trembling, and begging from people who passed by. Martin had nothing but weapons and clothes. He drew his sword, cut his coat into two pieces, and gave one to the beggar. That night in his sleep Martin saw Christ dressed in the half of the garment he had given away.

At 23 Martin went to be a disciple of St. Hilary of Poitiers, France, and was ordained a priest. He preached throughout the countryside for ten years.

The people of Tours demanded that he become their Bishop. He became the most celebrated Bishop of the 4th century, and one of the great Saints of France. He died in 397.

Saint Ambrose

December 7

AMBROSE was born in Gaul about the year 340. He studied in Rome and became an eloquent speaker. When he moved to Milan he was appointed Governor. At the age of thirty-four he became the Bishop of Milan.

Ambrose gave his riches to the Church and to the poor. He defended the Church against the Arian heretics of his time.

He witnessed the conversion of St. Augustine, whom he baptized in 387. He was an example of a zealous shepherd of souls and his heart was filled with a gentle love for the poor.

Ambrose left us many important writings on the doctrines of our Holy Faith. He is one of the four great Latin Fathers and Doctors of the Western Church.

The Church honors Ambrose as one of her greatest defenders. This is why he is pictured holding a church in his hand. The beehive means wisdom. He died in 397.

Prayer of the Church

God our Father,
  source of all holiness,
the work of Your hands is shown in Your Saints,
the beauty of Your truth is reflected in their
  faith.
We honor these holy men and women of every
  time and place.
May their prayers bring us Your forgiveness and
  love,
May we who aspire to have part in their joy
  be filled with the Spirit that blessed their lives.
May we share their faith on earth,
that we may also know their peace and joy in
  Your kingdom.
Grant this through Christ our Lord.

(Feast of All Saints, November 1)

Book of Saints

"SUPER-HEROES OF GOD"

By REV. LAWRENCE G. LOVASIK, S.V.D.
Divine Word Missionary

PART 9

CONTENTS

St. Fulgentius of Ruspe	— 3	St. Olga	18
St. Hildegund	5	Bl. Titus Brandsma	21
St. Miguel Cordero	7	St. Peter Julian Eymard	22
St. Cuthbert	8	Bl. Teresa (Edith Stein)	25
St. Benedict the Black	11	St. Hildegard of Bingen	27
St. Louis de Montfort	12	St. Galla	28
St. Mariana of Quito	14	St. Agnes of Assisi	30
St. Juliana Falconieri	17	Prayer	32

NIHIL OBSTAT: Francis J. McAree, S.T.D., *Censor Librorum*
IMPRIMATUR: ✠ Patrick J. Sheridan, D.D.,
Vicar General, Archdiocese of New York

The Nihil Obstat and Imprimatur are official declarations that a book or pamphlet is free of doctrinal or moral error. No implication is contained therein that those who have granted the Nihil Obstat and Imprimatur agree with the contents, opinions or statements expressed.

© 1996 by Catholic Book Publishing Corp., Totowa, N.J.

Printed in Hong Kong   ISBN 978-0-89942-504-7

Saint Fulgentius of Ruspe

January 1

BORN into a noble senatorial family of Carthage, Fabius Claudius Gordianus Fulgentius received an excellent education including Latin and Greek.

He was chosen lieutenant governor of Byzacena. But after reading a sermon of Saint Augustine, he decided to become a monk.

His austere lifestyle attracted many followers and he was elected Bishop of Ruspe (modern Kudiat Rosfa in Tunisia).

Shortly afterward, he was tortured and sent into exile by the Arian king. The Arians were heretics who denied the divinity of Christ. Fulgentius and the other exiles built a monastery and devoted themselves to prayer and study.

When a new king ruled in Carthage, the exiles returned home. Fulgentius won the people over to the true Faith by his powerful preaching and example of humility. He died on January 1, 533.

Although he suffered for the Faith, this holy man remained true. He based his teaching on the writings of Saint Augustine and has been called a "pocket Augustine."

Saint Hildegund

February 6

IT was in Germany in the twelfth century when Hildegund, wife of Count Lothair, was left a widow with young children when he died.

Later one of her sons died and the second son entered a monastery. So Hildegund, uncertain of her future, made a pilgrimage to Rome.

She then turned her efforts to establishing a house of prayer and praise to God. She dedicated all her possessions to Christ and converted her castle into a convent.

Hildegund and her daughter Hedwig assumed the Premonstratensian habit and began a new foundation with Hildegund as prioress. Her kindness and spirit of fervor attracted many others to a life of prayer and good works.

Both Hildegund's daughter Hedwig and her son Herman were known to the people as Blessed. Hildegund died in 1183 with a great reputation for sanctity, especially because of the example she gave in turning away from material possessions to seek only the honor and glory of God.

Saint Miguel Cordero

February 9

FRANCISCO Febres Cordero Muñoz was born in 1854 to a prominent family in Ecuador. He was not able to stand till age five. Then he saw a vision of the Blessed Mother and was cured.

He attended a school run by the Christian Brothers, and when he was of age, decided to join their Congregation. He was accepted and became known as Brother Miguel.

Miguel's first assignment was in Quito where he remained for thirty-two years. He was an outstanding teacher and wrote many books on education. The government of Ecuador adopted his texts for schools throughout the country. In 1892, Brother Miguel was elected to the national Academy of Letters.

Despite his fame in the field of education, Brother Miguel delighted in preparing the very young for their First Holy Communion. He also wrote manuals of piety, gave religious instruction, and conducted retreats.

Miguel died in 1910 in Spain and his body was returned to Ecuador with great public ceremony.

Saint Cuthbert

March 20

ALTHOUGH there is some confusion as to whether Cuthbert was born in Ireland, Scotland, or England, we know that he was orphaned at an early age. For a time he was a shepherd, and eventually became a monk at Melrose Abbey. Shortly afterward, he became the abbot there.

Later Cuthbert, with most of the monks of Lindisfarne, migrated to Ireland. Then he became prior of Lindisfarne or Holy Island. He loved God's creatures and was protector of the seabirds.

Cuthbert was also involved in missionary activities and attracted large crowds by his preaching. Then because of his desire for solitude, he became a hermit living on an island in seclusion.

Against his will Cuthbert was chosen Bishop of Hexam. He arranged to switch Sees and thus became Bishop of Lindisfarne.

The last years of his life were spent in ministering to his flock, caring for the sick, and working numerous healings. Cuthbert died at Lindisfarne in 687.

Saint Benedict the Black

April 4

AS a slave who was given his freedom, Benedict the Black, also known as Benedict the Moor, devoted his life to God. Born near Messina, Italy, in 1526, he became a hermit and later superior of a community of hermits.

When the community was disbanded, Benedict became a Franciscan lay brother at Saint Mary's Convent in Palermo.

At first he served as the cook, and later he was appointed superior. But preferring a life of service, he asked to be relieved of such responsibilities and became the cook again.

Benedict had a reputation for holiness, miracles, and generosity. He was also a skillful counselor, and many people sought his help. He died in 1589 and is the Patron of Blacks in the United States.

Refusing to allow his humble origins to keep him from his life's goal, Benedict pursued God's love and was richly rewarded. And the sting of slavery was turned into the glorious freedom of the children of God.

Saint Louis Mary Grignion de Montfort

April 28

LOUIS Mary Grignion is best known for spreading devotion to the Most Blessed Virgin Mary both through preaching and by the printed word.

He was born to a poor family at Montfort, France in 1673. Educated at the Jesuit College in Rennes, he was ordained a priest.

His first assignment was as chaplain to a hospital at Poitiers. During his stay there, Louis established a new congregation of nuns, the Daughters of Divine Wisdom.

Then Louis went to Rome and Pope Clement XI appointed him missionary apostolic, and he began to preach in Brittany.

His emotional style caused much reaction, but he was successful, especially in furthering devotion to the Most Blessed Virgin Mary through the Rosary. And he wrote a very popular book, *True Devotion to the Blessed Virgin.*

Later Louis founded the Missionaries of the Company of Mary known as the Montfort Fathers, and he died in 1716.

Saint Mariana of Quito

May 26

ATTRACTED to things religious from a very early age, Mariana dedicated herself completely to God.

She was born in Quito, Ecuador in 1618. Her parents were of Spanish nobility, but she was orphaned as a child. Then Mariana was raised with loving care by her sister.

At the age of twelve she became a recluse in her sister's house guided by her confessor a Jesuit priest. Mariana never left that house for the rest of her life, except to go to church.

She ate very little, slept only three hours a night, and spent much time in prayer. Drawing close to God, Mariana had the gifts of prophecy and miracles.

In 1645 when Quito was ravaged by an earthquake and epidemic, she offered herself publicly as a victim for the sins of the people. The quake ended, and as the epidemic began to subside, Mariana fell ill and died on May 26. She is known as the "Lily of Quito."

Saint Juliana Falconieri

June 19

JULIANA was born of a wealthy Florentine family in 1270. When she was very young her father died. She was raised by her mother and an uncle named Alexis who was one of the founders of the Servite Order.

At age fifteen Juliana refused her family's plan for marriage. She became a Servite tertiary and lived at home until her mother died.

Then Juliana gathered together a group of women dedicated to prayer and good works, and she was appointed superior. She is considered to be foundress of the Servite nuns.

She loved to serve the sick and gladly performed the most repulsive duties for them.

Her life was one of great self-denial, humility, and charity. And Juliana had a fervent devotion to the Eucharist.

In her last years Juliana was afflicted with painful diseases which she bore with joy and patience. Her saintly life ended in her convent at Florence in 1341.

Saint Olga

July 11

OLGA, also known as Helga, was born at Pskov, Russia, around 879. She married Igor, Duke of Kiev.

When Igor was assassinated, Olga reacted with vengeance on his murderers, ordering that they be scalded to death. And she had many of their followers put to death.

Then Olga ruled the country as regent for her son Svyastoslav until he came of age.

In 957 Olga became a Christian and was baptized in Constantinople. She was one of the first Russians to be baptized.

Turning from her former ways, she devoted the rest of her life to the spread of Christianity, and she requested missionaries from Emperor Otto I.

In this endeavor she did not achieve great success. Her son, Soyastoslav, did not become a Christian, but her grandson, Saint Vladimir, evangelized Russia and is its Patron Saint. Olga died at Kiev on July 11 at age ninety.

Blessed Titus Brandsma

July 26

BORN of a deeply religious family in the Netherlands in 1881, Anno Sjoera Brandsma became a Carmelite priest taking the name Titus.

He traveled widely speaking for many causes. Moreover, Titus was a journalist and author.

In 1935 he wrote a public protest condemning new laws against the Jews. And he said a Catholic newspaper could not accept Nazi propaganda and still be considered Catholic.

The courageous priest refused to hide from the Nazis. He was arrested and sent to the concentration camp at Dachau.

Titus was beaten nearly every day and harassed by the guards.

Soon he became so weak that he was sent to the prison infirmary. On July 26, 1942, he gave his Rosary to his nurse. She was a former Catholic who left the Church. She injected him with poison and he died in minutes.

Years later that nurse returned to the Faith. On her own accord she testified for Titus at the hearing for his canonization.

Saint Peter Julian Eymard

August 1

THE life of Peter Julian Eymard reminds us that all of us urgently need the nourishment of the Most Blessed Sacrament as we make our way on our pilgrimage in this world.

Peter was born in Grenoble, France in 1811. He was ordained a priest, and after five years of pastoral ministry, joined the Marist Fathers. He served as spiritual director of their junior seminary and later as provincial at Lyons.

In 1856 Peter was dispensed from his vows as a Marist and he organized a religious institute of priests dedicated to the Blessed Sacrament. They were engaged in perpetual adoration of and devotion to the Blessed Sacrament.

Peter also founded a congregation of nuns and a priests' Eucharistic league along with the Confraternity of the Blessed Sacrament.

By his writings, and especially by his example, Peter sought to make our Eucharistic Lord better known and loved. His works show that the Eucharistic presence in our lives is a foretaste of our union with the Father. He died in 1888.

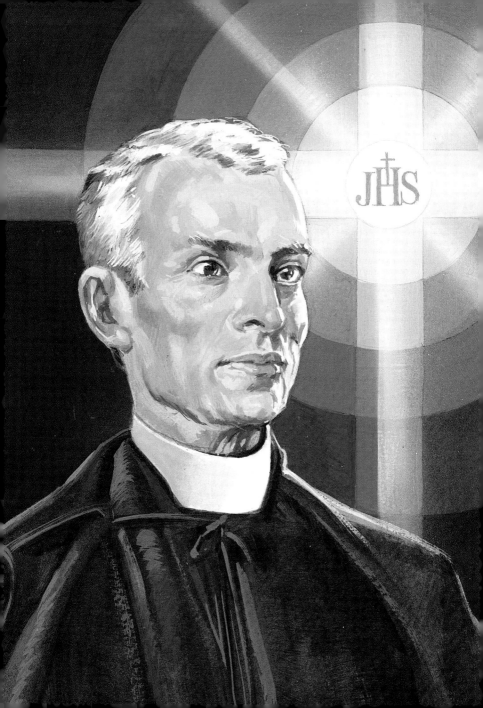

Saint Teresa Benedicta of the Cross (Edith Stein)

August 9

EDITH Stein, born in 1891 in Breslau, Poland, was the youngest child of a large Jewish family. She had a brilliant mind and became a doctor of philosophy at age twenty-five.

At a friend's house she saw an autobiography of Saint Teresa of Avila. She read it in a single night and soon after was baptized a Catholic.

Eleven years later Edith entered the Carmel at Cologne. She put behind her the years as a renowned scholar to become a simple nun seeking only closer union with God. She is remembered as a very warm and cheerful person.

Because of the situation in Germany Edith, whose name in religion was Teresa Benedicta of the Cross, was sent to the Carmel at Echt, Holland.

When the Nazis conquered Holland, Teresa was arrested because of her Jewish origin. She was sent to the concentration camp at Auschwitz with her sister Rosa who also became a Catholic. They died together in the gas chamber in 1942. Teresa was declared a Saint in 1998.

Saint Hildegard of Bingen

September 17

AFFLICTED with fragile health as a child, Hildegard, who was born in 1098 in Germany, was placed in the care of her aunt, Blessed Jutta.

Jutta had formed a community of nuns and Hildegard joined them. When Jutta died, Hildegard became prioress and moved the convent to Rupertsburg near Bingen.

Hildegard was favored with visions, prophecies, and revelations. At her spiritual director's request they were recorded in a work called *Scivias* (the one who knows the ways of the Lord) and approved by Pope Eugenius III.

Living in a turbulent age, Hildegard used her talents in the quest for true justice and peace. She corresponded with Popes, emperors, kings, and famous clergy.

Huge crowds sought to consult her and she was hailed as a Saint but some said she was a fraud.

This remarkable woman of God died in 1179. Miracles were reported at her tomb and she was proclaimed a Saint by the people.

Saint Galla

October 5

GALLA was the daughter of a noble patrician who had been a Roman consul in 485. After he was unjustly executed, she married, but within a year she was left a widow.

Though young and wealthy, Galla was determined not to marry again but to devote herself to Christ.

She joined a group of consecrated women who lived near Saint Peter's Basilica. For many years she served the poor, the sick, and the needy.

In later years Galla was afflicted with cancer of the breast. One night when she was unable to sleep, she saw a vision of Saint Peter.

Peter told her that she would be going home to heaven soon and that her friend Benedicta would follow in thirty days. And this happened just as predicted.

Saint Gregory recorded Galla's vision in his *Dialogues*. Galla died around the year 550.

The letter of Saint Fulgentius *Concerning the State of Widowhood* was probably addressed to Saint Galla.

Saint Agnes of Assisi

A GNES, born in Assisi in 1197, was the younger sister of Saint Clare. When Saint Francis sent Clare to the Benedictine convent of Sant' Angelo di Panzo, Agnes joined her there. Agnes was only fifteen years old.

Then Francis gave the sisters the Franciscan habit they desired and sent them to San Damiano to follow a life of poverty and penance. This marked the beginning of the Poor Clares.

Agnes led a life of detachment from the world's goods. In this way, she was able to become more absorbed in the life of God. Agnes became abbess of the Poor Clares convent at Monticelli. And later she founded convents at Mantua, Venice, and Padua. And Agnes firmly supported her sister's struggle for complete poverty in their Order.

In August 1253 Agnes went to Assisi to be with Clare in her last hours. Then Agnes died three months later on November 16.

The tomb of Agnes in the church of Santa Chiara at Assisi has been the site of numerous miracles.

Prayer

O GOD,
You have given us the Saints to be
our examples in this life,
our friends in the spirit,
and our helpers in heaven.

As we read the accounts of their holy lives,
teach us to imitate their words and actions,
so that one day we may be united with them
in Your heavenly dwelling.

Book of Saints

"SUPER-HEROES OF GOD"

By REV. LAWRENCE G. LOVASIK, S.V.D.
Divine Word Missionary

PART 11

CONTENTS

St. Alberic	2	St. Madeleine Sophie Barat	18
St. Mutien Marie Wiaux	4	St. John of Sahagún	21
St. Margaret of Cortona	7	Bl. Osanna of Mantua	22
Bl. Angela Guerrero	8	St. Macrina the Younger	24
St. Clement Mary Hofbauer	11	St. Grimonia	27
St. Hermenegild	12	St. Eulalia of Mérida	29
St. Wiborada	14	Bl. Jutta of Diessenberg	31
St. Epiphanius of Salamis	17	Prayer	32

NIHIL OBSTAT: Francis J. McAree, S.T.D., *Censor Librorum*
IMPRIMATUR: ✠ Patrick J. Sheridan, D.D.,
Vicar General, Archdiocese of New York

The Nihil Obstat and Imprimatur are official declarations that a book or pamphlet is free of doctrinal or moral error. No implication is contained therein that those who have granted the Nihil Obstat and Imprimatur agree with the contents, opinions or statements expressed.

Saint Alberic

January 26

ALBERIC, Robert, and Stephen Harding are considered the founders of the Cistercian Order that is known today as the Trappists.

Living as a hermit in France, Alberic invited other hermits to move to Molesmes in 1075 to establish a monastery with Robert as abbot and Alberic as prior.

As word spread about the monastery, their numbers grew rapidly. But some of the newer monks did not follow the strict monastic rule. As a result Robert left. When Alberic tried to reform the monastery, he was not successful.

Then he and Robert and Stephen Harding began the Cistercian Order at Citeaux near Dijon. Here the Benedictine Rule was strictly observed. Robert was the first abbot, and Alberic succeeded him. And he played a role in the growth of the place of the lay brother in the monastery.

Remembered as a father figure and "fellow-soldier" in fighting the "Lord's battles," Alberic died on January 26, 1109. He is remembered as one who truly loved his fellow monks, the Cistercian life, and the Word of God.

3

Saint Mutien Marie Wiaux

January 30

LOUIS Wiaux was given the name Brother Mutien Marie when he entered the Brothers of the Christian Schools in Belgium in 1852. This was the beginning of a teaching career that would last for sixty-six years.

As teacher, prefect of boarding students, and supervisor of recreation, Brother Mutien encouraged his students with a quiet but open manner. They knew that he cared.

And he prayed the Rosary constantly. His long visits to the chapel earned him the nickname "the praying Brother." As he grew older, he concentrated more and more on his work and prayer.

Brother Mutien died on January 30, 1917. His reputation for holiness began to grow within a short time, and he was canonized by Pope John Paul II in 1989.

Here is a modern Saint we can readily imitate. Brother Mutien's humility, kindness, and prayer-filled good example led many of his students to turn back to God.

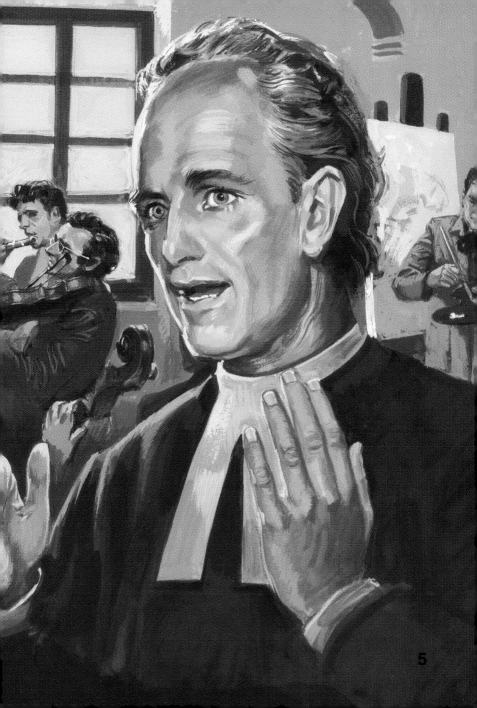

5

Saint Margaret of Cortona

MARGARET was born in Tuscany in 1247. Her mother died when she was seven. When her father remarried, she felt rejected at home, for her stepmother had little care for her.

So Margaret ran away with a young man and gave birth to a son without being married. When her partner died, she tried to return home.

Her father refused to accept her, but she was welcomed by the Friars Minor at Cortona. One Sunday at Mass, she confessed her sins before the whole congregation and asked pardon for her past scandal.

She joined the Third Order of Saint Francis, and her son became a Franciscan a few years later. Margaret advanced rapidly in prayer and was said to be in direct contact with Jesus.

She began to serve the sick poor without recompense depending only on alms. Then she established a hospital at Cortona and started a confraternity to assist the poor.

Through her words and example many returned to God. Margaret died on February 22, 1279, having spent twenty-nine years performing acts of penance.

Blessed Angela of the Cross Guerrero

March 2

FROM her earliest years Angela had a great devotion to Christ Crucified. Born in Seville, Spain, in 1846, she taught her religious daughters to imitate the poverty of Jesus Crucified in the Congregation of the Cross that she founded.

In her community the members were to live with and like the poor. They existed solely on free-will donations. And the sisters were to receive alms with gratitude and humility.

Angela's nuns were called upon to work with poor families, orphans, and the sick. And they were to educate children and adults in the fundamentals.

All the poor were to receive from the sisters money, housing, clothing, medicine, and instruction. And everything was to be given with love.

Angela died on March 2, 1932, and she was beatified in 1982 by Pope John Paul II.

Blessed Angela's life teaches us that we should share generously with our brothers and sisters who are most in need.

9

Saint Clement Mary Hofbauer

March 15

CLEMENT was born in Moravia in Austria-Hungary at a time when there was very little freedom of religion. For a while he lived as a hermit. Then he went to Italy when Emperor Joseph II abolished this way of life.

Later he studied at Vienna and Rome and was ordained a priest in the Redemptorist Order. At the request of the papal nuncio, Clement went to Warsaw and engaged in missionary work. He helped the poor, built schools, and sent Redemptorist missionaries to Germany and Switzerland.

In 1808, Clement and his companions were imprisoned when Napoleon suppressed religious orders in his territories. Each was expelled to his native country, and Clement settled in Vienna.

As chaplain of the Ursuline nuns he began to attract attention by his sermons, holiness, and spiritual direction.

Clement defeated efforts to establish a German national Church, and opposed secular domination of the Church. He died on March 15, 1820, and is called the "Second Founder of the Redemptorists."

Saint Hermenegild
April 13

WHEN we recite the Profession of Faith at Mass, we say "We believe in one Lord, Jesus Christ, . . . one in Being with the Father." Many years ago Arius denied the Divinity of Christ. His false teachings were called Arianism.

Hermenegild was the son of Leovigild King of Spain in the sixth century. Leovigild raised his children in the Arian heresy.

When Hermenegild married Indegundis the daughter of the king of Austrasia, he embraced the true Catholic Faith and renounced Arianism. Then Leovigild disinherited him, and he was deprived of all royal rights and privileges.

Later, Hermenegild led a revolt against his father but he was defeated. For a while father and son were reconciled. Then Leovigild tried to persuade his son to return to Arianism, but Hermenegild refused and was thrown into prison.

At Easter in 585 when Hermenegild refused to receive Communion from an Arian bishop, Leovigild sent soldiers to kill his son. Thus Hermenegild stood firm in the Faith and received a martyr's crown.

13

Saint Wiborada

May 2

WIBORADA was born of a noble family in Aargau, Switzerland, in the ninth century. When her brother Hatto became a priest, she turned her home into a hospital and served the patients her brother brought there.

After a pilgrimage to Rome she entered the Benedictine Monastery at Saint Gall. Later she withdrew to a life of solitude near Saint Gall. And finally she moved to a cell near the church of Saint Magnus where her brother was the pastor.

She spent long hours in prayer and practiced extraordinary penances. Blessed with the gift of prophecy and miracles, she exhibited great humility and did everything for God's honor and glory. And her holiness of life attracted many to seek her advice and counsel.

Wiborada foretold her death at the hands of invading Hungarians. She warned the clergy at Saint Magnus and Saint Gall so they escaped. But she refused to leave her cell and was martyred for her faith in 925. She was canonized by Pope Clement II in 1047.

15

16

Saint Epiphanius of Salamis

May 12

BORN in Palestine around 315, Epiphanius became a monk expert in languages and he spent many years studying the Scriptures. For a while he lived in desert communities in Egypt. When he returned to Palestine he was ordained and founded a monastery at Eleutheropolis where he was the superior for many years.

He had a widespread reputation for his learning, austerities, spiritual wisdom, and advice. Later he became Bishop of Constantia (Salamis) and then Metropolitan of Cyprus.

Epiphanius wrote many theological treatises—on the Trinity, the Resurrection, refuting heresies, and on ancient Jewish customs and measures. He was also an authority on Mary and encouraged a widespread devotion to our Blessed Mother. And he defended the primacy of Peter among the Apostles.

This great Saint wrote and preached against heresies, especially Arianism and was acclaimed as "the oracle of Palestine." He died in 403 while traveling from Constantinople to Salamis. Saint Jerome called him "a last relic of ancient piety."

Saint Madeleine Sophie Barat

May 25

ENDOWED by God with great natural beauty and many talents, Madeleine responded to the call for the Christian education of youth.

Born in France in 1779, she met Father Joseph Varin who wanted to found a congregation of women devoted to the Sacred Heart and dedicated to the education of girls. In 1800, Madeleine entered religious life and one year later established the first school of her new congregation of nuns, the Society of the Sacred Heart of Jesus.

Though she was only twenty-three, Madeleine was appointed superior and held that office for sixty-three years. Her society established convents and schools in twelve countries throughout the world, including the United States.

Madeleine exhorted her religious at all times to seek the glory of the Heart of Jesus in laboring for the sanctification of souls.

She died on May 25, 1865, at the age of eighty-six and was canonized in 1925. The good that her congregation has accomplished throughout the years speaks eloquently of her love for her Lord.

19

Saint John of Sahagún

June 12

IN many ways the life of a Christian calls for courage. Like Saint John we can expect to be treated with scorn if we speak out in favor of justice.

John was born in Sahagún, Spain, in the fifteenth century. He was educated by Benedictine monks and was ordained in 1445. After extended study at the University of Salamanca, he became renowned as a preacher and spiritual director.

Later, he joined the Augustinians and became prior of their monastery at Salamanca. John maintained its celebrated discipline by example rather than by authority.

John staunchly defended the rights of workers. And he had a special devotion to the Blessed Sacrament. He experienced visions and was famous for miracles. It was said that he had the gift of knowing the state of people's souls.

Because he preached against corruption in high places, John received threats against his life. But he was fearless and he caused a great change for the better in the lives of the people of Salamanca. This saintly priest died in 1479.

Blessed Osanna of Mantua

June 20

OSANNA had her first mystical experience at age five—a vision of Paradise. Later she had numerous visions of Christ in which she participated in the Passion. Although wounds did not appear on her body, she suffered physical pains as if they were there. And she also saw the Blessed Virgin Mary.

Born in 1449 at Mantua, Italy, Osanna rejected her father's plans for her to marry and became a Dominican tertiary at seventeen. She was not professed until many years later because she lovingly cared for her brothers and their families after the death of their parents.

Despite her intimate religious experiences, Osanna did not turn her back on the world. She expended much time and money to help the poor. She also made it a daily practice to visit the sick, comfort the afflicted, and give spiritual advice to all who flocked to her.

We know many details about her extraordinary visions since a record of her spiritual conversations with Girolamo de Monte Oliveto has been preserved. Osanna died on June 20, 1505.

23

Saint Macrina the Younger

July 19

MACRINA, the daughter of Saint Basil the Elder and Saint Emmelia, was born in Cappadocia around 330. Her mother provided her early education and she could read at a very early age, especially the Scriptures.

She was engaged to be married at the age of twelve. When her fiancé suddenly died, she refused further offers of marriage and dedicated her life to the service of God.

Then she turned her efforts to helping to educate her three brothers in the ways of God: Saint Basil the Great, Saint Peter of Sebaste, and Saint Gregory of Nyssa.

When her father died, Macrina and her mother retired to the family estate in Pontus. Other women came there to follow a community rule of prayer and self-denial with Saint Emmelia as Abbess.

After her mother's death Macrina became Abbess. She gave everything she owned to the poor and supported herself by manual labor, sleeping on a bed of boards. This generous and devout woman of God died on July 19, 379.

25

Saint Grimonia

September 7

GRIMONIA was the daughter of a pagan Irish chieftain who lived in the fourth century. At the age of twelve, she became a Christian.

At that time, she dedicated her life to God and took a vow of chastity. Her father was so enraged when Grimonia refused to marry that he threw her into prison.

Grimonia managed to escape and fled to France. She lived as a hermitess in a forest in Picardy—a life of prayer and severe self-denial. She received much strength from meditation on the Word of God and from her awareness of God's presence.

For she saw God everywhere—in the sky above, in the sun and clouds, in the trees and plants, in the birds and animals. She lived a solitary life, but she was never alone.

Her father sent his servants to try to find Grimonia and force her to return home. Eventually she was located, but when she refused to return home and marry, she was put to death. A chapel was built over her grave that became the site of numerous miracles.

Saint Eulalia of Mérida

December 10

EULALIA of Mérida is the most famous virgin martyr of Spain. She lived in Spain in the last decade of the third century. And she suffered martyrdom when she was twelve years old.

At that time the Emperor Diocletian led a cruel persecution of Christians. When someone was accused of being a follower of Christ, that person was ordered to offer sacrifice to false gods to save his or her life. By doing so, they would deny Christ; therefore, many Christians refused and gave up their earthly life so as to be assured of eternal life.

One day Eulalia was present at a trial when the Judge Dacian was trying to force Christians to worship false gods. Despite her mother's efforts to stop her, Eulalia denounced the judge and pleaded for the Christians.

As a result Eulalia was seized and told to worship false gods. And when she refused, she was tortured and finally burned at the stake. But nothing could make her deny the Savior she loved so much. She gained the crown of martyrdom around the year 304.

Blessed Jutta of Diessenberg

December 22

JUTTA was born in the eleventh century in Spanheim, Germany. For a while she lived as a recluse in a small house attached to St. Disibod's Monastery on the Diessenberg River.

She led an austere life spending long hours in prayer and meditation. And much time was devoted to studying the Scriptures.

Her niece, Saint Hildegard of Bingen, was entrusted to her care. Jutta raised her and was responsible for her education.

Because of Jutta's reputation for holiness, many people came to seek her advice and blessing.

Then she formed a community of women who followed the Benedictine Rule. Saint Hildegard joined the group and Jutta was the Prioress for over twenty years. Her nuns willingly followed her example of prayer and self-denial that led to such a joyful union with God.

When Jutta died in 1136, Saint Hildegard succeeded her as Prioress, and the community continued to flourish and expand for many years.

Prayer

O GOD,
You are the Source of all holiness.
You have made Your holiness shine forth
in many wonderful ways
through the lives of Your Saints.
As we read their lives,
help us to celebrate Your greatness.

Through Your Saints You have also given us
the courage to follow after Your Son.
Assist us to imitate the example of the Saints
for they show us the way to Christ.

Grant that by following the Saints
we may merit to join them
in everlasting happiness with You in heaven.

THE ANGELS

GOD'S MESSENGERS

AND

OUR HELPERS

By REV. LAWRENCE G. LOVASIK, S.V.D.
Divine Word Missionary

CATHOLIC BOOK PUBLISHING CORP.
NEW YORK, N.Y.

Nihil Obstat: Daniel V. Flynn, J.C.D., *Censor Librorum*
Imprimatur: ✠ James P. Mahoney, D.D., *Vicar General, Archdiocese of New York*
© 1978 *by Catholic Book Publishing Corp.*, N.Y. — Printed in Hong Kong
ISBN 978-0-89942-281-7

God Made the Angels

GOD made all things from nothing by His almighty power. He made the angels. Angels are spirits — they have no bodies. They have a mind and a will, for they can know and love God. God gave them great wisdom, power, and holiness. They are His messengers and servants.

The Good Angels Defeat The Bad Angels

BEFORE letting the angels join Him in heaven, God wanted to see if they would obey Him. Lucifer, whose name means "the carrier of light," was proud of his power. He turned against God and said: "I will not serve!"

But Michael — whose name means "Who is like God?" — arose to fight for God. The good angels joined him and they cast into hell Lucifer and the bad angels who followed him. The bad angels are now called devils.

An Angel Sends Adam And Eve Out of Paradise

GOD also made Adam and Eve. He gave them grace, which made them His dear children. But they disobeyed God and lost His Grace and the right to heaven.

God sent His angels to lead them out of paradise. The angel had in his hand a flaming sword, which was a sign that God is just and must punish sin.

But God promised to send them a Redeemer, who would save all people from their sins.

4

Abraham Welcomes God and Two Angels

PEOPLE began to forget God, but Abraham did not. So God promised to make him the father of a great people from whom would come the Savior of the World.

One hot day three strangers came to Abraham's tent. He gave them food. Abraham had no children. One of the strangers told him that in a year his wife Sarah would have a son. Abraham knew then that God Himself had come to him with two angels.

5

An Angel Stops Abraham
from Killing His Son Isaac

GOD said to Abraham, "Offer Me your son Isaac as a sacrifice." Abraham was ready to obey God. He made an altar and put wood upon it. He then tied Isaac upon the wood.

Just as Abraham was about to strike his son with the knife, an angel touched his hand and said, "Abraham, do not kill your son. God knows now that you truly love Him."

Then the angel told Abraham that God would bless him and that from his family the Savior of the world would one day be born.

6

The Angel of Death Punishes The Egyptians

BECAUSE the king of Egypt would not free the children of Israel, God sent an angel to punish the land of Egypt. At midnight the Angel of Death passed through the land, killing all the first-born sons of the Egyptians and also the first-born of all animals.

The Angel of Death spared the Israelites when he saw the blood of the lamb which God had commanded them to sprinkle on the doorposts. This was the first Passover.

An Angel Touches The Lips Of Isaiah

ISAIAH was one of the great-est prophets whom God sent to the people of Israel. He saw a throne upon which the Lord was sitting. Angels stood around the throne and sang, "Holy, holy, holy, Lord God of hosts, all the earth is full of His glory!"

The temple shook and Isaiah was afraid. One of the angels took a burning coal from the altar. with it he touched the lips of Isaiah and said, "Your sins shall be taken away."

Raphael Is A Guide For Young Tobiah

TOBIT sent his son, Tobiah, into a faraway country to collect a debt. God sent him the Angel Raphael to show him the way. On the journey a large fish leaped from the water after Tobiah. The angel told him to take the heart, gall, and liver of the fish to make a medicine.

When Tobiah returned home, the angel told him to put the medicine made from the fish on the eyes of his old father. At once his father was able to see. Then the angel said, "I am the Angel Raphael, one of the seven who stand before the Lord."

Raphael is the patron saint of the sick, of travelers, and of young people.

9

The Angel Appears to Zechariah

THE Jewish people were looking for the Redeemer. God sent an angel named Gabriel to Zechariah, a priest, who was burning incense in the temple. The angel said, "Do not be afraid, Zechariah, for your prayer has been heard. Your wife Elizabeth, shall bear a son and you shall call him John."

He shall be filled with the Holy Spirit, and he shall prepare for the Lord a perfect people."

Zechariah said to the angel, "How am I to know this? I am an old man, and my wife too is old."

The angel said, "I am Gabriel. I stand before God. I was sent to speak to you and bring you the good news. You will not be able to speak because you have not believed me."

Elizabeth gave birth to a son. Zechariah wrote down the words, "His name is John." At once he could speak again and he praised God. The child became St. John the Baptist who pointed to Jesus and said, "This is the Lamb of God Who takes away the sin of the world."

The Angel Gabriel Speaks To Mary

THE Angel Gabriel, sent from God, said to a young girl named Mary, "Hail, full of grace! The Lord is with you. Blessed are you among women."

Mary was surprised. The angel said, "Do not fear, Mary. You have found favor with God. You shall be the mother of a Son, and give him the name Jesus. He shall be great, and shall be called the Son of God."

Mary asked the angel, "How can this be?"

The angel said to her, "The Holy Spirit shall come upon you, and the Holy One to be born shall be called the Son of God."

Mary said, "I am the servant of the Lord. Let it be as you say." With that the angel left her. At that moment the Son of God became man and the Virgin Mary became the Mother of God.

The Second Person of the Blessed Trinity took to Himself a body and soul like ours. He became man and lived among us. This is called the Incarnation. Jesus is both God and Man.

The coming of the angel to Mary is called the Annunciation, because the angel announced the birth of Jesus.

The Angels Adore The Son of God

SOON after the birth of John the Baptist, Joseph had a dream. He saw an angel standing beside him. The angel said, "Joseph, son of David, do not be afraid to take Mary as you wife. She shall be the mother of a Son by the Holy Spirit. You shall call Him Jesus, for He will save His people from their sins."

14

Mary and Joseph traveled to Bethlehem to place their names upon a list by order of the Emperor because they were of the family of David. Because there was no room for them in the town, they had to spend the night in a stable. There Jesus, the Savior of the world, was born.

Mary wrapped her little son in soft clothes and laid Him in a manger. As she and Joseph adored the Divine Infant, hundreds of angels came to adore with them, for this was the Son of God Who became man for the love of people. The angels praised God for His mercy to a sinful world.

In this way God became man. He came down to earth and was born of the Virgin Mary for His love of us. Angels praise God for His mercy to us.

An Angel Appears To The Shepherds

ON THAT night some shepherds were watching their sheep in a field near Bethlehem. A great light shone upon them, and they saw an angel of the Lord standing before them. They were filled with fear as they saw how glorious the angel was.

"Do not be afraid," said the angel, "for I am bringing you good news of great joy for all the people. Today in the city of David is born a Savior, Who is Christ the Lord. You will find an infant wrapped in swaddling clothes and lying in a manger."

Many angels appeared singing: "Glory to God in the high heavens, peace on earth to those on whom His favor rests."

The shepherds said, "Lets us go over to Bethlehem and see what the Lord has made known to us." They hurried and found Mary and Joseph and the baby lying in the manger. They adored the Infant Jesus.

An Angel Appears To Joseph

GOD sent an angel to Joseph, who spoke to him in a dream saying, "Get up, take the Child and His mother and flee to Egypt. Stay there till I tell you, for Herod will try to kill the little Child." At once Joseph rose up in the night, and took his wife and her Child, to Egypt.

Some time later the angel again spoke to Joseph in a dream, saying, "You may now take the Child back, for the king who wanted to kill Him is dead."

Then Joseph took his wife and the little Child Jesus, and began his journey back to Nazareth.

The Angels Serve Jesus In The Desert

WHEN Jesus was thirty years old, He left Nazareth to begin His preaching. He first went to the desert. There the devil led Him in thought to Jerusalem to the top of a high tower and said to Him, "Now show the people that You are the Son of God by throwing Yourself down to the ground."

But Jesus said to him, "Away with you, Satan!"

Angels of God came to serve Jesus in the desert and gave Him food that He needed.

19

An Angel Gives Water Power To Heal

IN Jerusalem there was a pool beside which were lying a great crowd of sick, blind and crippled people. At certain times an angel came down to stir the water and gave it the power to heal. The first person to go down into the pool after the water was stirred was cured.

A man who had been a cripple for forty years said to Jesus, "I have no one to put me into the pool when the water is stirred."

Jesus said to him, "Rise, take up your mat and walk!" The man rose and walked away.

Jesus Teaches About Angels

WHEN Jesus was teaching the people, they brought little children to Him that He might bless them. He said, "Let the children come to Me. The kingdom of God belongs to such as these. See that you do no harm to one of these little ones; for their angels in heaven always see the face of My Father in heaven."

Jesus laid His hands on them and blessed them.

21

An Angel Comes To Comfort Jesus

IN THE Garden of Olives Jesus fell down upon the ground and prayed, "My Father, if it is possible, let this cup pass by. Still let it be as You will have it, not as I." Large drops of sweat like blood, caused by His suffering, fell from His face. Three times He prayed. Then an angel came and gave Him comfort and strength.

An Angel Announces The Resurrection of Jesus

ON Easter Sunday morning, Jesus rose from the dead by His own divine power, as He had promised. In this way He showed that He was the Son of God.

That morning some women went very early to the tomb of Jesus. They were bringing spices to put on His body, but they did not find the body of Jesus. They saw sitting at each end of the open tomb young men in white garments.

One of the angels said to them, "do not be afraid. You are looking for Jesus of Nazareth, Who was crucified. He is not here; He is risen. Go, tell His disciples that He will see them in Galilee."

23

Angels Speak To The Disciples

FORTY days after Easter, five hundred followers of Jesus met on a mountain. There Jesus showed Himself to them. After giving them His last commands, He blessed them, and then began to rise in the air until a cloud covered Him.

While the followers were looking up, they saw two men, like angels, standing by them. "Men of Galilee," they said, "why do you stand here looking up at the skies? This Jesus Who has been taken from you will return to earth, just as you saw Him Go up into the heavens."

An Angel Frees Peter From Prison

KING Herod arrested Peter and cast him into prison. An angel of the Lord stood beside him, and a light shone in the prison. The angel woke him, saying, "Get up quickly."

The angel told Peter to put on his sandals and cloak and to follow him. They passed by the guards and went through the gate of the city, though the gate was locked.

Peter was surprised and said, "Now I know for certain that the Lord has sent His angel and rescued me from the power of Herod."

When Peter came to his friends, they said, "It is His angel."

25

Angels Will Come With Jesus At The Last Judgment

JESUS will return at the Last Judgment. He once said, "When the Son of Man shall come in His majesty, and all the angels with Him, He will sit on the throne of His glory; and before Him will be gathered all the nations. The King will say to those on His right hand, 'Come, you have My Father's blessing.' To those on His left He will say, 'Out of My sight, you condemned, into everlasting fire prepared for the devil.'"

Angels Around The Throne Of The Lamb of God

IN HIS vision of heaven, St. John, the Apostle, saw many angels and men clothed in white robes with palms in their hands. They cried out with a loud voice, "Worthy is the Lamb that was slain to receive power and riches, wisdom and strength, honor and glory and praise!"

All the angels bowed before the throne and adored God, saying, "To the One seated on the throne, and to the Lamb, be praise and honor, glory and might, forever!"

The Good Angels Love And Help Us

THE good angels love us because they love God, Who wants them to love us and to help us. They protect us in soul and body. They keep us from sin and from all dangers. They pray for us and help us to do good deeds.

The good angels help us to fight against the temptations which the bad angels cause us. Bad angels try to lead us into sin and to make us lose our soul.

Saint Michael is the leader of the heavenly armies of angels. He is the mighty protector of the Church against all her enemies.

The Church prays:

"Saint Michael the Archangel,
defend us in battle.
Protect us against the wickedness of the devil.
O prince of the angels,
by the power of God,
cast into hell Satan
and all the evil spirits
who want to lead souls into hell."

29

You Have A Guardian Angel

GOD has given you an angel to be your faithful friend and to help you while you are on earth. This angel is God's messenger to tell you what God wants you to do. They will keep your soul from sin and will protect your body from harm. They are called your Guardian Angels because they guard you from evil.

Your Guardian Angel loves you because God loves you. They love you because your soul is so precious that Jesus shed His Blood on the cross to save it.

Ask your Guardian Angel to help you to save your soul so that you may see God in heaven forever.

Pray to him in these words:

"Angel of God, my guardian dear,
Through whom God's love protects me here;
Ever this day be at my side,
To rule and guide.
                                   Amen."

Love Your Guardian Angel

HONOR and love your Guardian Angel as your friend, for God has given them to you. Thank them and obey them when they tell you to do what is right and to stay away from what is evil.

Pray to your Guardian Angel each morning and night, and when you need their help.

The TEN COMMANDMENTS

By REV. LAWRENCE G. LOVASIK, S.V.D.
Divine Word Missionary

Nihil Obstat: Daniel V. Flynn, J.C.D., *Censor Librorum*
Imprimatur: ✠ James P. Mahoney, D.D., *Vicar General, Archdiocese of New York*
© 1978 by *Catholic Book Publishing Corp., N.J.* — Printed in Hong Kong
ISBN 978-0-89942-287-9

THE TEN COMMANDMENTS

JESUS said, "None of those who cry out, 'Lord, Lord,' will enter the kingdom of God but only the one who does the will of My Father in heaven." If we believe in God, we must do what God asks; we must keep His law.

Jesus also said, "Live on in My love. You will live in My love if you keep My commandments, even as I have kept My Father's commandments, and live in His love."

The Ten Commandments are:

1. I, the Lord, am your God. You shall not have other gods besides Me.
2. You shall not take the name of the Lord, your God, in vain.
3. Remember to keep holy the Sabbath day.
4. Honor your father and your mother.
5. You shall not kill.
6. You shall not commit adultery.
7. You shall not steal.
8. You shall not bear false witness against your neighbor.
9. You shall not covet your neighbor's wife.
10. You shall not covet anything that belongs to your neighbor.

WHEN the Israelites were in the desert on the way to the land that God promised them, God called Moses up to the top of Mount Sinai and gave him the Ten Commandments written on tablets of stone.

God gave Moses His Ten Commandments on Mount Sinai.

3

THE FIRST COMMANDMENT

I, the Lord, am your God. You shall not have other gods besides Me.

GOD has put us into this world to love and serve Him. The will of God must be put first in our life. We must always remember that we are children of God, Who is our all-good, all-loving Father. We owe Him our worship and true prayer. In this way we show that we belong to Him and want to love and serve Him every day of our life.

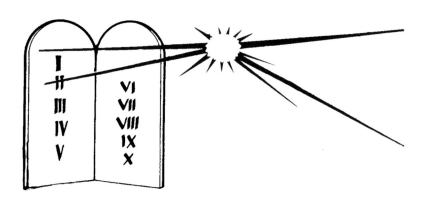

WE MUST offer to God alone the highest worship that He deserves.

We worship God:

by believing in God,
by hoping in God,
by loving God,
by adoring God,
by praying to God.

"Jesus, I love You!" Kathy and Brian always stop at the church to say a prayer.

5

THE SECOND COMMANDMENT

You shall not take the name of the Lord, your God, in vain.

Danny took Beth's doll, but he says, "Honest to God, I didn't take it!" He is not only taking God's name in vain, but also telling a lie.

THE second commandment tells us to love God's name.

We honor God's name when we make a promise in the name of God, when we say prayers to praise God.

WE SIN against the second commandment by profanity and cursing. Profanity means using God's name in words of anger. Cursing means to wish evil upon some person or thing, or to ask God to punish someone.

We also sin by making fun of God, the Saints or holy things.

Richard is making fun of Joan because she is reading her prayer book. Instead of getting angry, Joan says a prayer to herself, "Please help me, Jesus!"

THE THIRD COMMANDMENT

Remember to keep holy the Sabbath day.

THE third commandment tells us to go to Mass on Sunday (or Saturday evening). The Sacrifice of the Mass is the perfect act of worship, given to us by Jesus so that we may, with Jesus, offer the highest honor to God.

This family never misses Mass.

Steve is a farm boy. On Sunday afternoon he likes to take a walk in the fields and see the many beautiful things God has made.

WE MUST not do hard work on Sunday. It is a day of prayer and rest. Every Sunday say some extra prayers at home or read a book that will help you love God more.

THE FOURTH COMMANDMENT

Honor your father and your mother.

THE fourth commandment tells us to love and respect our parents, to obey them, and to help them when they are in need.

When you obey your parents, you obey God, because God wants your parents to take His place on earth.

As a boy, Jesus helped Saint Joseph with his work in the carpenter shop. He also helped His Mother at home.

Mary Ann is helping her mother with the wash, while Kevin is helping his father paint.

YOU obey your father and mother when you do at once what they tell you to do. You should try to help them in their work.

If you should disobey your parents, tell them that you are sorry, and will try hard to make them happy.

11

Your Parents Are Your Best Friends

REMEMBER that your mother and father also have the duty to teach you to love God and to serve Him. They cannot do this if you do not obey them when they tell you what is right and wrong. You disobey them when you will not do what they tell you to do, especially when they ask you to help them or say your prayers.

You will make them happy if you do things that will please them. God will bless you if you honor and love your parents for His sake. Jesus gave you an example when He obeyed and loved His Mother, the Blessed Virgin Mary, and His foster father, Saint Joseph.

BECAUSE your parents do so much for you to take care of you and to teach you, they are really your best friends. So love them and show them that you want to thank them for all the kind things they do for you. Let them see that you want to do the good things they tell you about, because they really want you to love God with all your heart.

Maria and Joseph listen to their Daddy talk about God.

THE FIFTH COMMANDMENT

You shall not kill.

THE fifth commandment tells us to do all that we can to take care of our own life and the life of our neighbor. Our life is not our own. It is a gift from God, and we must take care of our health. Most of all, we must take care of our soul by receiving the Sacraments often and by praying many times a day.

The fifth commandment tells us to take care of our body by eating nourishing food.

WE SIN against the fifth commandment when we do harm to others, when we show anger or hatred toward others and want to get even with them by causing them some injury. We also sin when we give a bad example by evil words or actions that may lead others into sin.

We sin also when we are lazy in doing our duty toward our parents, other people and even God, by not obeying our parents, by not helping others, or by not saying our prayers.

Billy is trying to make Jimmy fight, but Jimmy does not want to; he knows it is wrong.

15

THE SIXTH COMMANDMENT

You shall not commit adultery.

THE sixth commandment tells us to be pure in all we see and hear, say and do.

Pray to the Blessed Virgin Mary that she may help you to be pure and keep you from anything that is wrong.

Paul knows it is a sin to do anything impure. He confesses the sin as soon as he can.

NEVER speak impure words, or look at bad pictures, or touch yourself or anyone else in an impure way.

If you are pure and modest, God will be your Friend.

You can get help from God to keep your soul from sin if you go to Confession each month and receive Holy Communion at least once a week.

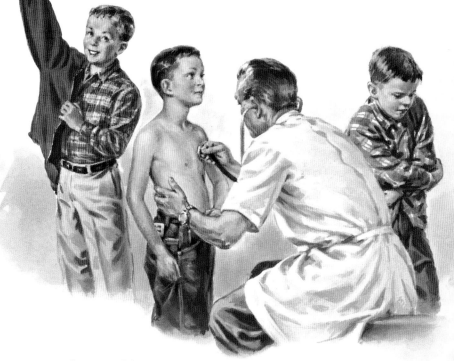

A good boy wants to keep his soul healthy and strong by being pure. Then he will really be a friend of Jesus and Mary.

SEVENTH COMMANDMENT

You shall not steal.

THE seventh commandment tells us to be fair, to give everyone what is his by right.

We must not steal or keep what belongs to others.

"Don't take that orange, Eddie! That's stealing!"

Jesus said that if God takes care of the birds and flowers, He will take care of us, too. We do not have to steal.

B E HONEST and fair in all things. It is wrong to cheat.

Do not damage the property of others, and do not keep what belongs to others.

You must return to the owner anything that has been stolen, or else pay for it.

The team that plays fair always wins in the eyes of God and people, even if it does not win the game.

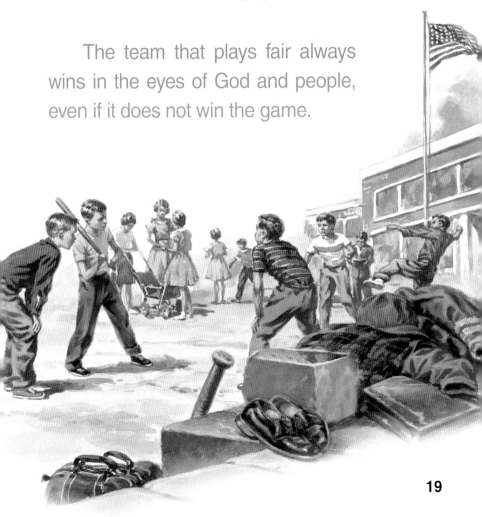

THE EIGHTH COMMANDMENT

You shall not bear false witness against your neighbor.

THE eighth commandment tells us not to hurt our neighbor's good name by lying about him or saying things that will make other people lose their respect for him.

Never harm others by saying unkind things about them. Never talk about their faults, because you have no right to judge people. Jesus said, "Judge not, and you will not be judged."

These children always pray for their neighbors. They do not talk about them.

THE eighth commandment also tells us not to tell a lie. You must be truthful even if you know you may be punished. You are really brave if you alway tell the truth.

When Johnny hit a car with a stone, he did not run away, but he said to the owner, "I threw the stone, sir, but I am very sorry."

THE NINTH COMMANDMENT

You shall not covet your neighbor's wife.

THE ninth commandment tells us never willingly to keep impure thoughts in our mind or to want to do anything that is impure with ourselves or with others.

Try to be pure in all that you think and want.

If your thoughts are pure, your actions will be pure.

When two people are married, they are allowed to think about and do certain things to show their love.

22

WHEN impure thoughts come to your mind, get busy and do something like work or play to keep yourself from thinking about them. Say a prayer to God and the Blessed Virgin Mary.

At Holy Communion, ask Jesus to help you to be pure in thought and word and deed.

Your mother and father love each other. They find great happiness in their home and family.

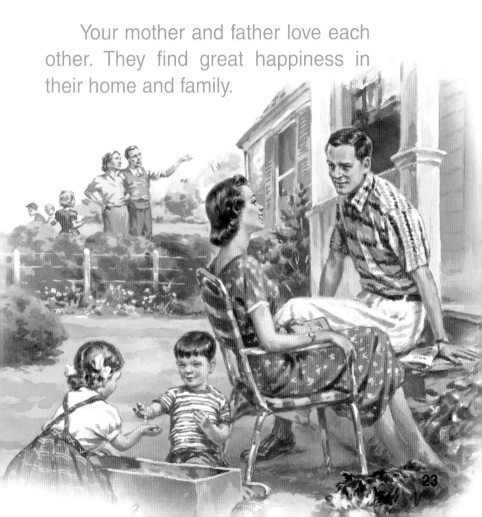

THE TENTH COMMANDMENT

You shall not covet anything that belongs to your neighbor.

THE tenth commandment tells us that we should not want anything that belongs to our neighbor. We are envious when we wish we had what other people have, instead of their having it.

Be satisfied with what you have, and do not want what does not belong to you.

Jesus said to the rich young man, "Sell what you have and give the money to the poor."

JESUS wants you to be kind to others, not selfish. Try to share your good things with others, even if they are not your friends. God will be good to you if you try to make other people happy by giving them what you can.

Michael got a new bicycle for Christmas and Bobby is sad because his friend is happy.

St. Peter's Basilica in Rome,
the center of the Catholic Church.

The
COMMANDMENTS of the CHURCH

JESUS Christ gave His Church power not only
to teach us what we must believe, but also to
command what we must do to save our souls.
Obedience to the Holy Spirit means that we
keep the commandments of God as well as the
laws of the Church.

Some of the duties expected of Catholics are:

1. To keep holy Sunday, the day of the Lord's Resurrection: to worship God by taking part in Mass every Sunday and Holy Day of Obligation; to avoid work that is not necessary.

2. To receive Holy Communion frequently and the Sacrament of Penance regularly.

3. To study Catholic teaching to prepare for the Sacrament of Confirmation, to be confirmed, and then to continue to study our holy Faith and help others to know about it.

4. To observe the marriage laws of the Church: to give religious training by example and word to one's children; to use parish schools and religious education programs.

5. To strengthen and support the Church: the parish and parish priests; the whole-wide Church and the Holy Father.

6. To do penance, including abstaining from meat and fasting from food on certain days.

7. To join in the missionary spirit and apostolate of the Church.

JESUS said, "God so loved the world that He gave His only Son, that whoever believes in Him may not die but may have eternal life. God did not send the Son into the world to condemn the world, but that the world might be saved through Him.

God has loved us by giving us His Son. We must love God in return by following His Son, obedient to His commandments, that we may reach heaven.

The Great Commandment of Love

GOD is love, and, in God's plan, that love reaches out to us in Jesus Christ, to unite us with God and with each other.

A lawyer once asked Jesus, "Teacher, which commandment of the law is the greatest?" Jesus said to him, "You shall love the Lord your God with your whole heart, with your whole soul, and with all your mind. This is the greatest and first commandment. The second is like it: You shall love your neighbor as yourself. On these two commandments the whole law is based."

The first three commandments of God tell us what we must do for God; the other seven tell us what we must do for our neighbor, and for ourselves.

The commandments of the Church tell us what is expected of a good Catholic. Jesus gave us His Church to teach us how we must live according to His teaching. He said to His Apostles, "He who hears you, hears Me."

By keeping the commandments of God and of the Church, we show our love for God and our neighbor.

Doing the Will of God

JESUS said, "None of those who cry out, 'Lord, Lord' will enter the kingdom of God but only the one who does the will of My Father in heaven." If we believe in God, we must do what God asks; we must keep His law.

Jesus also said, "Live on in My love. You will live in My love if you keep My commandments, even as I have kept My Father's commandments, and live in His love." If we really love Jesus, we will do what He commands us through the Catholic Church, which He founded. This is the way Jesus showed His own love for His Father—He was obedient in doing His will.

God made us to show His goodness and to make us happy with Him in heaven. He wants us to know and love and serve Him in this world.

We love and serve God by keeping His commandments and those of His Church, and also by our prayers and kind deeds.

This is a happy family because father, mother and children keep the commandments of God and of the Church.

A PRAYER TO JESUS

TEACH me, teach me, dearest Jesus,
In Your own sweet loving way,
All the lessons of *obedience*
I must practice day by day.

Teach me *meekness*, dearest Jesus,
Of Your Heart the gentlest art;
Not in words and actions only,
But the meekness of the heart.

Teach me generous *love*, dear Jesus,
To make use of every grace,
And to keep Your just commandments
Till I see You face to face.

Teach *obedience*, dearest Jesus,
Such as was Your daily bread
From the crib of Bethlehem
To the Cross on which You bled.

Teach *Your Heart* to me, dear Jesus,
Is my most important prayer;
For all grace and virtues
Are in richest beauty there.

Saint
ELIZABETH ANN SETON

By REV. LAWRENCE G. LOVASIK, S.V.D.
Divine Word Missionary

NIHIL OBSTAT: Daniel V. Flynn, J.C.D., *Censor Librorum*
IMPRIMATUR: ✠ Joseph T. O'Keefe, D.D., *Vicar General, Archdiocese of New York*

Birth of Elizabeth

ELIZABETH Ann Bayley was born in New York to Dr. Richard Bayley and his wife Catherine Charlton on August 28, 1774. She was baptized in the Protestant Episcopal Church.

Elizabeth remained a member of this Church until she reached the age of 30.

With the American Declaration of Independence on July 4, 1776, she became one of the first American citizens.

Elizabeth was only three years old when her mother died. One year later her little sister Kitty also died.

Elizabeth's Faith in God

ONE day Elizabeth and her little friend were looking out of a window. Turning toward the sky, Elizabeth said:

"Look, Emma, God lives there, in heaven. All good children will go to Him. Mommy and Kitty went to heaven. They are with God."

Elizabeth's Love for Her Father

ELIZABETH'S father was a Health Inspector of the Port of New York and a Professor of Anatomy at Columbia University.

Elizabeth lived alone with her father, whom she loved dearly. But she did not see him very much.

He was a doctor and he had to be in dangerous places on the war front.

The American colonies were trying to obtain their freedom from England and they needed the help of all their citizens.

Dr. Bayley did all he could to help his fellow Americans while the war continued. It lasted for seven years, but when it was over America was an independent country.

Elizabeth Imitates
Her Father's Kindness

ELIZABETH'S father was often called to help poor families when someone was sick.

He taught his little daughter to be kind to those who needed help.

Elizabeth's Love
for All God's Creatures

WHILE playing with some of her cousins at her uncle's home in New Rochelle, Elizabeth found a bird's nest.

Her cousins picked the little eggs and some of the chicks fell to the ground. Elizabeth took them into her hands. She cried and told her cousins not to touch the eggs.

She put the chicks on some leaves so that the mother could feed them.

When Elizabeth was four years old, her father married Charlotte Amelia Barclay. They later had seven children who were Elizabeth's step-brothers and sisters.

7

Elizabeth's Love for
Her Brothers

ELIZABETH was happy to have so many
brothers and sisters to play with. She
loved each of them.

Elizabeth Marries William Seton

ELIZABETH grew up to be a fine young woman. She was very beautiful and bright.

All who met her liked her and she made many friends.

Among her good friends was William Magee Seton who had just arrived from Europe where he was studying.

He fell in love with Elizabeth and married her in 1794. He was 26 years old, and she was 19.

A Happy Family

ELIZABETH and William wanted to have a family. They wanted to bring children into the world and make them children of God by Baptism.

In 1795, their first child was born and baptized as Anna Maria. Then four other children followed: William, Richard, Catherine, and Rebecca.

Elizabeth and William were kept busy in bringing up these active children. But they were very happy.

The Family Meets with Misfortune

WILLIAM was a handsome, wealthy businessman. He worked with his father who owned many ships.

When the French Revolution broke out in 1793, many American ships were seized or destroyed. His money in England was taken by the government.

After his father died, William was left with the business and the care of twelve brothers, besides his wife and his own children. The business failed.

Elizabeth Loses Her Husband

WILLIAM'S health was very poor. Doctors told him to take a trip to Italy, where the weather was mild. Elizabeth and her husband had to sell what they owned to pay for the trip.

They also had to leave behind four of their little children. Only Anna Maria, the oldest who was now eight years old, would go with them.

On October 2, 1803, they sailed for Livorno (Leghorn), Italy. After a month in the hospital of the Italian port, Elizabeth's husband died of tuberculosis.

The Filicchi brothers, Anthony and Philip, were friends of William during his student days. They welcomed the widow and the little child to their home and treated them as members of their own family.

Elizabeth Visits a Catholic Church

ELIZABETH wrote to her sister-in-law: "The Filicchi family is very kind to us. Truly, since we left our country, we have met with kindness and thoughtfulness.

"Anna Maria tells me: 'Mommy, how many good friends has God given us in this foreign land.' Their love means so much to me."

The Filicchi family took Elizabeth and her little daughter on a trip to Florence. For the first time in her life Elizabeth went to a Catholic church.

She wrote in a letter: "When I entered the church, I fell to my knees. I cried when I thought for how long I had been away from the house of the Lord.

"I prayed there a long time because I felt that God was really present there."

Elizabeth Learns about the Catholic Religion

ELIZABETH returned to Livorno with her friends. She saw the Catholic faith in action in the good example of her family friends.

They gave her books to study and they prayed for her.

Elizabeth Prays for the Catholic Faith

E LIZABETH herself prayed earnestly that God would give her the light to walk in the way that leads to Him.

She prayed: "O my God and Father. Your word is truth. I beg You to give me faith, hope, and love. This is what I need and what I want."

Elizabeth wrote to her sister-in-law: "My dear sister! How happy we would be if we could believe as these good people do.

"They have the faith in God in the Blessed Sacrament. They find Him in their churches. They see Him coming to them when they are sick.

"I cannot believe that there are any worries in this world if you believe the way Catholics believe."

Return to New York

IT was time to return to New York. Because of the danger on the trip, Mr. Filicchi accompanied them. They were very happy.

Anna Maria asked: "Mommy, are we going to go to a church like we did here when we are back in our own country?"

Elizabeth's Sadness on Leaving Her Friends

ND yet Elizabeth was sad to leave behind such good friends. She wrote:

"The closer a soul is to God, the more it grows in love for all creatures made by Him, and especially for those with whom we are so much in love."

Elizabeth Is Reunited
with Her Children

AFTER a voyage of fifty-six days, the ship arrived in New York on June 4. Elizabeth's four children were waiting for them at the pier, together with other members of her family.

Elizabeth wrote: "I have always had young children at home, loving them, waiting to help them, and make them happy.

"I pray that I may live long to be useful to my children. Whatever is the will of the Almighty, I hope I can do His will."

Elizabeth Becomes a Catholic

ELIZABETH was willing to make any sacrifice to do God's will. Five months of study with the kind and devout Filicchis had convinced Elizabeth of the truth of the Catholic Faith.

But the gift of faith and obedience to it came only after a long struggle. She was received into the Catholic Church in New York on March 14, 1805.

She cried out with joy: "Finally God is mine and I am His!"

Elizabeth wrote that the three things that led her to become a Catholic were: belief in the Real Presence of Jesus in the Blessed Sacrament, devotion to Mary the Mother of God, and conviction that the Catholic Church led back to the Apostles and to Christ.

Elizabeth Starts a School

MANY of her family and friends rejected Elizabeth because she became a Catholic. To support her children, she opened a school in Baltimore on the advice of Father Du Bourg, Rector of the Seminary of St. Mary at Baltimore.

God blessed her work. Soon the house was too small for the number of girls wishing to attend.

She was joined by other young women who wished to devote themselves to a holy life.

All the children loved Elizabeth

Elizabeth Becomes a Sister

IN 1809 Elizabeth took Religious vows, and as a Sister was allowed to raise her children. Several other women joined her, two of whom were sisters-in-law. They formed a Religious community.

In the summer they moved to Emmitsburg, Maryland, where they opened a private academy for the girls and a free school.

They were called the Sisters of Charity of St. Joseph. They followed the Rule of St. Vincent de Paul.

Doing the Will of God

ELIZABETH told her Sisters: "In our daily work we must do the will of God; do it in the way He wills it, and because He wills it."

Both the community and the school grew, even though the trials for Mother Seton were heavy.

Some of the Sisters died of tuberculosis. Her two daughters Anna Maria and Rebecca also died of the disease. Living conditions were poor. She accepted all with courage and hope.

Elizabeth's Trust in God

ONCE Mother Seton was asked about the greatest grace God had ever given her. She said: "The greatest grace was my having been led to the Catholic Church."

She also said: "Every morning at Mass I offer my work to God, whose blessed will can make me holy and make my work successful. I put myself in God's hands and tell my companions to do the same."

One of her prayers was as follows:

"I bow to You, my God,
in cheerful hope,
that confiding in Your infinite mercy,
assisted by Your powerful grace,
I shall soon arrive at that hour
of unspeakable joy.

But if it is Your will that the spirit
shall yet contend with its dust,
assist me so to conduct myself
through this life
as not to render it an enemy
but a conductor to that happy state."

Elizabeth's Trust in Jesus

ELIZABETH added:

"O my dearest Mother Mary!
How tight I hold her little picture
to show that I trust in her prayers.
How tenderly she loves our souls
bought by the Blood of her Son.

"I kneel before the crucifix
in silent prayer to Jesus.
He is our only hope."

Two Great Devotions

MOTHER Seton began the first American parochial school at Emmitsburg, an infirmary, an orphanage and school at Philadelphia, and an orphanage in New York City.

Mother Seton had two great devotions: doing the will of God and loving Jesus in the Blessed Sacrament and His Blessed Mother.

She said: "I never feel the presence of the Lord so much as when I have been ill. It is as if I were seeing the good Jesus and His holy Mother at my side to cheer me in all the hours of suffering."

She wrote: "God has given me a great deal to do, and I have always preferred, and hope always to prefer, His will to every wish of my own."

Elizabeth's Writings

IN the midst of her busy life, Elizabeth found time to write many letters, a Diary, and several other works, including translations of French books.

Elizabeth Becomes Ill

ONE day Elizabeth became ill. One of her pupils came to see her. Mother Seton said: "God bless you, my dear child. Remember my last lesson: Seek God in all things. Always ask yourself, 'Will God be pleased with what I am going to do?'

"If you do this, God will be with you, and will help you to keep the grace of your First Communion. You will never see me on earth again. We shall meet in heaven. Remember me in your prayers. God bless you."

Death and Sainthood

THE Sisters and all the children were very sad when they heard that Mother Seton was dying. Mother Seton said to her Sisters as they gathered at her bedside: "I am grateful, my Sisters, that you have come to me at this moment. Be children of the Church, looking to heaven! Be thankful to God!

"Soul of Christ, make me holy; Blood of Christ, wash me."

On January 4, 1821, at two o'clock in the morning, Elizabeth Ann Seton died at the age of 46. She was beatified by Pope John XXIII on March 17, 1963, the first American born citizen to become a saint. She was declared a saint by Pope Paul VI on September 14, 1975, and her feastday is January 4.

▬▬▬▬▬▬▬▬▬▬▬▬▬▬

Six North American religious orders trace their heritage to Mother Seton, the Sisters of Charity of St. Joseph in Maryland, the Sisters of Charity of St. Vincent de Paul of New York, the Sisters of Charity of Cincinnati, the Sisters of Charity of St. Vincent de Paul of Halifax, Nova Scotia, the Sisters of Charity of St. Elizabeth in New Jersey, and the Sisters of Charity of Seton Hill in Pennsylvania. Over 7500 Sisters in all.

Prayer in Honor of St. Elizabeth Ann

L ORD God, You blessed Elizabeth Ann Seton with gifts of grace as wife and mother, educator and foundress, so that she might spend her life in service to Your people.

Through her example and prayers may we learn to express our love for You in love for our fellow men and women. We ask this through Christ our Lord. Amen.

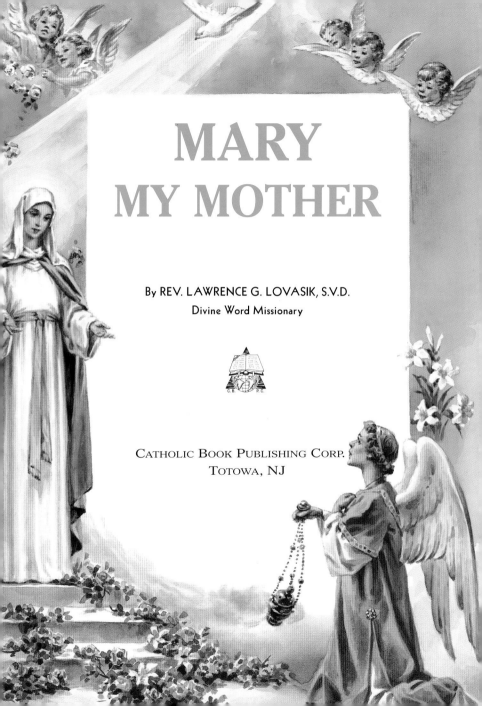

MARY
MY MOTHER

By REV. LAWRENCE G. LOVASIK, S.V.D.
Divine Word Missionary

CATHOLIC BOOK PUBLISHING CORP.
TOTOWA, NJ

MARY IS BORN

THE parents of the Blessed Virgin were Saint Joachim and Saint Anne. For a long time they were without children.

NIHIL OBSTAT: Daniel V. Flynn, J.C.D., *Censor Librorum*
IMPRIMATUR: ✠ James P. Mahoney, D.D., *Vicar General, Archdiocese of New York*
© 1978 by *Catholic Book Publishing Corp., NJ - Printed in Hong Kong*
978-0-89942-280-0

AT LAST God answered their prayers and granted them a daughter. They gave her the name Mary, which means Lady, or Star of the Sea.

Mary's soul was always in the grace and friendship of God. She is the Immaculate Conception because she never had original sin, the first sin committed by Adam and Eve, which all of us have when we come into this world.

Mary was chosen by God from all eternity to give us a Savior. The birthday brings to our minds the holiness of the Mother God has prepared from Himself.

MARY IS OFFERED
IN THE TEMPLE

WHEN Mary was three years old, her parents took her to the Temple in Jerusalem to offer her to God. They had made a promise before her birth to do so. Some say that Mary lived in the Temple from the age of three to the age of twelve, working as a servant girl.

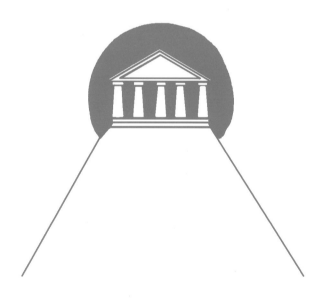

MARY gave her whole life to God. The Heavenly Father looked upon her as His beloved daughter. The Son of God loved her as the one chosen to become His Mother. The Holy Spirit made her beautiful with His grace as His holy Bride.

MARY WITH HER MOTHER

SAINT Anne was a good mother of her little daughter and taught her to pray and to read holy books. From Saint Anne, Mary heard the story of the chosen people and of the Messiah Who was to save the whole world. She did not think that God would choose her to be the Mother of His Son.

Mary was always kind, humble, and obedient to her parents. Everyone loved her.

6

MARY AND JOSEPH ARE MARRIED

WHEN Mary was about sixteen years old, she she was married to a young carpenter named Joseph.

God wanted His Son to be born of a pure and holy virgin. He wanted Saint Joseph to be the foster father of Jesus and the head of the holy Family.

THE ANGEL SPEAKS TO MARY

GOD sent the Angel Gabriel to Mary at Nazareth. He said, "Hail, full of grace! The Lord is with you. Blessed are you among women. Do not fear, Mary. You are to be a mother, and to bear a Son, and to call Him Jesus. He will be the Son of God, and King over all His people.

"How will that be?" Mary asked.

The Angel answered, "The Holy Spirit will come upon you and by His power the Child to be born of you will be the Son of God."

Mary said, "See, I am the servant-girl of the Lord. May all that you have said be done in me!"

At that moment the Son of God became man under her heart.

MARY VISITS ELIZABETH

THE angel also told Mary that her cousin Elizabeth was to have a child in her old age. Mary went at once to help her. The Holy Spirit let Elizabeth know that Mary was to be Mother of God, so Elizabeth greeted her, "Blessed are you among women, and blessed is the fruit of your womb."

Mary said, "My soul praises the Lord. All people shall call me blessed, for God has done great things for me."

10

JESUS IS BORN IN A STABLE

THE Emperor ordered all people to write their names on a list in the town where they were born. Mary and Joseph were of a family of David, so they went from Nazareth to the city of David, called Bethlehem.

Since there were many people in Bethlehem, there was no room for Mary and Joseph in the place where travelers stayed. They had to spend the night in a stable which was used for cattle. That night, Jesus was born. Mary wrapped Him in soft clothes and laid Him in a manger. With great joy Mary and Joseph adored this beautiful Child. He was the Son of God Who had come to save the world from sin. God gave us His Son on the first Christmas Day.

Some shepherds came to see the Child. They told Mary that an angel had appeared and told them to go to Bethlehem. They also heard many angels singing, "Glory to God in the highest heavens, and on earth peace to men of good will." They knelt down to adore the Infant Jesus.

MARY OFFERS JESUS IN THE TEMPLE

FORTY days after the birth of Jesus, Mary and Joseph took Him to the Temple in Jerusalem to offer Him to God. There they met a holy old man named Simeon, who took the Child into his arms and prayed, "You may take me out of this world, O Lord, because I have seen Him Who is our salvation and our light."

Then he said to Mary, "Because of this Child a sword of sorrow will pierce your heart." Mary remembered that her Son would one day die to save the world. She now offered Him to God as the Savior of us all.

Mary and Joseph offered a pair of young pigeons as a sacrifice to God.

13

THE MAGI VISIT JESUS AND MARY

SOME time later Mary saw three men, dressed in strange and rich clothing like kings, bow down before her Child to adore Him as King of the Jews. These Magi came from faraway lands, guided by a star that led them to Bethlehem. The star was a sign to them that a king was born to rule the world. They offered Jesus gifts of gold, incense, and spices, and then returned to their own country.

THE HOLY FAMILY
FLEES INTO EGYPT

A N ANGEL appeared to Joseph in his sleep and said, "Arise, take the Child and His Mother; flee into Egypt, and remain there until I shall tell you, for Herod wants to kill the Child." So Joseph took the Child and His Mother and left that very night for Egypt.

Herod killed all the boys in Bethlehem who were two years old or less. After Herod died, the angel told Joseph to return to Nazareth.

THE HOLY FAMILY AT NAZARETH

IN THEIR little home at Nazareth Mary's happiest moments were spent with her little Boy Whom she knew to be the Son of God. She loved and adored Him.

When Jesus was older, He helped His foster father in the workshop, where Mary often visited Him. The Holy Family worked and prayed and shared their joys together.

MARY FINDS JESUS
IN THE TEMPLE

WHEN Jesus was twelve, He went to the Temple with Mary and Joseph. After the feast, His parents left, but Jesus remained behind.

Three days later, they found Jesus in the Temple with the teachers of the law. Mary asked, "Son, why have You done this to us?" Jesus replied, "Did you not know that I had to be in My Father's house?"

Jesus returned to Nazareth and obeyed them.

17

MARY AT THE MARRIAGE FEAST

WHEN Jesus was thirty years old He began the work for which He was sent. He preached, healed the sick and worked miracles.

At a wedding feast in Cana Jesus changed water into wine when His Mother told Him there was no more wine. By His first miracle He showed us that He will not refuse His Mother's wishes.

MARY MEETS JESUS

AFTER three years of preaching and healing, Jesus was captured by the Jews and condemned to death, beaten and crowned with thorns.

Mary followed with John and some of the women as Jesus carried His Cross.

At one place Jesus and Mary met. She suffered very much because she loved Jesus and us.

MARY SEES JESUS
DIE ON THE CROSS

ON CALVARY Mary saw Jesus nailed to the Cross and raised between two thieves. She heard His words from the Cross, "Father, forgive them, for they do not know what they are doing," and His words to the good thief, "This day you shall be with Me in paradise."

As Mary stood beneath the Cross, she heard Jesus speak to her, "Woman, there is your son." Then He said to the disciple John, "There is your Mother." By these words Jesus gave Mary to the care of His best loved disciple, and we became children of Mary.

Mary heard the last words of Jesus: "My God, why have You forsaken me? It is finished! Father, into Your hands I give My soul." She saw Jesus bow His head and die. She watched the soldiers pierce the side of Jesus with a spear.

JESUS LIES IN MARY'S ARMS

THE friends of Jesus took Him down from the Cross and laid Him in the waiting arms of His sorrowful Mother. Our sins have made her suffer very much.

Then the body of Jesus was placed in a tomb near Calvary. When Mary left the tomb, the men rolled a stone before the opening. All left with sad hearts.

JESUS APPEARS TO HIS MOTHER MARY

AT DAWN on Easter Sunday Jesus rose by His divine power. He surely appeared to His Mother first. He had received from her the body that was now so glorious. Since she shared in all His sufferings, it was right that she should share in the joy and glory of His victory.

The Risen Jesus prepared His Mother for her part as Mother of the Church which He founded.

MARY
SEES JESUS
RISE
TO HEAVEN

JESUS also appeared to the holy women, and to the Apostles and disciples.

24

The Resurrection was the greatest sign that He was God and that the Church He began was the one true Church.

Mary saw Jesus for the last time when He appeared to His disciples on the Mount of Olives, forty days after He rose from the dead. After commanding them to go to teach all nations, He blessed His Mother and the disciples in farewell. He rose into the clouds to return to His Father in heaven. How Mary longed to go with Him! She teaches us to love Jesus with all our heart in joy and in pain.

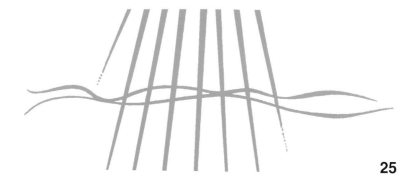

THE HOLY SPIRIT

COMES DOWN UPON

MARY AND THE APOSTLES

MARY returned with the disciples to Jerusalem to pray and await the coming of the Holy Spirit, Whom Jesus had promised.

On the tenth day, the feast of Pentecost, there came a sound from heaven like a great wind. Tongues of fire rested upon each of them, and they were filled with the Holy Spirit as they prayed.

The Holy Spirit came down upon the Blessed Virgin as He had at the Annunciation when He made her the Mother of God. Now He made her the mother of all of us on this birthday of the Church.

MARY IS TAKEN TO HEAVEN

MARY'S last years on earth were spent close to the Blessed Sacrament. Saint John said Mass each day in his own home, where Mary lived, and gave her Jesus in Holy Communion.

As Mary's love for Jesus grew greater, so also her desire to be with Jesus grew strong. One day Jesus came for His Mother. After she died, the Apostles took her body to a new tomb near the Garden of Olives. By the Assumption we believe that the Blessed Virgin Mary was taken up into heaven, body and soul. This was her reward for her love of God and all of us, and for her prayers and sufferings.

At the Annunciation Mary received Jesus on earth; at the Assumption Jesus received her in heaven.

JESUS CROWNS MARY QUEEN OF HEAVEN

JESUS led His Mother to a throne of glory in heaven, next to His own. As she felt pain and sorrow with Him on earth, she now feels joy with Him in heaven forever. As Jesus put a most beautiful crown upon her head, all the angels and saints praised her as their Queen. She bowed to the Most Blessed Trinity and again could say her prayer of praise: "My soul praises the Lord. All people shall call me blessed, for God has done great things for me."

The Blessed Virgin Mary now shares in the glory of her Son because she had a part in the great work of saving our souls. She is Queen of all of us. She obtains all graces for us through her prayers. As her children we should pray to her in all our needs.

MARY OUR MOTHER

MARY is our true Mother. Jesus gave her to us from the Cross when He said, "There is your Mother." In heaven she obtains many graces and blessings for us.

Mary loves us very much. We should love her as Jesus did and pray to her every day. Mary will keep us from sin and lead us to her loving Son and our Savior.

OUR LADY OF LOURDES
and
MARIE BERNADETTE SOUBIROUS
(1844-1879)

By Rev. Lawrence G. Lovasik, S.V.D.
Divine Word Missionary

NIHIL OBSTAT: Daniel V. Flynn, J.C.D., *Censor Librorum*

IMPRIMATUR: ✝ Joseph T. O'Keefe, D.D., *Vicar General, Archdiocese of New York*

Bernadette's parents were poor.

Bernadette's Home

BERNADETTE Soubirous was born on January 7, 1844, near Lourdes, in France. Her parents were very poor. Her father was a miller. He lost the mill and had to do odd jobs around town while his wife worked in the fields.

By this time Bernadette was five years old, and already looked after the house and cared for her younger brothers and sisters.

The family was forced to move to a rent-free single room of a very old building which once had been a town jail. It was here that Bernadette got asthma in the damp cell in Lourdes, so she was often sent to stay with friends, the Aravants, in the town of Bartres. There she helped with the housework and tended the sheep in the pasture. In return she received her board and lodging. In the evenings Madame Aravant taught her the catechism, the only education she ever received.

At the age of thirteen Bernadette was home again and being prepared for her First Holy Communion.

Bernadette Sees a Lady in the Grotto

BERNADETTE was a good-natured little girl, small for her age. She had big dark eyes and rather stubborn round face. She was very devout.

On Thursday, February 11, 1858, when Bernadette was fourteen, she dressed warmly, for it was a bitterly cold day, and went collecting wood with her small sister and playmate. The two smaller girls ran on ahead, leaving Bernadette behind trying to make up her mind whether or not to wade across the Gave River.

While she was taking off her shoes and stockings, she heard a sound of wind like a storm. She looked all around, but everything was still. There was no movement in the trees. She heard the wind again and looked toward the cave. Then she noticed that a wild rose which was growing below the cave was shaking. The cave was filled with golden light.

Bernadette went to collect wood with two companions.

Lifting up her eyes, she saw in the opening of the grotto nearby a lady of great beauty, dressed in a pure white robe with a blue sash, a veil over her head, a rosary clasped in her hands, and yellow roses at her feet. The lady smiled at Bernadette, and asked her to say her rosary.

Mary's purpose in appearing to Bernadette was to warn the child to pray and make sacrifices for sinners. The many miracles of body and soul performed at Lourdes are the proof that this message was a true warning from the Queen of heaven to her children and that she is deeply interested in their welfare.

As a nun, Bernadette wrote a letter describing her experience. "I had gone down one day with two other girls to the bank of the river Gave when suddenly I heard a kind of rustling sound. I turned my head toward the field by the side of the river but the tree seemed quite still and the noise was not from there. Then I looked up and saw a cave where I saw a lady wearing a lovely white dress with a bright blue belt. On top of each of her feet was a pale yellow rose, the same color as her rosary beads.

Bernadette saw a very beautiful lady.

This is the way Bernadette described her vision:

"I RUBBED my eyes, thinking I was seeing things, and I put my hand into the fold of my dress where my rosary was. I wanted to make the sign of the cross but I could not, and my hand just fell down.

"The lady made the sign of the cross herself and then I was able to do the same, though my hands were trembling. Then I began to say the rosary while the lady let her beads slip through her fingers, without moving her lips. When I stopped saying the Hail Mary, she vanished.

"I asked my two companions if they had noticed anything, but they said no. I told them that I had seen a lady wearing a nice white dress, though I didn't know who she was. I told them not to say anything about it. They said I was silly to have anything to do with it. I told them they were wrong. I came back next Sunday, feeling myself drawn to the place."

Bernadette was fourteen when she saw the lady.　**9**

"THE third time I went the lady spoke to me and asked me to come every day for fifteen days. I said I would. Then she said that she wanted me to tell the priests to build a chapel there. She also told me to drink from the stream. I went to the Gave, the only stream I could see. She pointed to a little trickle of water nearby. When I got to it I could find only a few drops of water. I began to scrape and was able to get a little water. Three times I threw it away, and the fourth time I was able to drink some. Then the lady vanished and I went back home.

"I went back each day for fifteen days and each time, except one Monday and one Friday, the lady appeared and told me to look for a stream and wash in it and to see that the priests build a chapel there."

The lady told Bernadette to wash in the stream. 11

12   The lady said, "I am the Immaculate Conception."

"I must also pray, she said, for the conversion of sinners. I asked her many times what she meant by that, but she only smiled."

On March 25, the Lady answered Bernadette's question as to who she was with the words, "I am the Immaculate Conception." This was said in the Lourdes dialect in which both Bernadette and her Vision spoke.

Bernadette continues:

"Finally, with outstretched arms and eyes looking up to heaven she told me she was the Immaculate Conception.

"During the fifteen days she told me three secrets but I was not to speak about them to anyone, and so far I have not."

Bernadette went back to the grotto every day for two weeks having been told to do so by her Vision, and she talked with the Lady whom she saw there. Thereafter she saw her Vision only a few more times, and after July never again.

Bernadette speaks with her pastor.

Bernadette Tells the Lady's Name

BERNADETTE at once hurried to the pastor's rectory and burst in on the surprised priest Abbé Peyramale. She said, "I am the Immaculate Conception!"

"What? What's that?"

"Monsieur le Curé, the Lady at Massabielle said, 'I am the Immaculate Conception.' "

"What are you talking about? No one can have a name like that. You are making it up. Do you know the meaning of those words?"

Bernadette shook her head.

"Then why say something you don't understand?"

"But I'm only telling you what the Lady told me . . . and I've said the words over and over again so that I would be sure to get them right."

As soon as the priest heard these words, he said to Bernadette, "My child, go home now. I will speak to you another time."

As soon as the door closed behind the girl, the Abbé fell to his knees, and with hands that shook, covered his face.

Crowds of People Go to the Grotto

BERNADETTE'S daily visits to the grotto during that February caused a great stir in the district. Day after day crowds of people from the surrounding countryside followed her to the grotto to watch as she was drawn into long ecstasies. They watched her strange movements as she obediently did the things the lady told her to do, known to her alone. They watched as she scraped away some soil from beside the grotto until a spring of water was trickling out, a spring which provided 27,000 gallons of pure fresh water a day, as it still does. This is the Lourdes water which, just occasionally, brings about miraculous cures.

Bernadette was questioned over and over by her crowd of curious followers as to just what she saw, what the Lady was like, what she said. Soon the police started questioning her, and all the civil authorities.

Little Bernadette kept to her first description, no matter how they tried to catch her in a lie to prove that the vision was only in her imagination.

Crowds of people followed Bernadette to the grotto. **17**

Bernadette at School

BERNADETTE was so pestered with questions that her family thought it better for her to leave home and go to the Sisters of Nevers, who had a school and a hospital in Lourdes. During her five years there she learned to read and write, and she grew a little, and she could answer the questions of the people whose questions had to be answered.

Bernadette was called to answer questions before the episcopal commission on December 7, 1860. Bishop Laurence who was in charge said, "Bernadette, tell us just once more what happened when you asked the Lady her name."

The face of the now sixteen-and-a-half year old girl changed. Extending her arms, she crossed them over her chest, lifted her eyes toward the ceiling and breathed: "She said, 'I am the Immaculate Conception.'"

As Bishop Laurence lookd at Bernadette's radiant face, tears rolled down his cheeks. He afterwards said to the other priests, "Did you see that child? Did you see her face?"

The Sisters of Nevers teach Bernadette.

20   **Bernadette becomes a novice.**

Bernadette Enters the Convent

SIX years later, so as to get away from the public eye, Bernadette became a nun of the Order of the Sisters of Charity of Nevers and moved to their convent in that city. She left Lourdes and the Pyrenees forever. Now she began to live a hidden life.

Three years later the Bishop put the novice's veil on Bernadette and gave her the name she would be known by in religion, Sister Marie-Bernard.

After this ceremony Bernadette was assigned to help out in the infirmary and in the sacristy. At the same time she followed the exercises of the novitiate with fervor. She had some free time; this she spent in prayer and reading.

She was humble enough to talk about her faults. She said, "I have a sharp tongue and a quick temper, and, of course, I want to give orders. Perhaps because I had charge of my little brothers at home. I have been stubborn all my life. Even at the Grotto I had to be told three times by Our Lady to drink the water."

22   Bernadette in the convent infirmary.

Bernadette Becomes Ill

THE Reverend Mother and the Mistress of Novices were often harsh with her because they tried to humble her. Some asked her whether she did not feel proud, but she answered, "But I was just used. The Virgin used me as a broom to remove dust. When the work is done the broom is put behind the door again."

Bernadette had always been delicate and had had the Anointing of the Sick three times. But in the last year of her life, when only thirty five years old, she developed a swelling and endured great suffering. Unable to sleep at night, gasping for breath, sick and full of pain, she prayed, "O Jesus, when I see Your cross, I forget my own." And by day, longing to be up and at work, she learned to say, "I am at my work." If she was asked, "What is it?" she would answer, "Being sick."

Bernadette said, "When one is a bride of Jesus Christ, in any physical or mental pain one must say only 'yes, my God,' without any 'ifs' or 'buts.' "

The Death of Bernadette

ON December 8, the feast of the Immaculate Conception, Bernadette went to the chapel for the last time; three days later she became bed-ridden. Asthma, tuberculosis, severe bleeding, and the tumor on the knee, all caused her great pain.

Bernadette said to the sister who was nursing her, "Do not pay any attention to my suffering. I suffer, but I am glad to suffer. I'm prepared to put up with anything for Jesus, anything to help save sinners."

On March 20 she was anointed. Afterwards she said to the Mother General: "Please Mother, please forgive me. Ever since I have been here I have caused trouble. Will you tell my companions that I am asking their forgiveness for the bad example that I have set them?"

Three sisters knelt at her side and prayed the "Hail Mary." At the words, "Holy Mary," Bernadette joined in. "Mother of God . . . pray for me . . . poor sinner . . . poor, poor sinner."

Then she breathed her last breath.

Bernadette dies saying, "Holy Mary, Mother of God." 25

The Incorrupt Body of Bernadette

BERNADETTE died, worn out with suffering, on April 16, 1879 at the age of thirty-six.

So deep was the memory of the beauty of Our Lady, that Bernadette, many years later in her sick bed at the convent, could still say, "When you have seen her once, you just long to die so that you can see her again."

Bernadette's longing had now come true. She could see again the beauty of the Immaculate Virgin Mary whom she loved so much on earth.

So many people filed past her body, as it lay in state in the convent chapel at Nevers, that funeral arrangements had to be delayed. Mother General insisted that Sister Marie-Bernard should be buried, not in the town cemetery, but in the chapel of St. Joseph which stood in the garden. It was beneath this chapel that a tomb was built for her.

Bernadette's incorrupt body in the convent chapel.   27

Bernadette Is Declared a Saint

ON August 20, 1908, an ecclesiastical court was set up to study the case for her beatification. One of the first tasks of the court was to exhume Bernadette's body. After being buried for over thirty years, it was found to be incorrupt.

Her head inclined slightly to the left. Her arms crossed over her chest, still clasped her crucifix and rosary. Both were tarnished and full of rust.

The flesh was white and intact, and her parted lips were smiling.

On May 13, 1913, Pope Pius X signed the decree introducing the cause of Bernadette's beatification. She was beatified on June 14th, 1925. Eight years later, on the feast of the Immaculate Conception, December 8, 1933 she was canonized by Pope Pius XI.

During the process of the canonization Pope Pius XI wrote: "We are pleased to say, for the greater glory of God, this life can be summed

up in three words. Bernadette was *faithful* to her mission, she was *humble* in glory, and she was *valiant* in her sufferings."

Now her incorrupt body can be seen as she lies in death in the side chapel of the mother-house of the Sisters of Charity at Nevers, where she lived and died as Sister Marie-Bernard.

Lourdes Today

LOURDES today remains one of the most frequented of Christian shrines. More than three million visitors, pilgrims and tourists, come each year to the Grotto of Massabielle, where the Virgin Mary appeared to Bernadette eighteen times in 1858. Many visitors devote a whole day or several days to their pilgrimage. They meet thousands of men, women, children, sick people, young and old from all nations and races, who help them in their search for God, and to bring their lives more in keeping with the message of poverty, prayer, penance, purity and dedication preached by Bernadette in her life.

Lourdes has three basilicas: the Basilica of the Immaculate Conception built over the grotto with its crypt, the Basilica of the Holy Rosary with its fifteen chapels and mosaics of the fifteen mysteries of the Rosary, and the Basilica of Pope St. Pius X built underground for large gatherings. Ten acres of buildings and religious monuments, hospital, museum and conference rooms are maintained by 150 people.

**The Basilica of the Immaculate Conception
and the Holy Rosary.**

Prayer of the Church

GOD, protector and lover of the humble,
  You bestowed upon Your servant,
  Bernadette,
the favor of beholding the Immaculate Virgin
  Mary
and of talking with her.
Grant that we may deserve
to behold You in heaven.

St. Francis of Paola

REV. JUDE WINKLER, OFM Conv.

Imprimi Potest: Michael Kolodziej, OFM Conv., Minister Provincial of St. Anthony of Padua Province (USA)
Nihil Obstat: Rev. Msgr. James M. Cafone, M.A., S.T.D., Censor Librorum
Imprimatur: ✠ Most Rev. John J. Myers, J.C.D., D.D., Archbishop of Newark

The Nihil Obstat and Imprimatur are official declarations that a book or pamphlet is free of doctrinal or moral error. No implication is contained therein that those who have granted the Nihil Obstat and Imprimatur agree with the contents, opinions or statements expressed.

2

Francis Is Born

WHEN one hears the name St. Francis, most people think of St. Francis of Assisi, but he was not the only St. Francis to come from Italy. There was another St. Francis, this one from the town of Paola in southern Italy, who sought humility above all things. He and his followers are called the Minims, a name taken from the Latin which means "the least." They wanted to be the least of the least, and yet he and his order had a great influence upon the Church and the world.

St. Francis of Paola was born in the part of Italy called Calabria in 1416. His father was named James and his mother Vienna. They were poor farmers who were not well educated, but they were wise in the ways of the Lord.

Their faith is especially seen in their devotion to St. Francis of Assisi. They had been married for many years and still they did not have any children. So they turned to their favorite Saint, Francis of Assisi. It was not long afterward, on March 27, 1416, that Vienna and James had their first child. They named their baby Francis in honor of St. Francis of Assisi, the Saint through whom they had received their great desire.

FRANCIS'S family was poor, as was almost everyone in that part of Italy. Because of this, they could not afford to give their son much education. He did live with the Franciscan friars for a year during which he learned to read.

And yet Francis's family taught him what was most important in life. They taught him to place God above everything else. For the rest of his life, he spent countless hours in front of the Cross, meditating on how much God loves us. He had a great devotion to the Sacrament of the Eucharist as well, never missing an opportunity to attend Mass. He also had a devotion to the Blessed Virgin Mary, praying the Rosary as he meditated on the Mysteries of our Faith.

Francis's family also took him on a number of pilgrimages to shrines throughout Italy. They took him to Rome and Assisi and a number of other places where his spiritual growth continued.

When he was only fifteen years old, Francis asked his parents for permission to live as a hermit. A hermit is someone who lives alone and spends many hours during the day and night praying.

The Beginning of an Order

ONE would not think that this type of lifestyle would draw many followers, but when he was nineteen years old two other young men joined Francis. At first they lived in a cave, but the local people were very impressed with their holy way of life, so they built them three small huts and a chapel. A parish priest would come to celebrate the Mass for these holy men each day.

Most religious orders, like the Franciscans or Dominicans, take three vows, promises to God to live the Gospel without property, in chastity, and in obedience. Francis added a fourth vow to these three. He promised to live a life of fasting. In those days, the fast during Lent was very serious. People would not eat meat, cheese, or eggs all through Lent. Francis and his followers promised to observe that fast all year long.

Francis did not make this promise because he hated the world. He did it because he wanted to devote himself entirely to the Lord. People sometimes misuse food, eating too much or too little or the wrong thing. They worry about what they are to eat or drink or wear. Francis remembered Jesus' instruction to be like the lilies of the field, trusting in God for everything.

The Founding of the Minims

THE number of those who wanted to live like Francis and his first two companions continued to grow. By 1452 there were enough of them to seek approval from the local Archbishop to become a religious order. He gave them his blessing. They were called "the Hermits of St. Francis of Assisi," but later on they changed their name to "the Order of Minims," the least brothers, meaning that they wanted to be the least important of all people.

Francis and his companions also built a new monastery for themselves as well as a new church for the many people who were beginning to visit them. The people of that region held them in such high esteem that they all helped them in their building project. It was most inspiring to see the rich working alongside the poor peasants as they built a house for God and His servants.

As the years went on, more and more people came to visit Francis and his followers. So many came, in fact, that the Holy Father, Pope Paul II, sent someone to check out this new group to make sure that they were faithful to the teachings of the Church. He found Francis laying stones for their new church building.

9

10

THE representative of Pope Paul II was so impressed with Francis that he reached out to kiss his hands. Francis pulled his hand back and said that it was he who should kiss his hands for he had celebrated Mass as a priest of God for thirty years. (In many countries people kiss priests' hands as a sign of respect.) This made it even clearer to the representative that Francis was a man of God, for no one had ever told Francis that he had been a priest for thirty years.

As much as he was impressed by Francis, he was not too sure about his way of life. He thought that eating no meat, cheese, or eggs all year long might make Francis and his followers sick.

At this point, Francis reached out into the fire and pulled out a handful of red hot coals. He held them in his hands for quite some time, and when he put them down and held up his hands to show the Pope's representative, there was absolutely nothing wrong with them. This convinced him that God was behind what Francis and his followers were doing.

In 1474 the Holy See officially approved of this new order.

Other Miracles

WHEN someone is as close to God as Francis tried to be, he often receives the power to perform miracles.

Once, while they were building the church near his monastery, the workers began to complain because of the long distance they had to travel to get water when they were thirsty. Francis struck a rock with a stick and water immediately began to flow out of it. This spring still produces water today.

Another time when he was traveling, his donkey needed to have new shoes. These shoes are nailed into the hoof of the animal to hold them in place (it doesn't hurt the animal). After the blacksmith finished putting the shoes in place, he asked to be paid for his work. Francis explained to the blacksmith that he didn't have any money. When Francis told the donkey to give back the shoes on its hoofs, the donkey stepped right out of them.

One of the most famous miracles is when he crossed the Straits of Messina from Italy to Sicily. He had no money to pay the boatman, so he took his mantle, laid it on the water, and floated across the Straits as if he were on the safest of boats.

FRANCIS also showed his openness to the Holy Spirit when he was able to tell the future on a number of different occasions.

In 1480, he was able to foretell that the Turks who were Muslims were going to capture the city of Otranto in Italy. He also predicted that the king of Naples would soon capture the city back, and this is just what happened.

Another time he was speaking with the Holy Father. Up to this time, the Holy See had not yet approved for the Minims to fast all year long. The Holy Father told Francis that he was still not ready to do so. Francis told him that it was all right, and pointing to one of the Cardinals said that he would do so when he became Pope. That Cardinal became Pope Julius II, and he gave official approval for the year-long fast of the Minims.

During that same visit, a powerful man named Lorenzo de Medici told his seven-year-old son to "kiss the Saint's hands." Francis predicted, "I will become a Saint when he becomes the Pope." This young boy grew up and became Pope Leo X, the Pope who canonized Francis as a Saint in 1519.

An Invitation for the King of France

AROUND this time, King Louis XI fell ill. He was not a very nice man. He even had a nickname, "the spider king," because people thought he was sneaky and as dangerous as a spider.

The king heard about the holy man Francis through some merchants who had come from Naples (a city not far from where Francis lived). Louis was afraid to die and desperate to be cured. So he sent an invitation to Francis to travel to France to cure him. He promised Francis all sorts of rewards if he would do this, but Francis just ignored the invitation. He was not going to seek the very riches that he had rejected all of his life.

Louis had great influence over Ferdinand, the king of Naples. He had Ferdinand repeat the invitation, but Francis once again just ignored it.

Finally, Louis went to the Holy Father, Pope Sixtus IV. The king of France and the Pope were not really all that friendly, but the Pope realized that if he could get Francis to go to France, then Louis would owe him a favor. So Pope Sixtus IV ordered Francis to travel to France so that he could heal the king, and Francis obeyed.

18

A Triumphant Journey

WHEN Francis left his monastery in Paola, he bid farewell to his brothers. He knew in his heart that he would never return to his homeland.

The first part of the trip was made on foot and by donkey. Whenever he passed through a village, the people would gather around him, begging him for his blessing.

When he reached Naples, he received a magnificent welcome. The king of Naples and crowds of people treated this humble man as if he were a great king.

Then, when he reached Rome, he was invited to meet with the Pope and the Cardinals. The Holy Father was so impressed with Francis that he offered to ordain him as a priest, but Francis turned down this honor for he wanted to remain a simple hermit.

When Francis finally reached France, the welcome was even more incredible. The king rewarded the first man who brought him news of Francis's arrival with a gift of ten thousand pieces of gold. He sent his son to accompany him to the palace. When he arrived there, the king bowed down to him and kissed his hands.

Will the King Be Healed?

FRANCIS had been invited to France to heal the king. He proved that he could heal people all along the way, for he entered cities that were suffering the plague and healed those who were ill with a blessing. Would he heal the king?

The king visited the holy man almost every day, and he often asked him to heal him, but he didn't get an answer. Rather, Francis kept advising him how to be a better Christian and ruler. Finally, the king's patience wore out, and he openly asked Francis whether he would heal him or not.

Francis's answer surprised the king. Rather than receiving the answer that the holy man would heal him, the king heard that his life was drawing to a close and he should get his soul in order.

One would have expected the king to be angry and possibly send Francis back to Italy, but the king knew that this was truly a holy man. Everyone had seen how he spent long hours in prayer and ate only the simplest of foods. Even though Francis and his companions were dwelling in a palace, they were really living as simply as they had in their monastery. And so the king followed Francis's advice and prepared his soul to meet the Lord.

AFTER the king died, there was no lessening of Francis's importance. Because the new king was too young to rule on his own, his sister Princess Anne acted as his regent. (Regents are people who rule in the place of kings or queens when they are too young or ill to rule themselves.) She asked Francis to pray that she might have a child, and sometime later she gave birth to a daughter.

He also advised Charles, the new king, to marry a princess of Brittany. The two royal families of these lands had been fighting for a long time, and this marriage brought peace to their regions. Earlier he had brought peace to France and Spain when he advised King Louis XI of France to return some disputed territory to Spain.

Here was a simple, humble hermit, an uneducated man, who was giving advice to the royal families of Europe. He might have been uneducated according to the standards of the world, but he was wise according to the judgment of God.

Even people from the great University of Paris recognized his talents and sought his advice. This was also true of many members of religious orders.

All Things to All People

FRANCIS'S wisdom was especially seen in the way that he treated people. He did not treat them all the same way but in the way that he thought would be most useful for them to come to God. With some of them he was gentle and understanding, with others he was harsh as he condemned their evil deeds.

We see an example of him being gentle when he crossed the Straits of Messina on his cloak. At first he had asked a boatsman to carry him across, but the man had refused to do so unless he were paid. When the boatsman saw the miracle of his crossing on his cloak, he begged for forgiveness from Francis. The holy man readily forgave him.

It was also said that when he would return from a trip and he was told that one of his brothers had not been living up to his vows the way that he was supposed to, Francis was always ready to forgive him.

But he could also be quite harsh with people who deserved it. He disliked people who would tell lies to hurt others. He even condemned the rich and powerful when they abused people.

MUCH of Francis's spiritual advice is found in the many letters he wrote to his followers, to rulers, and to anyone who sought his advice.

To his followers he wrote, "My beloved sons, whom I love so much in Christ, I am already leaving you for France. I remind you first of all to love our merciful Father in Heaven, Whom you should love and serve with all your strength and purity of heart; secondly, I counsel mutual love. You shall mortify your body with a fruitful and reasonable penance, by which you will be freed from falling into the snares of the devil."

In another letter he advised, "Be peace loving. Peace is a precious treasure to be sought with great zeal."

He also wrote, "Take pains to avoid sharp words. Pardon one another so that later on you will not remember the injury."

He stated that our greatest source of spiritual strength is reflecting upon the sufferings and death of Jesus, "Fix your minds upon the Passion of our Lord Jesus Christ. Inflamed with love for us, He came down from heaven to redeem us."

The Spread of the Minims

EVEN though Francis and the Minims did not seek power or fame, their holiness brought them many friends and followers. Francis saw his order spread throughout southern Italy and Sicily.

When Francis came to France, the order began to spread there as well. Part of the expansion was due to Francis's influence in the royal court. Part of it was simply the people's recognition of how God was working through this humble hermit.

In the meantime, King Ferdinand of Spain received a piece of advice from Francis (that he should not let his troops retreat in a battle that they were fighting against the Moors). He followed that advice and quickly won a great victory. In gratitude, King Ferdinand invited Francis to establish the Order of Minims in Spain as well. From there, one of the Minims even accompanied Columbus on his second trip to the New World.

Meanwhile, the emperor of Austria invited the Minims to come. They opened three houses in his empire, two in southern Germany and one in Bohemia.

King Charles of France also helped the Minims to establish a church in Rome.

29

Francis's Passion Week

FRANCIS, in spite of his many penances, lived a long life. About three months before his death at ninety-one, he received a revelation from God that he would soon die. He spent the next three months alone so that he could dedicate himself totally to prayer and contemplation.

Then, on Palm Sunday, he developed a high fever. Even though he was weak, he wanted to attend all of the services during Passion Week to commemorate the Passion of our Lord.

On Holy Thursday, he attended the Holy Eucharist. Later, all of his brothers gathered together for a ceremony that is called the Chapter of Faults (during which they confess their sins and shortcomings to each other). Francis asked his brothers' forgiveness for when he might have been too strict with them. He hugged them and kissed each of them goodbye.

Then, on Good Friday, he asked someone to read the Passion from the Gospel of John. His last words were a prayer for good people and sinners, among whom he included himself. He then seemed to be staring at something glorious, and he went home to the Lord.

Francis, Saint and Patron

IT did not take long for Francis of Paola to be declared a Saint. He died on April 2 of 1507, and he was canonized by Pope Leo X only twelve years later. (Remember, this was the same person whom Francis had predicted would become a Pope and canonize him when he was only a boy of seven years old.) His feast day is April 2.

Many people have sought his intercession, and he has become the patron of sailors, of those suffering from epidemics, of travelers, and those seeking protection from fires. Many couples also pray for his intercession so that they might receive the same favor he had received for Princess Anne of France: a healthy child.

The Mass for Children

By REV. JUDE WINKLER, OFM, Conv.

Imprimi Potest: Daniel Pietrzak, OFM Conv., Minister Provincial of St. Anthony of Padua Province (USA)
Nihil Obstat: James T. O'Connor, S.T.D., Censor Librorum
Imprimatur: Patrick J. Sheridan, Vicar General, Archdiocese of New York

The Nihil Obstat and Imprimatur are official declarations that a book or pamphlet is free of doctrinal or moral error. No implication is contained therein that those who have granted the Nihil Obstat and Imprimatur agree with the contents, opinions or statements expressed.

THE MASS

A GIFT FROM JESUS

JESUS loved his apostles so much that he promised them he would never leave them alone. Because he was going to ascend to sit on the right hand of God the Father, he wanted to leave the apostles and us a sign that he would always be with us.

And so, on the night before he died on the cross, Jesus gathered his apostles together for a very special meal. The meal was special for two reasons.

The first reason was that he was celebrating a Passover meal with them. Passover was a feast that the Jews celebrated every year to remember how the Lord had led Israel out of Egypt and how he had freed them from their slavery.

The second reason why this meal was so special was that Jesus was changing it. During the meal he took the bread and told the apostles that it was now his body. He took a cup of wine and told them that it was now his blood. He then told His apostles to continue to do what he was doing in this meal.

This is why we celebrate the Mass. We want to continue to do what Jesus told us to do. This is how we will know that he is always with us until the day he comes back in all his glory.

INTRODUCTORY RITES

STAND

ENTRANCE SONG — As the priest and ministers go to the altar, the people sing the Entrance Song which begins our celebration of the Mass.

3

SIGN OF THE CROSS

We Call upon the Holy Trinity

We begin our Mass as we begin any prayer, with the sign of the cross. We are calling upon God to be with us as we pray to Him.

Priest: In the name of the Father, and of the Son, and of the Holy Spirit.

People: **Amen.**

GREETING

We Are Welcomed in God's Name

The priest then greets us and welcomes us to church. He is speaking not only in his own name, but also in God's name. He uses one of these forms:

A

Priest: The grace of our Lord Jesus Christ and the love of God and the fellowship of the Holy Spirit be with you all.

People: **And also with you.**

B

Priest: The grace and peace of God our Father and the Lord Jesus Christ be with you.

People: **And also with you.**

C

Priest: The Lord be with you.

People: **And also with you.**

PENITENTIAL RITE

We Express Sorrow for Our Sins

The priest now invites us to think of our sins and to tell God that we are sorry for them. We want to apologize for having been selfish and for having sinned so that we can listen to God's word and receive His body and blood with a pure heart.

To show our sorrow, we can say:

I confess to almighty God,
and to you, my brothers and sisters,
that I have sinned through my own fault

We strike our own breasts:

in my thoughts and in my words,
in what I have done,
and in what I have failed to do;
and I ask blessed Mary, ever virgin,
all the angels and saints,
and you, my brothers and sisters,
to pray for me to the Lord our God.

The priest says a short prayer asking for God's mercy.

KYRIE

We Ask Jesus for Mercy

Priest: Lord, have mercy. **People: Lord have mercy.**

Priest: Christ have mercy. **People: Christ have mercy.**

Priest: Lord have mercy. **People: Lord have mercy.**

Sometimes, instead of saying these prayers, the priest asks for God's mercy by calling upon God three times. He finishes his prayer with "Lord, have mercy; Christ, have mercy; Lord, have mercy." We repeat those last words each time he says them.

GLORIA

We Praise God

Now we are so happy God has promised us his forgiveness that we have to celebrate. We do this by saying or singing the song that the angels sang so long ago when they celebrated the birth of Jesus in Bethlehem.

Glory to God in the highest.
and peace to his people on earth.
Lord God, heavenly King,
almighty God and Father,
  we worship you, we give you thanks,
  we praise you for your glory.
Lord Jesus Christ, only Son of the Father,
Lord God, Lamb of God,
you take away the sin of the world:
  have mercy on us;
you are seated at the right hand of the Father:
  receive our prayer.
For you alone are the Holy One,
you alone are the Lord,
you alone are the Most High,
  Jesus Christ,
  with the Holy Spirit,
  in the glory of God the Father. Amen.

OPENING PRAYER

We Join in Prayer Together

This is followed by the Opening Prayer. There are different prayers for each day of the year. In this prayer, the priest asks God to be with us in a very special way as we open our hearts to him.

Priest: For ever and ever.

People: Amen.

OPENING PRAYER — *The priest prays in the name of all who are present. He asks the Lord to guide our thoughts, our prayers, and our love.*

7

LITURGY OF THE WORD

READINGS — In this part of Mass, we hear the Word of God. Readings taken from the Bible are proclaimed to the people of God. These readings come from both the Old Testament and the New Testament. They speak of God's love for us throughout history and especially of God's love shown to us in Jesus.

FIRST READING

SIT

God Speaks to Us through the Prophets

We sit and listen to the Word of God as it was spoken in the Old Testament, especially through his prophets. The reader takes their place in speaking to us.

At the end of the reading:

Reader: The Word of the Lord.

People: **Thanks be to God.**

RESPONSORIAL PSALM

We Respond to God's Word

The people repeat the response said by the reader or sung by the cantor.

SECOND READING

God Speaks to Us through the Apostles

We now listen to readings taken from the letters of Paul and the other apostles.

At the end of the reading:

Reader: The Word of the Lord.

People: **Thanks be to God.**

ALLELUIA VERSE

STAND

We Praise Jesus Who Comes to Speak to Us

Jesus will speak to us in the gospel. We rise now out of respect and prepare for his message with the alleluia verse.

9

GOSPEL — *The priest or deacon reads the gospel in the name of Jesus, and Jesus himself becomes present among us through his word.*

GOSPEL

The priest or deacon greets us in the name of Jesus.

Deacon (or priest): The Lord be with you.
People: And also with you.

Deacon (or priest):
A reading from the holy gospel according to N.
People: Glory to you, Lord.

We listen to the priest or deacon read the Gospel.

At the end of the Gospel:

Deacon (or priest): The Gospel of the Lord.
People: Praise to you, Lord Jesus Christ.

HOMILY

These readings are God's message to us, but sometimes they can be difficult to understand. This is why the priest or deacon explains the meaning of the readings to us in a homily. The homily also tells us how to live God's word in our own lives.

PROFESSION OF FAITH

We Profess Our Faith

Having heard God's word in the readings and having heard an explanation of those readings in the homily, we now want to proclaim before everyone that we believe. We believe what God has told us; we believe that he has called us; we believe that he loves us. To say all of this, we profess our faith with the creed.

THE NICENE CREED

WE believe in one God,
    the FATHER, THE ALMIGHTY,
maker of heaven and earth,
of all that is seen and unseen.

We believe in one Lord, JESUS CHRIST,
the only Son of God,
eternally begotten of the Father,
God from God, Light from Light,
true God from true God,
begotten, not made, one in Being with the Father

Through him all things were made.
For us men and for our salvation
    he came down from heaven:

All bow at the following words up to: and became man.

by the power of the Holy Spirit
    he was born of the Virgin Mary, and became man.

For our sake he was crucified under Pontius Pilate;
    he suffered, died, and was buried.
    On the third day he rose again
        in fulfillment of the Scriptures;
    he ascended into heaven
        and is seated at the right hand of the Father.

He will come again in glory to judge the living and the dead,
and his kingdom will have no end.

We believe in the HOLY SPIRIT, the Lord, the giver of life,
who proceeds from the Father and the Son.
With the Father and the Son he is worshiped and glorified.
He has spoken throught the Prophets.
We believe in one holy catholic and apostolic Church.
We acknowledge one baptism for the forgiveness of sins.
We look for the resurrection of the dead,
and the life of the world to come. Amen.

———— OR   THE APOSTLES' CREED ————

I BELIEVE in God, the Father almighty,
creator of heaven and earth.

I believe in Jesus Christ, his only Son, our Lord.
He was conceived by the power of the Holy Spirit
and born of the Virgin Mary.
He suffered under Pontius Pilate,
was crucified, died, and was buried.
He descended to the dead.
On the third day he rose again.
He ascended into heaven,
and is seated at the right hand of the Father.
He will come again to judge the living and the dead.

I believe in the Holy Spirit,
the holy catholic Church,
the communion of saints,
the forgiveness of sins,
the resurrection of the body,
and the life everlasting. Amen.

GENERAL INTERCESSIONS

We Pray for Our Brothers and Sisters in Christ

We then close the first part of the Mass by saying the General Intercessions, also known as the Prayer of the Faithful. When we go to Mass, we pray not only for ourselves but also for all who need God's help.

The priest usually begins and ends the General Intercessions and someone else reads the intentions for which we are praying. We add our voices to this prayer by repeating the response that has been chosen. Very often, our response is:

People: Lord, hear our prayer.

We begin by praying for the Church. We pray for the Pope, the bishops, priests, all deacons, and all of the people of God. We pray that we might all answer God's call in a loving manner.

We pray for public authorities, the leaders of our nation, and all the people of the world.

We also pray for those who have a special need. We pray for the poor, for those who are sick, for those who are sad, and for anyone else who might need our prayers.

We pray for those who have died. We remember them because we want to share our love with them and pray that they might be with God in heaven.

Finally, we pray for our own local community and our particular needs.

The Prayer of the Faithful closes the first part of the Mass, which is called the Liturgy of the Word.

LITURGY OF THE EUCHARIST

SIT

PREPARATION SONG — *While the gifts of the people are brought forward to the priest and are placed on the altar, a song is sung. The gifts are bread and wine and whatever else we offer for the needs of the Church and for the poor.*

15

PREPARATION OF THE GIFTS

We Place the Bread on the Altar

The priest takes the bread and says in a quiet voice:

Blessed are you, Lord, God of all creation.
Through your goodness we have this bread to offer,
which earth has given and human hands have made.
It will become for us the bread of life.

If there is no singing, we may respond.
Blessed be God for ever.

We Place the Wine on the Altar

He then takes the wine and says in a quiet voice:

Blessed are you, Lord, God of all creation.
Through your goodness we have this wine to offer,
fruit of the vine and work of human hands.
It will become our spiritual drink.

If there is no singing, we may respond.

Blessed be God for ever.

The priest washes his hands, asking God to wash away his sins.
He then says,

INVITATION TO PRAYER `STAND`

We ask God to Accept Our Sacrifice

Priest: Pray, brethren, that our sacrifice
may be acceptable to God, the almighty Father.

People: **May the Lord accept the sacrifice at your
hands
for the praise and glory of his name,
for our good, and the good of all his Church.**

PRAYER OVER THE GIFTS

We pray for God's Grace

*When we have offered our gifts, the priest says the Prayer over
the Gifts. Like the Opening Prayer, there is a special one for each
day of the year.*

At the end:

People: **Amen.**

EUCHARISTIC PRAYER

The priest now begins the Eucharistic Prayer. This is the prayer that will change the bread and wine into the body and blood of our Lord.

Priest: The Lord be with you.

People: And also with you.

Priest: Lift up your hearts.

People: We lift them up to the Lord.

Priest: Let us give thanks to the Lord our God.

People: It is right to give him thanks and praise.

The priest then calls upon the Lord with a prayer called the Preface. We respond to that prayer by singing or saying the same prayer that the angels sing before God's throne:

HOLY, HOLY, HOLY

We Praise God in Union with the Angels

Priest and People:

Holy, Holy, Holy Lord, God of power and might,
heaven and earth are full of your glory.
  Hosanna in the highest.
Blessed is he who comes in the name of the Lord.
  Hosanna in the highest.

18

HOLY, HOLY, HOLY — *The priest and people unite with all the angels to praise God the Father and Jesus whom he has sent.* **19**

THE BREAD BECOMES THE BODY OF CHRIST — *The priest recalls Jesus' words at the Last Supper and by God's power the bread becomes the body of Christ.*

WORDS OF INSTITUTION

The Bread and Wine Becomes Christ's Body and Blood

There are a number of different Eucharistic Prayers that the priest can use, but they all use the words that Jesus said over the bread and wine. The priest takes the bread and says,

B efore he was given up to death,
a death he freely accepted,
he took bread and gave you thanks.
He broke the bread,
gave it to his disciples, and said:

"Take this, all of you, and eat it:
this is my body which will be given up for you."

The priest holds up the body of Christ for all the people to see.

The priest then takes the cup filled with the wine and says,

W hen supper was ended, he took the cup.
Again he gave you thanks and praise,
gave the cup to his disciples and said:

"Take this, all of you, and drink from it:
this is the cup of my blood,
the blood of the new and everlasting covenant.
It will be shed for you and for all
so that sins may be forgiven.
Do this in memory of me."

The priest holds up the cup that contains the blood of Christ for all the people to see.

THE WINE BECOMES THE BLOOD OF CHRIST — *The priest recalls Jesus' words at the Last Supper and by God's power the wine becomes the blood of Christ.*

22

MEMORIAL ACCLAMATION

We Proclaim the Mystery of Our Faith

We are so happy that God is giving us this very special gift that we feel like crying out for joy. The priest invites us to do this in the Memorial Acclamation. This prayer is a short profession of faith. There are four different ones that we can use:

Priest: Let us proclaim the mystery of faith.

People:

A Christ has died,
Christ is risen,
Christ will come again.

———————— OR ————————

B Dying you destroyed our death,
rising you restored our life,
Lord Jesus, come in glory.

———————— OR ————————

C When we eat this bread and drink this cup,
we proclaim your death, Lord Jesus,
until you come in glory.

———————— OR ————————

D Lord, by your cross and resurrection
you have set us free.
You are the Savior of the world.

GREAT AMEN

We Give Our Assent to All That Has Taken Place

At the end of the Eucharistic Prayer, we join the priest in giving glory to the Father through Jesus:

Through him,
   with him,
in him,
in the unity of the Holy
   Spirit,

all glory and honor is
   yours,
almighty Father,
for ever and ever.
People: Amen.

COMMUNION RITE
LORD'S PRAYER

STAND

We Speak to God our Father in the Words
Jesus Taught Us

*After the Eucharistic Prayer is finished, we prepare to receive
Jesus in communion by saying the prayer that Jesus taught us. We
praise God, ask for our daily bread, and beg forgiveness for our
sins.*

Priest and People:

Our Father, who art in heaven,
hallowed be thy name;
thy kingdom come;
thy will be done on earth as it is in
heaven.
Give us this day our daily bread;
and forgive us our trespasses
as we forgive those who trespass
against us;
and lead us not into temptation,
but deliver us from evil.

LORD'S PRAYER — Our preparation for receiving Jesus in Holy Communion continues with the "Our Father," the prayer that Jesus taught us to say.

Priest: Deliver us, Lord, from every evil,
and grant us peace in our day.
In your mercy keep us free from sin
and protect us from all anxiety
as we wait in joyful hope
for the coming of our Savior, Jesus Christ.

People: **For the kingdom, the power, and the
glory
are yours, now and for ever.**

SIGN OF PEACE

We Offer a Sign of Peace to Each Other

*Before we receive the body and blood of Jesus, we have to
make peace with each other.*

The priest says a prayer for peace and unity that ends with:

Priest: For ever and ever.

People: **Amen.**

Priest: The peace of the Lord be with you always.

People: **And also with you.**

Priest: Let us offer each other the sign of peace.

We give a sign of peace to those around us.

27

BREAKING OF THE BREAD

We Ask for Mercy and Peace

We then call upon Jesus to prepare us so that we might be ready to receive communion. We say,

People:

Lamb of God, you take away the sins of the world:
   have mercy on us.

Lamb of God, you take away the sins of the world:

Lamb of God, you take away the sins of the world:
   grant us peace.

COMMUNION

We Ask God to Make Us Worthy to Receive Communion

The priest invites us to receive Jesus our Savior who comes to us in communion. He prays with us, asking God to make us worthy to receive his great gift.

Priest and People:

Lord, I am not worthy to receive you, but only say the word and I shall be healed.

He then receives communion.

It is very important that we remind ourselves of what we are about to do when we receive communion. We do not want to go up to receive it just because everyone else is going or just because we do it every Sunday. We should remind ourselves that this is the body and blood of our Lord. We should receive it because we want to be one with Jesus and we want to be like him.

COMMUNION — *We receive the bread that has become the body (and blood) of our Lord. This is God's most special gift to us.*

We Receive Jesus

We then go up to receive the body and blood of Jesus. The priest or the minister of the eucharist says:

Priest: The body of Christ.

Communicant: Amen.

Priest: The blood of Christ.

Communicant: Amen.

This response means that we really want to be one with God.

The Communion Song is sung while communion is given to the faithful.

PERIOD OF SILENCE OR SONG OF PRAISE   `SIT`

We Praise God

After communion there may be a period of silence, or a song of praise may be sung.

PRAYER AFTER COMMUNION

We Ask for the Grace of Communion

Priest: Let us pray.

When everyone has finished receiving communion, the priest says a prayer called the Prayer after Communion. Like the Opening Prayer and the Prayer over the Gifts, it is different for each day of the year. The prayer usually asks that we might be able to live with our whole heart and our entire love the things that we have promised to do when we received communion.

At the end:

Priest: Through Christ our Lord.

People: Amen.

CONCLUDING RITE

The Mass closes with a sign of the cross, just as it began with one. This time the sign of the cross is a blessing.

BLESSING

We Receive God's Blessing from the Priest

Priest:　The Lord be with you.

People: And also with you.

Priest:　May almighty God bless you,
　　　　the Father, and the Son, and the Holy Spirit.

People: Amen.

DISMISSAL

We Are Sent Out to Bring Christ to Others

Deacon (or priest):

A　　Go in the peace of Christ.

─────────── OR ───────────

B　　The Mass is ended, go in peace.

─────────── OR ───────────

C　　Go in peace to love and serve the Lord.

People:　Thanks be to God.

The Recessional Song ends our celebration.

As we go forth from the Church, we realize that we have been changed. We have received the body and blood of our Lord, and this has made us his apostles. We now go forth into the world to carry the love of Jesus to everyone whom we will meet.

32

Scriptural Rosary for Children

REV. JUDE WINKLER, OFM Conv.

Imprimi Potest: Michael Kolodziej, OFM Conv., Minister Provincial of St. Anthony of Padua Province (USA)
Nihil Obstat: Rev. James M. Cafone, M.A., S.T.D., Censor Librorum
Imprimatur: ✠ Most Rev. John J. Myers, J.C.D., D.D., Archbishop of Newark

© 2005 by CATHOLIC BOOK PUBLISHING CORP., Totowa, N.J.
Printed in Hong Kong   ISBN 978-0-89942-532-0

"Whatever you ask through the Rosary shall be granted."

Promise of Our Lady to St. Dominic

How the Rosary Began

There are a number of different stories about how the Holy Rosary began. Two of the oldest stories tell us why people needed the Rosary and who helped spread its use throughout the world.

In the early days of the Church, people wanted to make their daily lives more holy. When they would ask spiritual leaders how they could do this, the leaders would tell them that they should meditate on the Mysteries of God's love. They asked these spiritual guides how long they should meditate on these Mysteries (for they had no clocks or watches). The answer was that they should meditate for as long as it would take to pray one Our Father and ten Hail Marys.

Even if this is how the Rosary began, it was St. Dominic, the founder of the Dominicans, who spread the practice of praying it every day. He preached at the beginning of the thirteenth century, a time when many people had turned away from God. Dominic devoted himself to preaching the Word of God to those who had lost their Faith.

There is a legend that the Blessed Virgin Mary appeared to St. Dominic and gave him a Rosary, telling him to pray it so that sinners would be converted.

Lourdes and Fatima

There have been a number of signs and appearances throughout the ages that show us the importance of the Rosary.

When the Blessed Virgin Mary appeared in Lourdes, France, in 1858, St. Bernadette prayed the Rosary with her. After they had finished praying it, Mary revealed to Bernadette that she was "the Immaculate Conception." Bernadette did not even understand what this meant for this truth of the Faith had only just been declared. It means that Mary was protected from the damage of sin from the moment of her conception.

Then, in 1917, the Blessed Virgin Mary appeared to three young children in Fatima, Portugal. This was a very difficult time in the world. World War I was tearing apart nations. The Communists, who deny that God exists, were about to take power in Russia.

Mary told the children that they should pray the Rosary. She called it a powerful weapon against selfishness and sin. This message is just as true today as it was when Mary appeared at Lourdes and Fatima.

How to Pray the Rosary

One can pray the Rosary with a group of people or alone. One can pray this devotion in church, at home, or anywhere.

We begin the Rosary with the Sign of the Cross (for this is the way that we begin all of our prayers).

After this, we pray the Apostles' Creed. This is a very ancient prayer that proclaims the important truths of our Faith.

After the Apostles' Creed, we pray one Our Father, three Hail Marys, and one Glory be.

We now come to the most important reason why we pray the Rosary: to meditate on the Mysteries of our Faith. We proclaim each of the five Mysteries, followed by one Our Father, ten Hail Marys, and one Glory be.

Remember, the reason for praying the Rosary is not to tally how many prayers we can say. It is to meditate on God's love as shown in the lives of Jesus and Mary. This is why we hold the Rosary while we pray, so that we can keep track of the number of prayers we have said without having to count them.

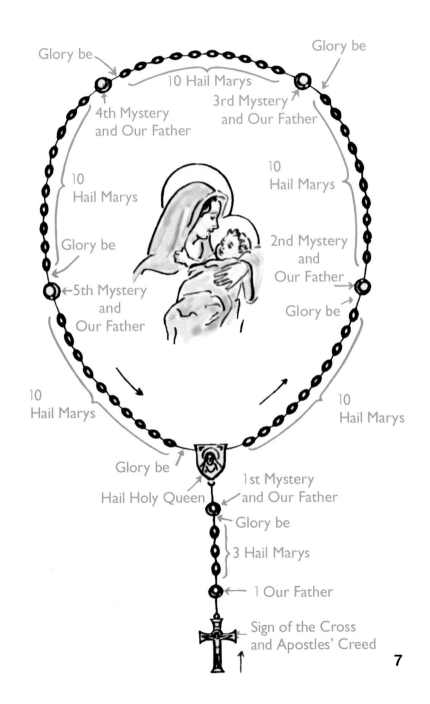

Glory be

Glory be

10 Hail Marys

3rd Mystery
and Our Father

4th Mystery
and Our Father

10
Hail Marys

10
Hail Marys

Glory be

2nd Mystery
and
Our Father

5th Mystery
and
Our Father

Glory be

10
Hail Marys

10
Hail Marys

Glory be

1st Mystery
and Our Father

Hail Holy Queen

Glory be

3 Hail Marys

1 Our Father

Sign of the Cross
and Apostles' Creed

The Joyful Mysteries

These are the Mysteries that we pray on Mondays and Saturdays, the Sundays of Advent, and Sundays from Epiphany until Lent:

1. The Annunciation

2. The Visitation

3. The Birth of Jesus

4. The Presentation of Jesus in the Temple

5. The Finding of Jesus in the Temple

To help us meditate upon them, we will read some verses from the Bible that tell us what happened. If there is no such passage from Scripture, we will read some thoughts that help us reflect on the Mystery.

The First Joyful Mystery: The Annunciation

Luke 1:26-28, 30-31, 38

In the sixth month, the Angel Gabriel was sent by God to a town in Galilee called Nazareth, to a Virgin betrothed to a man named Joseph, of the house of David. The Virgin's name was Mary.

The Angel came to her and said, "Hail, full of grace! The Lord is with you." The Angel also said, "Do not be afraid, Mary, for you have found favor with God. Behold, you will conceive in your womb and bear a Son, and you will name Him Jesus." Mary said, "Behold, I am the servant of the Lord. Let it be done to me according to your word."

The Second Joyful Mystery: The Visitation

Luke 1:39-43

Mary set out and journeyed in haste to a town of Judah where she entered the house of Zechariah and greeted Elizabeth, her cousin who was with child. When Elizabeth heard Mary's greeting, the baby leaped in her womb.

Then Elizabeth exclaimed with a loud cry, "Blessed are you among women, and blessed is the Fruit of your womb. And why am I so greatly favored that the Mother of my Lord should visit me?"

The Third Joyful Mystery: The Birth of Jesus

Luke 2:1, 4, 6-7

In those days, a decree was issued by Caesar Augustus that a census should be taken throughout the entire world. Joseph therefore went from the town of Nazareth in Galilee to Judea, to the city of David called Bethlehem, because he was of the house and family of David.

While Joseph and Mary were there, the time came for her to have her Child. She wrapped Him in swaddling clothes and laid Him in a manger, because there was no room for them in the inn.

The Fourth Joyful Mystery:
The Presentation of Jesus in the Temple

Luke 2:22, 27-30, 38

When the days for their purification were completed according to the Law of Moses, they brought the Child up to Jerusalem to present Him to the Lord.

Prompted by the Spirit, Simeon came into the Temple. He took Jesus in his arms and praised God, saying, "Now, Lord, You may dismiss Your servant in peace, for my eyes have seen Your salvation."

At that moment, Anna came forward and began to praise God, while she spoke about the Child.

The Fifth Joyful Mystery:
The Finding of Jesus in the Temple

Luke 2:42-43, 46, 49

When Jesus was twelve years old, the Holy Family made the journey for the feast of Passover. When the days of the feast were over and they set off for home, the Boy Jesus stayed behind in Jerusalem.

After three days Mary and Joseph found Him in the Temple, where He was sitting among the teachers, listening to them and asking them questions.

Jesus said to Mary and Joseph, "Why were you searching for Me? Did you not know that I must be in My Father's house?"

13

The Luminous Mysteries

These are the Mysteries that we pray on Thursdays:

1. The Baptism of Jesus
2. The Wedding Feast at Cana
3. The Proclamation of the Kingdom of God
4. The Transfiguration
5. The Institution of the Eucharist

To help us meditate upon them, we will read some verses from the Bible that tell us what happened. If there is no such passage from Scripture, we will read some thoughts that help us reflect on the Mystery.

The First Luminous Mystery: The Baptism of Jesus

Matthew 3:13-15, 16-17

Jesus arrived from Galilee and came to John at the Jordan to be baptized by him. John tried to dissuade Him, saying, "Why do You come to me? I am the one who needs to be baptized by You." But Jesus said to him in reply, "For the present, let it be thus."

After Jesus had been baptized, as He came up from the water, suddenly the heavens were opened and He beheld the Spirit of God descending like a dove and alighting on Him. And a voice came from heaven, saying, "This is My beloved Son, in Whom I am well pleased."

15

The Second Luminous Mystery:
The Wedding Feast at Cana

John 2:3, 6-7, 8-9, 11

When the wine was exhausted at a wedding, the Mother of Jesus said to Him, "They have no wine." Now standing nearby there were six stone water jars, each holding twenty to thirty gallons. Jesus instructed the servants, "Fill the jars with water."

The servants brought some of the water to the steward. The steward tasted the water that had become wine. Jesus performed this, the first of His signs, at Cana in Galilee.

The Third Luminous Mystery:
The Proclamation of the Kingdom of God

Matthew 13:31-32, 45-46

The kingdom of God is like a mustard seed that a man took and sowed in his field. It is the smallest of all the seeds, but when it has grown it is the greatest of plants and becomes a tree large enough for the birds to come and make nests in its branches.

The kingdom of God is like a merchant searching for fine pearls. When he found one of great value, he went off and sold everything he had and bought it.

The Fourth Luminous Mystery:
The Transfiguration

Matthew 17:1-3, 5

Jesus took Peter and James and his brother John and led them up a high mountain by themselves. And in their presence He was transfigured; His face shone like the sun, and His clothes became dazzling white. Then Moses and Elijah appeared to them, conversing with Him.

Then a cloud came and cast its shadow over them. A voice came out of the cloud, saying, "This is My Son, My Chosen One. Listen to Him."

The Fifth Luminous Mystery:
The Institution of the Eucharist

Matthew 26:26; Luke 22:19; Matthew 26:27-28

While they were eating, Jesus took bread, and after He had pronounced the blessing, He broke it and gave it to His disciples, saying, "Take this and eat; this is My Body, which will be given for you. Do this in memory of Me."

Then He took a cup, and after offering thanks, He gave it to them, saying, "Drink from this, all of you. For this is My Blood of the covenant, which will be shed on behalf of many for the forgiveness of sins."

19

The Sorrowful Mysteries

These are the Mysteries that we pray on Tuesdays and Fridays throughout the year, and daily from Ash Wednesday until Easter Sunday:

1. The Agony in the Garden

2. The Scourging at the Pillar

3. The Crowning with Thorns

4. Jesus Carries His Cross

5. Jesus Dies on the Cross

To help us meditate upon them, we will read some verses from the Bible that tell us what happened. If there is no such passage from Scripture, we will read some thoughts that help us reflect on the Mystery.

The First Sorrowful Mystery:
The Agony in the Garden

Mark 14:32-33, 35-36; Luke 22:43

Jesus and the disciples went to a place that was called Gethsemane, and Jesus said to His disciples, "Sit here while I pray." He took with Him Peter and James and John, and He began to suffer distress.

Moving on a little farther, He threw himself on the ground and prayed that, if it were possible, the hour might pass Him by, saying, "Abba, Father, for You all things are possible. Take this cup from Me. Yet not My will but Yours be done." Then an Angel from heaven appeared to Him and gave Him strength.

The Second Sorrowful Mystery:
The Scourging at the Pillar

Matthew 27:24-26; 1 Peter 2:23

When Pilate saw that a riot was about to occur, he took some water and washed his hands in full view of the crowd, saying, "I am innocent of this Man's Blood." He then released Barabbas to them, and had Jesus scourged.

When Jesus was abused, He did not retaliate. When He suffered, He made no threats, but He placed His trust in the One Who judges justly.

The Third Sorrowful Mystery:
The Crowning with Thorns

Matthew 27:27-30

The governor's soldiers took Jesus inside the praetorium and gathered the whole cohort around Him. They stripped Him and put a scarlet robe on Him, and after twisting some thorns into a crown, they placed it on His head and put a reed in His right hand.

Bending the knee before Him, they mocked Him, saying, "Hail, King of the Jews!" The soldiers spat upon Jesus, and taking a reed, used it to strike Him on the head.

The Fourth Sorrowful Mystery: Jesus Carries His Cross

Luke 23:26-27, 32

As they led Jesus away, they seized a man from Cyrene named Simon, who was returning from the country. They put the Cross on his back and forced him to carry it behind Jesus. A large number of people followed Jesus, among them many women who were mourning and lamenting over Him.

There were also two others, both criminals, who were led away to be executed with Him.

The Fifth Sorrowful Mystery:
Jesus Dies on the Cross

Mark 15:25, 29, 33-34, 37

It was around nine o'clock in the morning when they crucified Him. Those people who passed by jeered at Him, shaking their heads.

Beginning at midday, there was darkness over the whole land until three in the afternoon. At three o'clock, Jesus cried out in a loud voice, "My God, My God, why have You forsaken Me?" Then Jesus cried out in a loud voice and breathed His last.

The Glorious Mysteries

These are the Mysteries that we pray on Wednesdays and Sundays from Easter until Advent:

1. The Resurrection

2. The Ascension

3. The Descent of the Holy Spirit

4. The Assumption

5. The Crowning of the Blessed Virgin Mary

To help us meditate upon them, we will read some verses from the Bible that tell us what happened. If there is no such passage from Scripture, we will read some thoughts that help us reflect on the Mystery.

The First Glorious Mystery: The Resurrection

Luke 24:1-6

At daybreak on the first day of the week, the women came to the tomb with spices they had prepared. They found the stone rolled away from the tomb, but when they went inside, they did not find the Body of the Lord Jesus.

Suddenly two men in dazzling clothes appeared at their side. They said to the women, "Why do you look among the dead for One Who is alive? Jesus is not here. He has been raised."

The Second Glorious Mystery: The Ascension

Acts 1:9-11

Jesus was lifted up as the disciples looked on, and a cloud took Him from their sight.

While He was departing as they gazed upward toward the sky, suddenly two men dressed in white robes stood beside them, and they said, "Men of Galilee, why are you standing there looking up into the sky? This Jesus Who has been taken from you into heaven will come back in the same way you have seen Him going into heaven."

The Third Glorious Mystery:
The Descent of the Holy Spirit

Acts 2:1-4

When the day of Pentecost arrived, they were all assembled together in one place. Suddenly, there came from heaven a sound similar to that of a violent wind, and it filled the entire house in which they were sitting.

There appeared tongues of fire, which separated and came to rest on each one of them. All of them were filled with the Holy Spirit, and they began to speak in different languages, as the Spirit enabled them to do.

The Fourth Glorious Mystery:
The Assumption

Luke 1:46-54

M ary said, "My soul proclaims the greatness of the Lord, and my spirit rejoices in God my Savior. For He has looked with favor on the lowliness of His servant; henceforth, all generations will call me blessed.

"The Mighty One has done great things for me, and holy is His Name. His mercy is shown from age to age to those who fear Him. . . . He has come to the aid of Israel His servant, ever mindful of His merciful love."

30

The Fifth Glorious Mystery:
The Crowning of the Blessed Virgin Mary

Romans 8:14-15, 17, 30

Those who are led by the Spirit of God are children of God. You did not receive a spirit of slavery leading to fear; rather, you received the Spirit of adoption. . . . If we are children of God, then we are heirs—heirs of God and joint heirs with Christ.

Those whom He predestined He also called, and those whom He called He also justified, and those whom He justified He also glorified.

After one has prayed all five decades of the Rosary, one can say the following prayer.

O God, whose only-begotten Son, by His life, death and resurrection, has purchased for us the rewards of eternal life; grant, we ask You, that, meditating upon these Mysteries of the Most Holy Rosary of the Blessed Virgin Mary, we may imitate what they contain and obtain what they promise, through the same Christ our Lord. Amen.

We then close our recitation of the Rosary with the Sign of the Cross.

RECEIVING HOLY COMMUNION

How to Make
A Good Communion

JHS

By REV. LOVASIK, S.V.D.

Nihil Obstat: James T. O'Connor, S.T.D., Censor Librorum
Imprimatur: ✠ Patrick J. Sheridan, D.D., Vicar General, Archdiocese of New York

The Nihil Obstat and Imprimatur are official declarations that a book or pamphlet is free of doctrinal or moral error. No implication is contained therein that those who have granted the Nihil Obstat and Imprimatur agree with the contents, opinions or statements expressed.

2

THE INSTITUTION OF THE HOLY EUCHARIST

ON the night He was betrayed, Jesus took bread and gave it to His disciples, and said: **"Take this, all of you, and eat it: this is My Body which will be given up for you."**

When supper was ended, He took the cup. Again He gave thanks and praise, gave the cup to His disciples, and said: **"Take this, all of you, and drink from it: this is the cup of My Blood, the Blood of the new and everlasting covenant. It will be shed for you and for all so that sins may be forgiven. Do this in memory of Me."**

Our Lord changed bread and wine into His Body and Blood and offered Himself to God. This was a sacrifice. This was His Body to be offered on the Cross. This was His Blood to be shed for the forgiveness of sins. He told the Apostles that He would die on the next day. That would be the **bloody** sacrifice on the Cross.

Jesus wanted this **unbloody** sacrifice to continue on earth till the end of time. When He told the Apostles to do as He had done, He made them priests with the power to offer this sacrifice.

JESUS OFFERS HIMSELF
IN THE MASS

AFTER our Lord returned to heaven, the Apostles continued to offer this Eucharistic Sacrifice. They ordained other priests. In this way Jesus gave us the priesthood and the Mass.

In the Mass Jesus gives Himself to His Heavenly Father, as He did on the Cross, but now in an unbloody manner in the Sacrament of the Eucharist, for He cannot suffer anymore.

The Sacrifice of the Mass is the same Sacrifice that Jesus offered on the Cross. In every Mass Christ is present, acting through His priest, under the appearances of bread and wine.

In every Mass His Death becomes present, offered as our sacrifice to God in an unbloody and sacramental manner. As often as the Sacrifice of the Cross is celebrated on an altar, the work of our redemption is carried on.

At Mass we offer Christ, our Passover Sacrifice, to God, and we offer ourselves along with Him. We then receive the risen Lord, our Bread of Life, in Holy Communion.

5

THE MASS—OUR GREATEST GIFT TO GOD

THE Mass is a true sacrifice because in it Jesus continues His Sacrifice of the Cross, and He gives us the graces He won for us when He died for our salvation.

There is nothing that we can give God as a gift that is greater than His own Son. We offer Jesus to His heavenly Father in the Mass as our Greatest Gift to God.

We join with Jesus and the priest in offering to God this highest form of worship:

1. To give God the highest adoration and glory.
2. To thank Him for all His blessings.
3. To make up for all our sins.
4. To obtain all the blessings we need.

In the Mass it is Jesus Christ, the God-Man, Who is our High Priest and our Victim, praying for us to His heavenly Father.

HOLY COMMUNION HELPS US TO LOVE GOD AND EACH OTHER

HOLY Communion makes sanctifying grace grow in our soul. That grace helps us to love God. That same grace helps us to love our neighbor for the love of God.

Jesus also strengthens us through actual or sacramental grace when we receive Him in Holy Communion. That grace gives light to our mind and strength to our will to do good and to avoid evil. Through Holy Communion we receive the grace to overcome temptation and avoid sinning against God and our neighbor.

Only by the help of this sacramental grace can we truly live in a life of love and fulfill God's greatest commandment: "You shall love the Lord your God with all your heart . . . and your neighbor as yourself" (Matthew 22:37). And our Lord's own commandment: "I give you a new commandment: Love one another " (John 13:34).

The Eucharist is a sacrament of unity because it unites us more closely with God and with one another.

9

10

CONDITIONS FOR RECEIVING COMMUNION

To receive Holy Communion you must:

1. Have your soul free from mortal sin.
2. Not eat or drink anything for one hour before Holy Communion. But water may be taken at any time before Holy Communion.

Before Holy Communion you should:

1. Think of Jesus.
2. Say the prayers you have learned.
3. Ask Jesus to come to you.

After Holy Communion you should:

1. Thank Jesus for coming to you.
2. Tell Him how much you love Him.
3. Ask Him to help you.
4. Pray for others.

EXAMINING YOUR CONSCIENCE

In order to be as holy as possible when you receive Communion, ask yourself some questions such as:

- Did I obey my parents?
- Did I always tell the truth?
- Did I try to help others?
- Did I say my prayers?
- Did I fight with anyone?
- Did I make fun of anyone?
- Did I take anything that does not belong to me?
- Did I do my homework and my chores?

After you have finished asking yourself these and other questions, ask God for forgiveness by saying an ACT OF CONTRITION, such as:

O MY God, I am sorry for all my sins with my whole heart.
I will try to be better in the future.

Sometimes you may wish to go to Confession before receiving Communion.

GETTING READY AT HOME TO RECEIVE COMMUNION

Although we can receive Communion on any day, we usually receive it on Sunday. Sunday is a special day. It is the day set aside for us to give thanks and praise to God, especially by participating in the Holy Mass. On Sunday, we rest from the usual things we do every day and think about God and the things of God.

Sunday is also a special day for the family. We dress in our best clothes and enjoy a family dinner. We may go on a picnic or take a drive or visit our relatives. We should have a special happiness all day and be good to others.

We should also say a special prayer in honor of the Blessed Trinity:

Thank You, GOD THE FATHER.
 You made me to know, love, and serve You and to be happy forever in heaven with You.

Thank You, GOD THE SON.
 You died and rose from the dead to save me.

Thank You, GOD THE HOLY SPIRIT.
 You were sent by the Father and the Son to make me holy.

AT MASS — JOIN IN THE SINGING

At Mass, we think about God. We talk with God. We even sing to God.

So, when you are at Mass, be sure to do the following things:

- Join in the singing to celebrate the wonderful opportunity you have to meet Jesus in this Mass even though you cannot see Him.

- Do everything you can to be united with the priest and people in offering the Mass to God.

- Think of the Father, Who made us.

- Think of Jesus Who died so that we might live forever.

- Think of the Holy Spirit, Who is always giving us His help.

- Think of our Blessed Mother, Mary, who prays for us to her Divine Son Jesus.

- Most of all, be thankful that you can receive Jesus in Communion.

AT MASS — LISTEN TO THE READINGS

At Mass, the Word of God is read to us. God's Word tells us how to live as followers of Jesus.

So, when you are at Mass, be sure to do the following things:

- Listen to the First and Second Readings.
  They come from the Bible.
  They speak of God's love for us
  throughout history
  and especially of God's love
  shown to us in Jesus.

- After the First Reading,
  join in the response that is said or sung
  by everyone.

- When you rise to hear the Gospel,
  remember that the priest or deacon reads it
  in the name of Jesus.
  It is Jesus Himself
  Who becomes present among us
  through His word.

- Then listen to the homily,
  which shows us how to live God's word
  in our lives.

19

20

AT MASS — RESPOND TO THE PRAYERS

At Mass, the priest says many prayers. We have special responses to make to some of these prayers.

So, when you are at Mass, be sure to do the following things.

- Make the responses to the prayers.
- Say the proper response when the priest says, "Let us proclaim the mystery of faith."

A Christ has died,
   Christ is risen,
   Christ will come again.

B Dying you destroyed our death,
   rising you restored our life,
   Lord Jesus, come in glory.

C When we eat this bread and drink this cup,
   we proclaim your death, Lord Jesus,
   until you come in glory.

D Lord, by your cross and resurrection
   you have set us free.
   You are the Savior of the world.

AT MASS — PRAY SILENTLY
BEFORE COMMUNION

Before receiving Communion, the priest prays silently for a few moments. You too can say a silent prayer as final preparation before receiving Jesus in Communion.

JESUS, I believe in You.
Jesus, I hope in You.
Jesus, I love You with all my heart.

Jesus, I want so much to receive You
into my heart.

I long for You.

Jesus, I am sorry for all my sins.

I am not good enough for You to come to me.

But I know You want me to come to You
that You may make me good.

Jesus, give me Your grace
that I may always please You.

Holy Mary, my dearest Mother, pray for me
and make my heart ready for Jesus.

AT MASS — PRAY ALOUD
BEFORE COMMUNION

The priest now invites all to receive Communion.

Say with all the people:

Lord, I am not worthy to receive you,
but only the say the word and I shall be
healed.

The priest then receives Communion.

AT MASS — RECEIVE JESUS
WITH DEVOTION

After the priest receives Communion, it is time for us to receive Jesus. So be sure to do the following:

- **Join the Communion Procession and sing the hymns that tell of your love for Jesus.**

- **Bear in mind that you are going to receive the Body and Blood, Soul and Divinity of the Lord.**

- **Make the proper response when you reach the priest or minister of Communion.**

Priest or other minister: **The Body of Christ.**

- **Answer: Amen.**

- **Receive the Sacred Host on your tongue or in your hand.**

If the Precious Blood is to be received from the Cup, then one again answers Amen when the minister says: "The Blood of Christ."

Priest or other minister: **The Blood of Christ.**

- **Answer: Amen.**

- **Receive the Precious Blood from the Cup.**

AT MASS — THANK JESUS
AFTER COMMUNION

During the Time of Silence that follows Communion, you may say private prayers of thanks to Jesus.

JESUS, I believe in You.
Jesus, I hope in You.
Jesus, I love You with all my heart.
Jesus, I thank You for having come to me.
Welcome to my heart and bless me.

You are the same Jesus
Who loved little children
and let them come to You.

You are the same Jesus
Who gave Your life for us on the Cross
and rose from the dead.

And now that You are so close to me,
I ask You to help me
to love You more
and to serve You as You want me
to serve You.

JESUS IS WITH US IN THE TABERNACLE

Jesus is present under the appearances of the Consecrated Bread and Wine. The Church expresses this presence of Jesus in the Eucharist by preserving the Consecrated Bread in the tabernacle that is found in every Catholic church.

JESUS, I thank You
　　for staying in the tabernacle
　day and night to be with me
　and to hear my prayers
　when I need Your help.

You are my best Friend.

I want to come to visit You often.

I want to show You how much I love You,
　　and to ask You to help me
　　and those I love.

O Sacrament most holy,
　O Sacrament divine!

All praise and all thanksgiving
　be every moment Thine!

PRAYERS TO OUR LADY
OF THE BLESSED SACRAMENT

Since Mary is the Mother of Jesus, she is also known as Our Lady of the Blessed Sacrament. It is good for us to pray to her from time to time.

O VIRGIN Mary,
  we pray to you
  as our Lady of the Blessed Sacrament.

You are the glory of the Christian people,
  the joy of the Universal Church,
  and the salvation of the whole world.

Pray for us,
  and awaken in all believers a deep devotion
  for the most Holy Eucharist.

In this way,
  they may be worthy to receive often
  this holy Sacrament of the Altar.

31

JESUS IS "GOD WITH US"

WE should adore, love, and thank Jesus in the Blessed Sacrament by our visits to the tabernacle in our churches and in Benediction. Benediction is a ceremony in which the Blessed Sacrament is exposed to the people for adoration. It ends with the priest blessing the people with the Consecrated Bread.

God is really with us in the Mass, in Holy Communion, and in the tabernacle.

The Sacramentals
of the Church

By REV. LAWRENCE G. LOVASIK, S.V.D.
Divine Word Missionary

NIHIL OBSTAT: Daniel V. Flynn, J.C.D., *Censor Librorum*
IMPRIMATUR: Joseph T. O'Keefe, *Vicar General, Archdiocese of New York*

Through His Church Jesus teaches us and helps us to
become holy through the Seven Sacraments and many
Sacramentals.

SACRAMENTALS

SACRAMENTALS are holy things or actions which the Church uses to obtain for us from God, through her prayers, favors for our body and soul.

Sacramentals are like Sacraments, but there is a difference: A **Sacrament** is a sign that we can see, instituted by Christ to give grace. The Sacraments receive their power to give grace from God, through the merits of Jesus Christ.

There are seven Sacraments: Baptism, Confirmation, Holy Eucharist, Penance, Anointing of the Sick, Holy Orders, and Matrimony.

The **Sacramentals** were instituted by the Church and obtain graces for us by helping us to practice acts of virtue which draw down God's graces on us.

The Sacramentals obtain favors from God through the prayers of the Church offered for those who make use of them, and through the devotion they inspire.

Sacramentals do not give sanctifying grace but make us ready to receive it. Sacramentals prepare our souls to receive whatever grace God wishes to give us.

The Holy Trinity—Father, Son, and Holy Spirit—one true God in three Persons, lives in our soul by grace. Sacramentals prepare us to receive that grace from God.

HOW SACRAMENTALS HELP US

1. Sacramentals prepare us to receive *actual graces*.

Actual grace is a help given to us by God to offer light to our mind and strength to our will that we may do good and avoid evil.

"Sacramental" means "something like a Sacrament." Sacramentals do not of themselves give grace. Rather, they make us ready to receive grace by arousing in us feelings of faith and love.

2. Sacramentals help us to receive *forgiveness of our venial sins,* which are less serious offenses against the law of God.

3. Sacramentals obtain for us the *forgiveness of the punishment* we deserve for our sins.

4. Sacramentals obtain for us *health of body and other blessings* that we need in our daily life.

5. Sacramentals *protect us* from the power of the devil and temptations to do evil.

Jesus lives in us by His grace and helps us to live in Him by giving us the Sacramentals. They prepare us to receive blessings for soul and body.

BLESSINGS

IN her blessings the Church shows how much she values the things of this world, which are God's gifts to us.

A blessing is a ritual ceremony by which a priest makes persons or things holy for divine service, or calls down the favor of God on what he blesses. The Church's ritual has over two hundred such blessings.

There are *blessings* for fields and gardens, cattle and schools, cars, houses, wine, water, fire and vegetables. All manner of persons and things are blessed.

Since the coming of the Son of God among us, all the world is consecrated to God's service. The Sacramentals extend Christ's presence to every part of our daily life. Things are blessed not only to ask God's protection on their use, but also to remind us that the life of Christians is to consecrate all that they use to the glory of God.

Karen and Tommy pray silently with their parents as Father John blesses the family car.

BLESSING OF THROATS

ST. Blase, Bishop of Sebaste, was beheaded after terrible torments in 317. Among his miracles is one in which he cured a boy who was choking from a fishbone. So he is venerated as the patron saint against diseases of the throat.

When the priest blesses throats on his feast-day, February 3, holding a candle and making the sign of the cross, he says, "Through the intercession of Saint Blase, Bishop and Martyr, may you be protected from all diseases of the throat and every other evil."

Mary, Joan, Pat, and Tony have their throats blessed.

Brigid and Timmy follow Father Andrew as he blesses a room of their home.

THE BLESSING OF A HOME

THERE is a custom of blessing homes during the Christmas Season especially among the German and Slavic people. This blessing is usually given by the pastor. He sprinkles the rooms with holy water and incenses them, then recites the prayers.

Exorcism is a prayer in which the priest commands the devil to leave a possessed person or forbids him to harm someone.

ACTIONS

MOST of the Sacramentals are *sacred actions, words, and objects,* to which the Church gives a blessing or by which she teaches the people that they can obtain certain graces from God.

Sacramental actions are movements of the body that the Church uses when honoring the Holy Eucharist and giving the Sacraments. Some of them are: kneeling, folding one's hands, making the sign of the cross, and bowing.

Kathy, Linda, Bobby, and Johnny kneel in prayer before an outdoor statue of Jesus on the Cross.

Children make the sign of the cross at the start of a new school day.

THE SIGN OF THE CROSS

WE usually begin and end our prayers with the sign of the cross. It expresses two important mysteries of the Christian religion: the Blessed Trinity and the Redemption.

When we say "in the name," we express the truth that there is only one God. When we say "of the Father, and of the Son, and of the Holy Spirit," we express the truth that there are three distinct Persons in God. When we make the form of the cross on ourselves, we express the truth that the Son of God, made man, redeemed us by His death on the cross.

Anna and Ralph make the Way of the Cross by going from station to station in the church.

THE WAY OF THE CROSS

THE heart of salvation is that Jesus Christ entered the glory of Resurrection through His suffering, Death and burial. Every Mass is the best Way of the Cross a Christian can share.

But piety inspired the Church of Jerusalem to celebrate the Mass at the very places where the scenes of the Passion of Christ happened, from the trial of Jesus to the grave. There are fourteen stations of the Cross.

1. **Jesus is condemned to death**
2. **Jesus takes up His cross**
3. **Jesus falls the first time**
4. **Jesus meets His afflicted Mother**
5. **Simon of Cyrene helps Jesus carry His cross**
6. **Veronica wipes the face of Jesus**
7. **Jesus falls a second time**
8. **Jesus meets the women of Jerusalem**
9. **Jesus falls a third time**
10. **Jesus is stripped of His garments**
11. **Jesus is nailed to the cross**
12. **Jesus dies on the cross**
13. **Jesus is laid in the arms of His Mother**
14. **Jesus is laid in the tomb**

BLESSED OBJECTS

SACRED objects are Sacramentals because the Church has performed a special blessing on them. A blessed object can mean a person, a building, and various things.

Some blessed *objects of devotion* are: holy water, candles, ashes, palms, incense, crucifixes, medals, rosaries, scapulars, images of Jesus, Mary, and the Saints, the clothing worn by men and women religious, the vestments worn by the priest at the altar, rings exchanged by a couple at marriage, the Bible and prayerbooks.

Father Vincent puts on the blessed vestments for Mass.

Clare dips her finger in holy water and prepares to make the sign of the cross before entering church.

HOLY WATER

WATER is a symbol of purity of body and soul. It is used in the ceremony of baptism, to show the cleansing from sin.

Before entering and leaving a church we bless ourselves with holy water as we make an act of faith in the Holy Trinity and thank Our Lord for having died on the cross for our redemption.

Sprinkling with holy water is done before the solemn Mass on Sunday and during the Mass on special occasions, such as weddings, funerals, and blessings.

CANDLES

THE candle is a Sacramental used in the Church's Liturgy. Candles were first used to give light in early morning services. They are an emblem of God, giver of life and enlightenment. Being pure, they remind us of Christ's spotless body, the flame signifying His Divine Nature.

Candles are required at the public administration of the Sacraments, at Mass and Benediction, at funerals and at other church ceremonies.

Candles burn brightly on the altar at Mass.

Philip and Ned light vigil lights at a shrine of the Sacred Heart of Jesus.

Candles are blessed on the feast of the Presentation of the Lord, February 2. They remind us of the words of holy Simeon concerning Christ: "A light of revelation to the Gentiles."

A procession of the people with lighted candles is held to remind us of the entry of Christ, the Light of the World, into the temple of Jerusalem.

The lighting of *vigil lights* is but a symbol of a person's devotion and a means of making an offering to the church.

THE CRUCIFIX, RELICS, AND SACRED IMAGES

WE honor Christ and the Saints when we pray before the crucifix, relics, and sacred images because we honor the persons they represent. We adore Christ, but we venerate the Saints and Our Lady.

When we pray to the Saints we ask them to offer their prayers to God for us because they are with God and have great love for us.

Before their soccer game, a team of boys from St. Aloysius School prays by an outdoor statue of the Saint.

Deacon Ray incenses the Book of Gospels before proclaiming the Gospel at Mass.

INCENSE

INCENSE is an aromatic gum in the form of powder or grains that give off a fragrant smoke when they are burned. When blessed it is a Sacramental. Its burning means zeal; its fragrance, virtue; its rising smoke, our prayer going to God.

It is used at Mass, for the Gospel book, the altar, the people and ministers, and the bread and wine; before consecration; at benediction of the Blessed Sacrament; during processions; at funerals.

Boys and girls receive ashes from Father Louis on Ash Wednesday.

ASHES

WHEN blessing and giving ashes on Ash Wednesday, the priest says, "Lord bless the sinner who asks for your forgiveness and bless all those who receive these ashes. May they keep this lenten season in preparation for the joy of Easter."

Ashes are used as the mark of our repentance. When the priest places ashes on those who come forward, he says to each one: "Turn away from sin and be faithful to the gospel." Or "Remember, man, you are dust and to dust you will return."

PALMS

ON Palm Sunday, when the priest blesses the palm branches, he says, "Almighty God, we pray, bless these branches and make them holy. Today we joyfully acclaim Jesus our Messiah and King. May we reach one day the happiness of the new and everlasting Jerusalem by faithfully following Him. May we honor You every day by living always in Him for He is Lord for ever."

By using blessed palms we also ask God to protect and help us.

Connie and Angela leave Mass on Palm Sunday, holding their palm branches.

HOLY OILS

HOLY oil stands for strength, sweetness, and spiritual activity. Christians are sometimes called "athletes of Christ," and so they are anointed with holy oil in order to remain spiritually strong.

Holy oil symbolizes Christ's priestly and kingly power in which all who are baptized share—His royal priesthood. It also symbolizes the imparting of the grace of the Holy Spirit.

The Church uses three types of holy oil: (1) "Oil of the Catechumens" at Baptism and Holy Orders; (2) "Holy Chrism" at Baptism, Confirmation, and Episcopal Ordinations; and (3) "Oil of the Sick" at the Anointing of the Sick.

WORDS

WORDS, too, can be sacred. They become Sacramentals when what is said has been made holy by the Church. Such words are *indulgenced prayers*. An indulgence is the forgiveness granted by the Church of the punishment which we deserve for the sins already forgiven.

At noon Carl and Carmela stand in the open fields and say an indulgenced prayer to Mary: the Angelus.

THE ROSARY

THE Rosary is a devotional prayer honoring the Mother of God. It is said on a string of beads made up of five sets each of one large and ten smaller beads, called decades. On the large beads the Our Father is said; on the small ones, the Hail Mary.

While saying twenty decades, we think about the joyous, luminous, sorrowful, or glorious parts of Our Lord and Our Lady's life, called the Mysteries of the Rosary.

At Lourdes, France, in 1858, the Blessed Virgin appeared to Bernadette and said the Rosary with her. At Fatima, Portugal, in 1917, she said the Rosary with the three children to whom she appeared, and said, "I am the Lady of the Rosary, and I have come to warn the faithful to amend their lives and ask pardon for their sins. People must not continue to offend the Lord, who is already so deeply offended. They must say the Rosary."

The Rosary is a Sacramental. The Rosary is a devotion most pleasing to our Blessed Mother and to Our Lord, because during the recitation of the Our Father and Hail Mary we think about their lives and the love they showed for us.

THE MYSTERIES OF THE ROSARY

THE JOYFUL MYSTERIES

1. The Annunciation
2. The Visitation
3. The Nativity
4. The Presentation in the Temple
5. Finding of the Child Jesus in the Temple

THE LUMINOUS MYSTERIES

1. Christ's Baptism
2. The Wedding at Cana
3. Proclamation of the Kingdom
4. The Transfiguration
5. Institution of the Eucharist

THE SORROWFUL MYSTERIES

1. The Agony in the Garden
2. The Scourging
3. The Crowning with Thorns
4. The Carrying of the Cross
5. The Crucifixion

THE GLORIOUS MYSTERIES

1. The Resurrection
2. The Ascension
3. The Descent of the Holy Spirit
4. The Assumption
5. The Coronation of the Blessed Virgin

RELICS AND SCAPULARS

WE honor *relics* because they are the bodies of the Saints or objects connected with the Saints or with Our Lord.

The Church has also approved a number of blessed scapulars as two small pieces of cloth joined by strings and worn around the neck and under the clothes. The best known is the brown scapular of Our Lady of Mount Carmel.

The scapular medal is a blessed medal, worn or carried on the person, instead of one or more of the small scapulars. It bears on one side a picture of the Sacred Heart, and on the other an image of the Blessed Virgin Mary.

While Betty kisses the relic of St. Frances Cabrini, Jennie puts on her scapular.

Mark reads the bible at his desk while Andy uses his prayerbook.

THE BIBLE AND PRAYERBOOKS

THE *Bible* is the Word of God. Inspired by the Holy Spirit it is the written story of God's actions in the world and the teachings of Jesus, His Son, and of His Apostles.

Prayerbooks are used to help us speak to God. We say prayers from a prayerbook or use our own words. Prayerbooks also teach us about God and His Church and her teachings.

A *Missal* is a prayerbook containing the prayers recited by the priest at Mass, the Scripture Readings that are proclaimed, and the parts that are to be recited by the people.

THE LITURGICAL YEAR

There are three cycles in the Church year according to the most important mysteries of Our Lord's life: Christmas, Easter, and Pentecost. All are called to share in the liturgical prayer of the Church. Liturgical seasons and feasts are Sacramentals given to us by the Church.

SACRED TIMES

THE *liturgical seasons, feasts, and fasts of the Church* are Sacramentals which are given to us by the Church to make our faith stronger and to prepare our souls to serve God more generously.

Seasons of the Church: In Advent we look forward to the coming of the Lord by remembering the prophecies that foretell His birth, and we look forward to His coming on the last day.

In the Christmas Season we think of the earthly birth of the Savior and also His childhood and hidden life at Nazareth.

During the Lenten Season we think about the Passion and Death of Jesus to help us carry our daily cross by following Him.

In the Easter Season we think of the Resurrection and Ascension of Christ, and the coming of the Holy Spirit at Pentecost.

In the series of weeks from Pentecost to Advent we think of our salvation by following Christ in His teaching and example.

Feastdays of the Saints. The feasts of the Saints proclaim the wonderful works of Christ in His servants, and offer us examples to imitate.

Pilgrims come from all over the world to visit the shrine of Our Lady of Lourdes.

SACRED PLACES

BESIDES sacred times, there are sacred places. These places are set aside for Divine Worship. This means God is there in a presence that is more grace-filled than His usual presence in creation.

All churches are sacred places. The activities that Catholics carry out in them will be more open than any other place to God's grace and beneficial to their own salvation and that of the world.

There are also many **shrines** in different parts of the world, where God grants special favors on those who come to pray there. Some of these shrines are: Lourdes, in France; Fatima in Portugal; Guadalupe in Mexico City; Assisi in Italy; St. Anne de Beaupre in Canada; Czestochowa in Poland; and the Holy Places in Palestine.

In some countries, the shrines become national symbols of the devotion of the people, in which they show their deep faith in God, Our Lady, and the Saints.

Through Sacramentals we share in the life of Jesus.

FAITH IN THE USE OF SACRAMENTALS

SACRAMENTALS are not some kind of charm that works magically by just being had or worn or said. We must use the sacramentals with faith that they may help us as the Church wants them to help us.

This also calls for hope that what the Church encourages, Christ also blesses with His heavenly grace. For the Sacramentals carry with them the promise of God's help for soul and body, on the authority of the Church.

Using the Sacramentals should help us to serve God better.

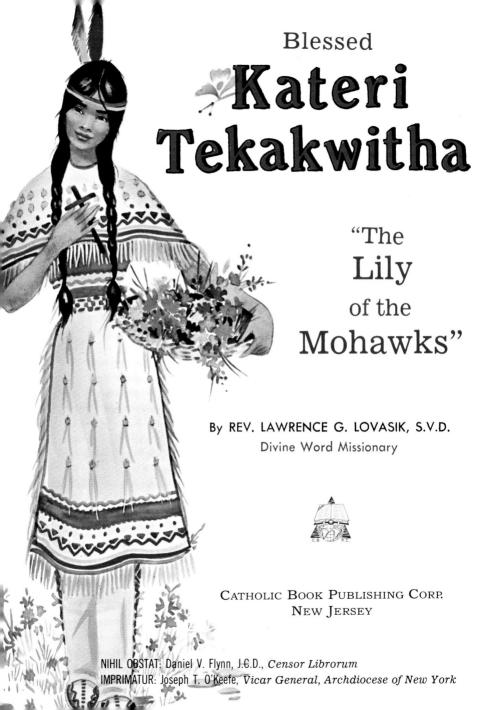

Blessed

Kateri Tekakwitha

"The
Lily
of the
Mohawks"

By REV. LAWRENCE G. LOVASIK, S.V.D.
Divine Word Missionary

CATHOLIC BOOK PUBLISHING CORP.
NEW JERSEY

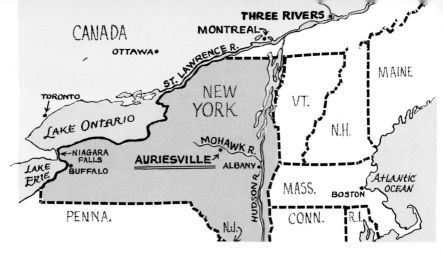

A Girl from New York State

KATERI Tekakwitha was born in 1656, a mile from the town of Auriesville, New York. This was ten years after the brave Jesuit Isaac Jogues was put to death nearby.

As a girl, she watched friendly traders and the Blackrobes, priests of New France, enter and leave the fort. The fort was known as Caughnawaga, meaning "at the rapids," because the Mohawk River runs swiftly as it passes this spot.

The Iroquois were enemies of the Huron and Algonquin tribes, as well as of the French. Kateri's mother Kahenta (Flower of the Prairie) was an Algonquin. Her mother had been brought up and baptized at an Indian village near the French colony of Three Rivers in Canada.

© 1981 by *Catholic Book Publishing Corp.*, N.J. — Printed in Hong Kong   978-0-89942-298-5

Kateri's Mother—
A Christian from Canada

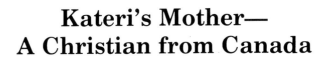

ON one of the Mohawk raids into Canada, Kateri's mother was taken through the woods and across the lakes to the shore of the Mohawk River in northeastern New York.

There Kateri came to learn about the famous "longhouses" of the Mohawks. These were made from the bark of birch trees.

Kateri's Father— A Mohawk Chief

KATERI'S mother was saved from the torture and the fire by a fierce pagan Mohawk warrior, Kenneronkwa (which means "Beloved"). She became his wife.

4

Like all the Mohawks, he was very tall, with fine lips, dark complexion, and straight black hair.

He was also a great hunter and warrior, skilled in using a rifle and a bow and arrow, and in riding a canoe.

Birth of Kateri

THE young couple was soon blessed with a son and a daughter. The girl came later to be called Kateri Tekakwitha.

Some think the name Kateri means "Eye of the Sun."

The family lived in an Iroquois longhouse at Gandawague, a little village of the Mohawks.

6

Death of Kateri's Parents

WHEN the Jesuit Father LeMoyne visited the Mohawks in 1656, he found Kateri tied to her mother's cradleboard. A few years later her mother died of small-pox.

Kateri was only four years old. Her father and brother also died of small-pox, which spread like wild-fire through the Mohawk nation.

Kateri herself became ill with small-pox, but she escaped death. She was then adopted by her two aunts and uncle.

When she was ten years old, war broke out between the French and the Mohawks. She fled from the village together with the other Mohawks to escape the horrors of war.

After the war, the French missionaries began to bring the Catholic Faith to the Mohawks.

8

Kateri's Dress and Her Works

KATERI had the well-known Indian features —high cheek bones, dull red skin, and soft dark eyes. Well-oiled and neatly parted hair in a long plait behind. For binding up the hair, she made ribbons and bands out of eel skins, and, for her waist, large beautiful belts.

She wore leggings and moccasins. Her dress was made of deer and moose skins. Beads of many colors adorned her neck. Over all she wore a red blanket.

Kateri was quiet and shy, perhaps because small-pox had made marks on her face and harmed her eyesight. When she had to go out, she shaded her eyes with a blanket.

But she was cheerful and busy. She showed special skill in making wooden things that were used in the village.

She was thin and weak from the time her mother died, and yet she was always the first one at work. She pounded the Indian corn and made the soup and gave food to the family.

Kateri Learns about Jesus

KATERI did not want to marry though her aunts tried to force her. They began to treat her as a slave and made her do all the work that was hard.

She suffered all these insults with patience and served everybody with gentleness.

Kateri first learned about Jesus from the Jesuit missionaries. It was her duty to serve them during their visit in her uncle's cabin.

Through fear of her uncle or through shyness, she never told any missionary of her desire for Baptism for eight years.

When Kateri was nineteen years old, she injured her foot and could not leave the cabin. The missionary, Father de Lamberville, came to see her and she opened her heart to him.

*Father de Lamberville
and Kateri*

11

Kateri is Baptized

AFTER kateri was well she began to attend the morning and evening prayers at the chapel, and to prepare for her Baptism.

She was baptized on Easter Sunday, April 5, 1676 in the chapel of St. Peter. The Indians were watching the celebration of the Great White Feast and the Baptism of the niece of a great Mohawk chief.

Kateri was now a Christian at the age of twenty, and received the name Kateri (Katherine).

Kateri's Devotion

TWICE each day she went to the chapel where the Blackrobe said morning and night prayers with his people.

On Sundays she assisted at Mass at this beautiful bark-covered chapel of St. Peter.

She also joined the Christian Indians who were chanting the prayers of the Rosary.

13

Kateri Bears Insults for Her Faith

KATERI'S religion was put to many tests, but she never grew weak in her faith.

Some children would pull her hair, others would point their finger at her and call her "Christian" as though they meant "dog."

Kateri's Courage in Suffering

KATERI had much to suffer from drunkards, witchdoctors and enemies of Christianity, and even her uncle.

They threw stones at her and called her a witch. But she was fearless.

Voyage to a Safer Place

THe priest and some Christians of her village were Kateri's only friends, and he told her to leave the country as soon as possible. She was to go to the Praying Castle in Canada, the new Caughnawaga on the St. Lawrence River.

Having spent a year and a half in her home as a Christian, Kateri set out for the new Christian colony of Indians in Canada, which was three hundred miles away. A Christian Oneida Indian chief, known as Hot Ashes, and his wife arranged for the trip, assigning a Mohawk and a Huron brave to be her guide.

Kateri Escapes from Her Uncle

KATERI'S uncle learned that she had left and went after her to bring her back.

When Hot Ashes saw the uncle coming, he made Kateri get out of the canoe and hide in the bushes until the uncle gave up the chase. Then he put Kateri in the canoe again and paddled up the Mohawk River toward Canada.

17

Caughnawaga —
A Christian Indian Colony

CAUGHNAWAGA lay on the south bank of the St. Lawrence River several miles west of Montreal.

The Indian colony had about one hundred fifty families. There were sixty cabins in all with at least two families in each cabin.

Kateri Reaches Her New Home

KATERI arrived in Canada in the autumn of 1677. She gave herself to God, asking Him to do with her whatever He pleased. She was to live in the cabin of Anastasia, her mother's friend, and her brother-in-law and his wife.

Kateri brought with her a letter from Father de Lamberville to the missionaries. He had written:

"I send you Kateri Tekakwitha. Will you kindly direct her? You will soon know what a treasure we have sent you. Guard it well!

"May it profit in your hands, for the glory of God, and the salvation of a soul that is certainly very dear to Him."

The people of the village were very good Christians. Kateri enjoyed meeting the new converts. Many of them had left the country of the Iroquois. She was an example to all of them.

Kateri Makes A Friend

MARY Teresa became a close friend of Kateri. Both watched the third chapel being built, and Kateri said: "A chapel of wood is not what God wants; He wants our souls to make a temple of them."

Teresa and Kateri prayed together and did penance and shared their most secret thoughts.

Kateri was simple, humble, kind, and cheerful. She spent much time in prayer. She was obedient to the priest who was the director of her soul, but, most of all, to the Holy Spirit, Who made her soul holy.

Every morning, even in the bitterest winter, she stood before the chapel door until it opened at four and remained there until after the last Mass. There were three Holy Masses. The people prayed aloud together, especially the Rosary.

Kateri's Daily Work

KATERI kept very busy around her home. She made nets and buckets to draw water, and mats out of bark. She made clothes from skins, and leather belts covered with beads.

Kateri's Devotion to Jesus in the Eucharist and on the Cross

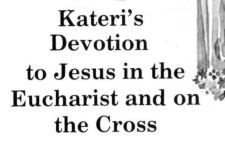

KATERI made her first Holy Communion on Christmas 1677 after she reached the St. Francis Xavier Mission.

Kateri was devoted to the Holy Eucharist and to Jesus Crucified. She carved the sign of the cross on a tree in the woods where she did her praying.

She said: "I offer my soul to Christ the Lord in the Blessed Sacrament and my body to Christ in the Lord, hanging on the Cross."

23

Kateri's Works of Kindness

THE people in the village liked Kateri because she was kind and cheerful in her quiet way.

Kateri walked her simple way among the people, helping with the sick, caring for the little children, and doing other works of kindness.

Kateri's Great Love for God

WHEN Kateri, a child of the forest, found God, she loved Him with her whole heart. She did everything she could to please Him, and stayed away from anything that would keep her from loving Him.

Kateri Offers Her Life to God

KATERI proved her love for Jesus by prayer and sacrifice. She would cry out: "My Jesus, I must suffer for You; I love You, but I have offended You. I am here to make up for my sins."

Kateri offered her life to God by a vow. She said to the priest: "I have dedicated myself to Jesus, Son of Mary. I have taken Him for my Spouse, and only He shall have me as a spouse."

While giving herself as a bride to Jesus, she also offered her life to the Blessed Virgin Mary, whom she loved dearly.

In memory of her consecration she changed her scarlet blanket to blue and wore the braids of an unmarried Iroquois maiden.

She was considered a Saint by her fellow Christians because of her great love for God and all people.

Kateri Becomes Very Sick

KATERI'S health was poor. She was always in pain. She had a sickness which left her with the sweat of a slow fever and stomach pains.

Two months before Holy Week of 1680, after suffering almost a year, she felt chest pains and severe headaches. She kept herself in the same position day and night. She wanted to suffer with Jesus on the Cross.

Her greatest joy was the Holy Communion brought to her by the priest. She lived only for the love of Jesus and now she was ready to die for Him.

On Tuesday of Holy Week Kateri began to be very sick. She received the Holy Anointing and the Eucharist. Her friend Teresa, who was at her side, heard Kateri whisper: "I am leaving you, Teresa. I am going to die.

"Keep up your courage. Listen to the Fathers. Never give up your penances.

"I will love you in heaven. I will pray for you. I will help you."

Death of Kateri

ON April 17, 1680, Kateri died. Her last words were: "Jesus, Mary, I love You!" She was only twenty-four years old.

The Indians came to kiss her hands as she lay in death. They all said: "We have lost our Saint."

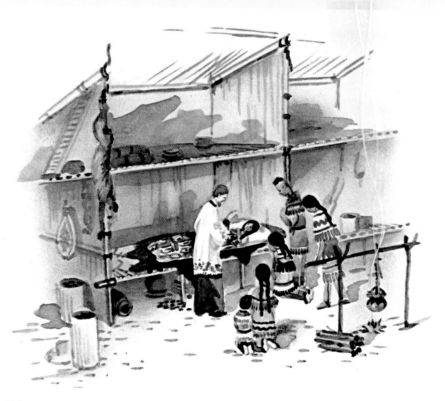

Favors Granted by Kateri

KATERI was buried at three o'clock on Holy Thursday afternoon. One of the priests said: "She loved the Holy Eucharist and the Cross, and now she can spend Holy Week in heaven."

Kateri granted many favors to those who prayed to her. The sick were cured, sinners converted, and miracles sprang up. Many Indians tried to imitate Kateri's example.

Many favors have been reported by her friends through the years. They call her the "Lily of the Mohawks."

On June 22, 1980, Pope John Paul II declared her Blessed. This is the last step before a person is declared a Saint.

She will be the first native North American saint. Kateri of the Mohawks is the Indians' undying gift to America and the fruit of the blood of the North American Martyrs.

Prayer to Kateri

KATERI, loving child of God and Lily of the Mohawks, I thank God for the many graces He gave you. Help me to be more like you in my love for God and for people.

Give me a great love for the Holy Eucharist and the Mother of Jesus. Make me ready to make sacrifices for Jesus that I may save my soul and be happy with you in heaven.

Kateri, I love you. Always be my friend!

CELEBRATING ADVENT
with the Jesse Tree

REV. JUDE WINKLER, OFM Conv.

Imprimi Potest: Daniel Pietrzak, OFM Conv., Minister Provincial of St. Anthony of Padua Province (USA)
Nihil Obstat: James T. O'Connor, S.T.D., Censor Librorum
Imprimatur: ✠ Patrick J. Sheridan, D.D., Vicar General, Archdiocese of New York

PREPARING FOR CHRISTMAS

CHRISTMAS is one of the happiest days of the year. It is the day when we celebrate how much God loves us. We rejoice because God sent His only Son into our world to be born as a baby in Bethlehem.

Because it is such an important day, there are many things we have to do to prepare for it. Months before it arrives we begin to think about the presents that we will receive from our parents. We must ask to go to the toy store or talk to our friends to decide what we should ask them to buy for us.

As the day approaches, there are all kinds of preparations to do at home. We help Dad and Mom get ready for our celebration. We help them clean the house, bake cookies, decorate the Christmas tree, and all the other things that have to be done. There is really a lot to do to get ready for Christmas.

Yet, we have to be careful that we do not spend all our time preparing our homes and then forget to prepare our hearts. That is why we have a special time of the year called Advent. It is when we look at our hearts to make sure that we are ready to welcome the baby Jesus into our lives and our love.

THE JESSE TREE

ADVENT is a good time to think back on how God prepared the hearts of His people for the birth of His only Son. That way, when we have heard how they grew closer to God all throughout their history, we might be encouraged to draw close to God ourselves.

It would be impossible to look at every single thing that God did for His people before Jesus was born, but maybe we can look at a few of those things. We will be looking at the Jesse tree. This is the name given to the promises that God made throughout the Old Testament concerning the birth of His only Son.

Just like our Christmas tree, the Jesse tree has beautiful decorations. But instead of having stars and lights on it, it has the promises that God made to us and to His people, promises made out of love.

The tree is named after Jesse, the father of David, the great king of Israel. The reason for this is that some of the most important promises of all were made to Jesse and to his son David. They were promised that God's only Son would be born in their family.

GOD CREATES ADAM AND EVE

THE first branch of this tree is very old, for it dates back all the way to the first days of the world.

In the beginning God created the heavens and the earth and all the things that are in them. The greatest of all the things that He created were the first man and woman. God loved Adam and Eve and He put them in charge of all His creation.

God placed Adam and Eve in the Garden of Eden. He told them that they could eat the fruit of any tree in the garden except the tree of the knowledge of good and evil. They were not to eat the fruit of that tree.

One day, while Eve was walking in the garden, a serpent spoke to her and convinced her to eat some of the fruit that she was not supposed to eat. When she had tasted the fruit, she gave some to Adam, her husband. As soon as they finished, they realized that they had sinned against God.

When God came to walk in the garden that evening, they hid from Him, for they knew that they had done something very bad. He called them out from hiding and spoke to them.

THE PROMISE OF A SAVIOR

WHEN they finally came out, God told the man, the woman, and the serpent that they would be punished for the bad thing they had done. He told the man that from then on he would have to work very hard to earn a living for his family. He told the woman that she would be punished by having much pain when she was giving birth to her children.

God gave the most serious punishment to the serpent for it had tempted the woman to turn against the Lord. He told it that it would no longer have any legs but would have to crawl on its belly for the rest of its life.

One part of the punishment is actually a promise to us. God told the serpent that the child of the woman would step on the head of the serpent. This was a promise that the devil would not be powerful forever. God was promising to send a Holy One who would crush the power of the evil one and free us from sin.

Then, to show us that He still loved Adam and Eve and all of us in spite of our sins, He made some clothes for Adam and Eve to protect them from the cold. This is the story of God's first promise to send Jesus into the world.

9

NOAH AND THE FLOOD

IN spite of the love that God had shown Adam and Eve, men and women continued to turn against the Lord. They sinned more and more until God finally decided that He would have to punish the whole world.

God decided that He would send a great flood to destroy all life upon the earth. He would only save one very good family from the flood, Noah and his family.

One day God called to Noah and told him to build a large boat, an ark. When he was finished, he was to collect all kinds of animals and to put them on board the ark. Noah did just as the Lord commanded him.

When Noah was finished and had all the animals on board the ark, God sent a great flood that destroyed all people and animals upon the earth. The flood lasted a long time, but all throughout it God kept Noah and his family safe.

Then, when the flood was over, God promised Noah that He would never again flood the whole earth. He gave us the rainbow as a sign of His promise. Once again, in spite of the fact that we had sinned, God gave us a sign of His mercy and His love.

ABRAHAM AND SARAH

THE next branch on our Jesse tree is the promise that God made to Abraham and Sarah. God promised that, even though they were very old, they would still have a son. Their children and grandchildren and other descendants would be as many as the stars in the sky. He also promised them a fertile land in which they could dwell.

Abraham and Sarah waited for a long time, but still they had no children. Then, one day, God visited them along with two angels in the form of three desert travelers. Abraham and Sarah were so kind and generous to them that God repeated His promise and then added that He would fulfill it within one year. Sarah soon became pregnant and gave birth to a son, Isaac.

Some time later, God asked Abraham to give Isaac back to Him in sacrifice. Although Abraham could have wondered whether God was taking back His promise, he trusted God. When God saw Abraham's great faith, He stopped him from sacrificing his son and greatly rewarded Abraham and Sarah. They were to become the father and the mother of God's holy people, Israel. It would be to this people that God would send His only Son, Jesus.

13

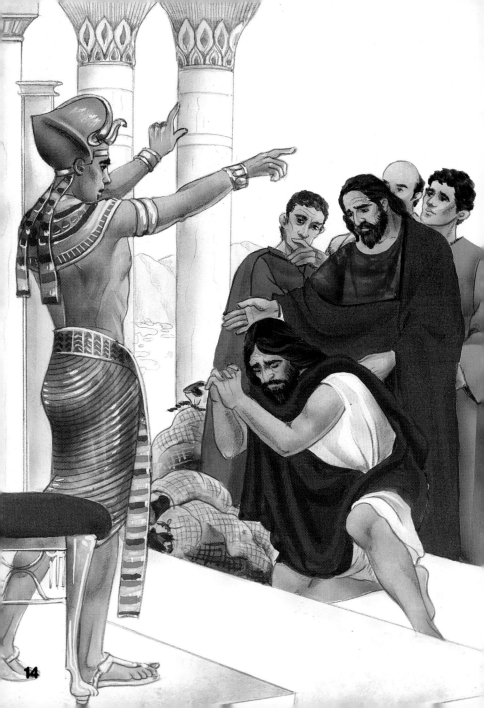

THE SONS OF JACOB

GOD continued to fulfill His promise to Abraham and Sarah. Isaac, their son, married Rebekah and they had two sons, Esau and Jacob. God chose Jacob as the son of His promise. Jacob and his wives, Leah and Rachel, had twelve sons and one daughter.

These twelve sons were to become the founders of the twelve tribes of Israel. Two of the most famous sons were Joseph and Judah.

Joseph was one of the youngest sons and he was a favorite of his father. His brothers hated him for that and sold him into slavery in Egypt. God cared for him there and made him an important official in the court of Pharaoh, the king of Egypt. When a great famine broke out over all the earth, Joseph was able to give grain to his family and to save them from death. He forgave his brothers and brought them and their father Jacob to Egypt where they could live in safety.

Judah, the second oldest son, was to become famous because of a promise that Jacob made to his son before he died. He told Judah that he would be as strong as a lion and would be the father of great kings. One day, the King of kings, Jesus, would be born from his tribe.

MOSES THE LIBERATOR

THE people of Israel grew very strong in Egypt, so strong that the Egyptians became frightened of them. They made them into slaves and treated them very badly.

God heard the cries of His people and He sent them a prophet, Moses, to lead them to freedom. Moses told Pharaoh to let his people go, and when Pharaoh refused, God sent a series of plagues against Egypt. Finally, God sent a terrible plague in which all the first sons of Egypt died, and Pharaoh let the people of Israel go.

When the army of Pharaoh chased after the people of Israel, God had Moses part the Red Sea and lead the people across. He drowned Pharaoh and his army in the Red Sea.

Israel dwelt in the desert for forty years. God cared for them there, giving them bread from heaven, which is called manna, and water from a rock. He also gave them a gift through Moses, the Ten Commandments, so that they would know how to serve God and to love each other. Before he died, Moses promised that God would send another prophet greater than he ever was. That prophet was Jesus, God's only Son.

YOUR GOD WILL BE MY GOD

O NE of those who was part of God's promise was Ruth, a woman from a foreign land.

There was a good woman from Israel named Naomi who moved from her home in Bethlehem to Moab, a pagan land, with all of her family. While she was there, her two sons married women from Moab. Eventually her husband died as well as her two sons. She told her two daughters-in-law that they should return to their families and she would return to Jerusalem.

One of the daughters-in-law returned to her family, but Ruth, the other one, refused to do this. She told Naomi that she would go with her wherever she went. Naomi's people would be her people and Naomi's God would be her God.

Naomi and Ruth traveled to Bethlehem. When they arrived there, Ruth cared for Naomi by picking up the loose grain in the fields that had been harvested. God rewarded Ruth for her goodness to Naomi. He sent a good man of Israel, Boaz, into her life. They married and had a son named Obed, who was to be the grandfather of David, the great king of Israel. Thus, Ruth was also one of the ancestors of Jesus, our Lord.

DAVID, THE SON OF JESSE

G OD does not always make the same choices that we would probably make, and this is seen most clearly in the story of David.

The people of Israel had asked God and the prophet Samuel for a king, and God had given them Saul. But Saul did things that were evil in the sight of God, so God told the prophet Samuel that he should go out and anoint a new king.

Samuel traveled to Bethlehem, to the house of Jesse, as God had ordered. He told Jesse to bring all his sons before him. But as each son passed in front of him, Samuel knew that the Lord was not choosing that man to be the future king of Israel.

When all Jesse's sons had passed in front of the prophet, Samuel asked Jesse if there were any others. Jesse said that the youngest son, David, was out tending sheep. Samuel had him called, and the minute he saw David he knew that God had chosen him.

God chose David not because he was the oldest or the tallest or the most handsome. He chose him because he was pure of heart, for God judges us according to our hearts. So Samuel took out his oil and anointed David the king of Israel.

A HOUSE FOR DAVID

DAVID became a great hero in Israel. He defeated the giant Goliath and many of the other enemies who were attacking his people. Then, when king Saul was killed in battle, David became the king of all of Israel.

One of the first things that David did as king was to capture the city of Jerusalem and to make it his capital. He built a great palace for himself. He also brought the Ark of the Covenant, the holiest of all the things that God had given to His people, into Jerusalem.

One day David called Nathan the prophet to his palace. David told Nathan that he felt guilty, for here he was living in a great palace while the Ark of the Covenant was still in a tent. He wanted to build a great temple to house the Ark.

God spoke to Nathan, sending him to speak to David. Nathan told David that God did not want him to build Him a house. Rather, God was going to give David a house that would never end.

This was a promise that David's descendants would rule over Israel for all time. It would be fulfilled when Jesus, the son of David, would become the King of Israel and the King of all kings.

EMMANUEL

THE descendants of David, however, did not follow the Lord with all their hearts. So God sent them prophets to call them back to His ways.

One of the prophets whom God sent was Isaiah. The people of Israel had sinned against the Lord and God had allowed their enemies to attack them. God then sent Isaiah to the king and told him to trust in the Lord, for God would defeat all of Israel's enemies.

Isaiah told the king to ask for a sign from the Lord as an assurance that they would be delivered, but the king refused to ask for a sign. The prophet told the king that God would give a sign anyway, for a maiden would bear a child who would be named Emmanuel, a name that means "God is with us."

The prophet also promised that when this child would reign, there would be a time a peace in Israel and over the whole world. The peace would be so great that even the wolf would lie down with the lamb and the lion with the calf. There would be a great peace on God's holy mountain. Jesus is the fulfillment of this promise, for He truly is "God with us"; He truly is the Prince of Peace.

LITTLE TOWN OF BETHLEHEM

S TILL the kings who lived in Jerusalem continued to sin against the Lord. And so God sent another prophet, Micah, who would make still another promise to the people of Israel.

Micah realized that the people of Jerusalem had forgotten the Lord. They were too rich and too important, so they did not have time to pray or to turn to the Lord. They were not humble enough to admit that they needed God's help.

But people of the small towns were always turning to God. Micah saw this and realized that the poor people and the unimportant are really the chosen ones of God. He remembered how God had chosen David, a small and unimportant child from Bethlehem, to be His great king.

So Micah spoke to Bethlehem and promised that another King would arise out of it. This King would reign over Israel just as David had done. He would be pleasing to God and turn all the people back to justice. He would rule forever.

When the Magi came to Herod to ask where the new King of Israel was born, the wise men of Israel turned to this promise to tell Herod that the Messiah was to be born in Bethlehem.

A NEW JERUSALEM

EVEN though God had sent many Prophets to Israel to turn His people away from their sins, they refused to listen to them. Finally, God sent a terrible punishment upon His people. He allowed the enemies of Israel to conquer the land and to take them off into exile.

The people of Israel were now living in a foreign land, and they began to wonder whether God had forgotten them or whether He was taking back His promises to them. God sent them a number of Prophets to reassure them that this was not the case.

These Prophets spoke of how God would restore His beloved land. He would build a new Jerusalem that would be much better than the one that had been destroyed. He would give His people a time of peace and prosperity.

God also promised that He would send one of His servants to His people. This Servant would preach the Word of God to all the nations and turn their hearts to the Lord. He would suffer for the sake of the people and take their sins upon Himself. He would die for His people, and then the Lord would raise Him from the dead. That Servant of the Lord was Jesus Himself.

29

JOHN THE BAPTIST

THE people of Israel tried to believe in the promises that God had made, but they waited for a long time and suffered a great deal.

Then, one day, a priest named Zechariah was in the temple burning incense before the altar of God. An angel appeared to him and told him that he and his wife, Elizabeth, would soon have a son. They were to name their son John and he would be a powerful messenger of the Lord. He would turn the people back to the Lord and prepare them for the coming of the Messiah.

Zechariah and Elizabeth were both very old, and Zechariah wondered how this could happen. The angel Gabriel replied that he had been sent from God Himself. Because Zechariah had doubted the promise of the Lord, he would be unable to speak until the child was born.

Zechariah returned to his home and soon afterward Elizabeth became pregnant. In her pregnancy she was helped by her cousin, the Virgin Mary, who was to be the Mother of God's Son, Jesus. The son whom Elizabeth bore was John the Baptist who would go out into the desert and baptize the people so that they might be ready to greet Jesus with their whole hearts.

THE JESSE TREE

D URING the Season of Advent we can think of the people and events of the Jesse Tree.

First Week — Numbers 1, 2, and 3
Second Week — Numbers 4, 5, and 6
Third Week — Numbers 7, 8, and 9
Fourth Week — Numbers 10 and 11

5 MOSES
(Exodus)
p. 16

4 JOSEPH AND HIS BROTHERS
(Genesis 37-50)
p. 15

6 RUTH
(Book of Ruth)
p. 19

3 ABRAHAM AND SARAH
(Genesis 12—25)
p. 12

7 DAVID
(1 Samuel 16—1 Kings)
pp. 20-23

2 NOAH
(Genesis 6—9)
p. 11

EMMANUEL
(Isaiah 2—11)
p. 24
8

10 NEW JERUSALEM
(Isaiah 40—66)
p. 28

9 MICAH
(Micah 5:1-3)
p. 27

1 ADAM AND EVE
(Genesis 1—3)
p. 7-8

JOHN THE BAPTIST
(Luke 1—3)
p. 31
11

OUR LADY OF FATIMA

By

REV. LAWRENCE G. LOVASIK, S.V.D.

Divine Word Missionary

NIHIL OBSTAT: Daniel V. Flynn, J.C.D., *Censor Librorum*

IMPRIMATUR: ✠ James P. Mahoney, D.D., *Vicar General, Archdiocese of New York*

© 1984 *by Catholic Book Publishing Corp., N.Y.* — Printed in Hong Kong

ISBN 978-0-89942-387-6

An Angel Appears to Three Children

IN the Spring of 1916, an angel appeared to three children tending sheep in a pasture in the village of Fatima, Portugal. The older girl, Lucia Santos, was nine, and her two cousins Francisco and Jacinta Marto were eight and six. The angel taught them special prayers and told them that he was the Angel of Peace, the Guardian Angel of Portugal.

The angel taught them to say: "My God, I believe, I adore, I hope, and I love You. I ask forgiveness for those who do not believe, nor hope, nor love You."

The angel asked them to pray for sinners and for peace, and to bear the suffering the Lord would send them.

The next year Sunday, May 13, 1917, the children were with their flock of sheep in a field called the Cova. They said the rosary after lunch and then they played. They were frightened by two flashes of lightning out of the clear sky.

The children said an angel gave them Communion. 3

4   **The children saw a beautiful young woman.**

A Beautiful Lady Appears

THE children saw a beautiful young woman standing over a small oak tree surrounded by a bright light. Her clothing was pure white, and a mantle edged with gold covered her head and flowed around her body. A gold cord ending in a tassel hung around her neck. Her hands were joined, and from her right arm hung a white rosary of pearly beads.

With a smile of motherly tenderness, but somewhat sad, she told the children to come near, saying, "Have no fear, I will do you no harm. I come from heaven. I want you children to come here on the thirteenth of each month, until October. Then I will tell you who I am."

"Do you come from heaven? Will I go there?" asked Lucia.

"Yes," replied the Lady, "but you must say the rosary, and say it devoutly."

After the vision the children returned to their homes.

The Children Tell Their Secret

AT supper that evening, Jacinta told her mother what had happened, but she did not believe her story. Her brothers and sisters—all home for Sunday night supper—spread the story throughout the village the next day. Relatives and friends gathered in their home demanding to know why the children were telling such lies.

Lucia's mother was angry with her when she told her secret. Within twenty-four hours after the children had seen the Lady the prediction she had made— "You will have much to suffer"—started coming true.

Only the father of Jacinta and Francisco believed the things that were happening at Fatima. He did not think that his children would lie to him. The priest said to him: "Let the children go to the Cove. Then bring them to me and I'll question them one by one."

When the people heard about the story, they made fun of the children. They thought that they were lying.

Lucia's mother was angry when Lucia told her secret.

8 The Lady asked the children to say the Rosary.

The Lady Comes Again

THE Lady's second visit happened on June 13. The children knelt down near the oak tree and began to say the rosary. A flash of lightning came from the clear sky. Lucia cried out: "Our Lady is coming."

The Lady appeared in a bright light and asked the children to say the rosary every day and to say after each mystery: "O Jesus, forgive us our sins, save us from the fire of hell. Take all souls to heaven, and especially those most in need of Your mercy."

Lucia asked the Lady if she would take the children to heaven. She said: "Francisco and Jacinta soon, but you must remain on earth to spread the devotion to my Immaculate Heart."

On July 13, 5000 people were present when the children came to the Cova with their flocks. The Lady appeared for the third time.

The Virgin Mary foretold the Second World War and the coming of Communism. She asked for the consecration of Russia to her Immaculate Heart.

The Promise of a Miracle

ON August 13, the mayor of the town came in his carriage and took the children away as they were leaving for the Cova. After asking them many questions, he put them in jail. He tried to make them change their story. Since they would not do so, they were released from the jail.

Although the children were not at the Cova, over 15,000 people were on hand and said the rosary. At noon there was a flash of lightning and a clap of thunder; then a glowing cloud settled over the little tree where the Lady usually appeared.

On September 13, more than 30,000 people gathered at the Cova. The Lady appeared again and asked the children to pray for peace.

Lucia asked for a miracle that would prove what the children had seen. The Lady promised a miracle that would happen on October 13.

During the vision, the whole crowd saw a shower of white petals fall from the sky, only to melt a few inches from the ground.

The mayor asked the children many questions. 11

12   **The children knelt in the mud and prayed.**

The Lady of the Rosary

O N the morning of October 13, when the children arrived at the Cova, 70,000 people filled the field hoping to see the Lady. But they never did.

Rain began to fall heavily. At noon the three children knelt down in the mud to pray the rosary. A sharp flash of lightning stilled the great crowd. A dim cloud rested on the oak tree.

The beautiful Lady appeared in radiant brightness. Lucia asked the question: "Who are you and what do you want?"

The Lady said: "I am the Lady of the Rosary, and I have come to warn the faithful to amend their lives and ask pardon for their sins. People must not continue to offend the Lord, Who is already so deeply offended. They must say the rosary."

The Virgin Mary then asked that a church be built on the spot and promised the war would end in a year if people would amend their lives.

The Miracle of the Sun

THE Virgin Mary then rose from the tree and showed her beauty and power. The children saw her first with St. Joseph. Mary was covered with a blue mantle. Then she appeared as the Mother of Sorrows. Beside her stood Jesus in a red robe, His hand raised to bless.

Finally, Mary stood alone in the sky. She wore the dress of Our Lady of Mt. Carmel and held the scapular in her hand.

The rain kept falling heavily. Suddenly the clouds parted and the sun was seen shining brightly. It seemed to revolve three times within ten minutes, and cast off great shafts of colored light which fell upon the sky and earth. It seemed to be coming toward the earth. Then it stopped and seemed to go back into the sky.

The great crowds of people were afraid. They cried out: "Forgive us our sins. Save us, O Jesus!" The people walked away slowly, their minds filled with the thought of God's Mother.

The sun seemed to revolve three times. 15

Francisco made his First Communion on his deathbed.

16

The Deaths of
Francisco and Jacinta

ON April 4, 1919, Francisco died of influenza,
making his First Communion on his deathbed. He had been faithful to the wishes of the
Blessed Virgin and had said many rosaries each
day and made sacrifices to make up for the sins
of people since the first vision.

Jacinta also became ill, and the Blessed
Mother appeared to her a number of times.
She, too, was faithful to the requests of Our
Lady of Fatima and died in a Lisbon hospital
on February 20, 1920.

When her body was taken out of the grave
September 13, 1935, it was found to be incorrupt.

The cause for the beatification of Francisco
and Jacinta has begun. Both children are buried
in the large basilica of Our Lady of Fatima,
Francisco on the right and Jacinta in the left
transept.

Lucia in a Convent

LUCIA, whom the Blessed Mother made her messenger and on whom she placed the burden of making known her wishes, left Fatima in 1921 and worked in an orphanage.

Lucia ever remained faithful in carrying out the wishes of the Blessed Virgin Mary. She knew that Our Lady of Fatima wanted her to live a life of holiness to be an example to the whole world of the spirit of the message given her by Mary.

In 1925 she entered the Convent of the Sisters of St. Dorothy and received the name of Sister Mary Lucia of Sorrows. In 1948 she became a Carmelite nun.

Lucia was asked by her spiritual director to put into writing certain graces that she had received. Our Lord made known to her that she should now make known what the Blessed Mother had told her about devotion to her Immaculate Heart.

Lucia became a nun. 19

Devotion to Our Lady Approved

THE close of the First World War and the rise of Communism had proved that what the Blessed Virgin foretold was really true.

In 1930 the bishop of Leira declared the apparitions to the three children at Fatima as worthy of belief. 215 cures took place in the 13 years since the Virgin Mary appeared.

Pope Pius XII approved the devotion to Our Lady of Fatima and consecrated the world to her Immaculate Heart, October 31, 1943.

In 1945 Pope Pius XII approved the feast of the Immaculate Heart of Mary to promote this devotion for the peace of the world. He also consecrated Russia to her Immaculate Heart.

Pope Paul VI, in the Vatican Council, again consecrated the world to the Immaculate Heart of Mary on November 21, 1969.

Pope John Paul II visited Fatima and urged all Catholics to say the Rosary each day.

Pope Pius XII approved devotion to Our Lady of Fatima. 21

The Basilica at Fatima

TODAY there is a large basilica at the place where the Virgin Mary appeared to which hundreds of thousands of pilgrims come from all over the world each year.

There Holy Masses are offered and Holy Communion given, confessions are heard and people say the rosary.

From May 13 to October 13 special pilgrimages and devotions are held at the Basilica. A crowd of more than 200,000 people fill the large area called the esplanade, in front of the Basilica.

In the middle of the esplanade is a high pillar on which stands the Sacred Heart. A small wooden chapel in the esplanade with the statue of Our Lady of Fatima marks the place where Mary appeared.

The large golden statue of the Sacred Heart of Jesus in the middle of the esplanade reminds all the pilgrims that Mary's mission is to lead us to her Son.

Special devotions are held at the Basilica. 23

Through Mary to Jesus

WE owe special veneration by word and example to Mary as Mother of Christ, Mother of the Church, and our spiritual Mother. In doing this we imitate her Son Who loved and honored His Mother more than any other human being that ever lived.

Jesus made His Mother holier and more beautiful than any other member of His Church, for she is truly the Mother of the Church.

Some of the special gifts Mary received from God are: being Mother of God, being preserved from all stain of original sin, and being taken body and soul to heaven.

By honoring the Mother of Jesus we show our love for her Son, who made her so holy and beautiful. He made her so powerful as Queen of Heaven that she may help us, her children, in all our needs.

Through her prayers we can receive the grace we need to be more like Jesus and to save our souls. By following her example and by seeking her help in prayer we can be sure of reaching her Son in eternal life.

In honoring Mary, we imitate her Son.

The apparitions at Fatima call to mind Mary as Queen of heaven and her interest in the salvation of mankind on earth. Through the rosary and penance she brings blessings upon her needy children. She appeals for peace in the world.

Our Lady asked for devotion to her Immaculate Heart.

The Immaculate Heart of Mary

OUR Lady told the children at Fatima that her heart is the hope of the world. In a vision to Sister Mary Lucia, she asked for the spread of devotion to her Immaculate Heart: "To save souls God wishes to establish in the world the devotion to my Immaculate Heart." She also appealed for the daily rosary.

She promised: "If people do what I tell you, many souls will be saved and there will be peace."

"I come to ask the consecration of Russia to my Immaculate Heart and I ask that the Communion of Reparation be made in atonement for the sins of the world on the five first Saturdays of every month. Please say the rosary."

The Virgin Mary promised: "If my wishes are fulfilled, Russia will be converted, and there will be peace; if not, then Russia will spread her errors throughout the world, bringing new wars and persecutions of the Church; the good will be martyred, and the Holy Father will have much to suffer. But in the end, my Immaculate Heart will triumph."

We should answer our Lady's requests by a great love for her Son in the Holy Eucharist at Holy Mass and Holy Communion. We should consecrate ourselves to her Immaculate Heart and pray the rosary that God may forgive sinners and grant peace to the world.

If we do what our Blessed Mother asks, we can be sure of coming closer to Jesus and reaching eternal life in heaven.

Prayer to the Immaculate Heart of Mary

MARY, Virgin Mother of God and our Mother, at Fatima you asked us to honor your Immaculate Heart. In honoring your Immaculate Heart we honor your person and the love you have for us.

The heavenly Father prepared you, Virgin Mary, to be the worthy Mother of His Son. He let you share beforehand in the salvation Christ would bring by His death, and kept you sinless from the first moment of your conception. Help us by your prayers to live in His presence without sin.

Almighty God gave you, a humble virgin, the privilege of being the Mother of His Son, and crowned you with the glory of heaven. May your prayers bring us to the salvation of Christ and raise us up to eternal life.

You stood beneath the cross when your Son entrusted us to your care and made you our Mother also. We, your children, turn to you with confidence.

Our Lady of Fatima, pray for us.

The heavenly Father raised you, the sinless Virgin, Mother of His Son, body and soul to the glory of heaven. May we see heaven as our final goal and come to share your glory. May we follow your example in reflecting your holiness in our life and join in your hymn of endless joy and praise in heaven.

Prayer to Mary, Queen of Peace

MARY, Virgin Mother of God and Queen of Heaven, your loving Son Jesus has offered Himself as a perfect sacrifice for all mankind to reconcile us with His Father and to bring us the peace of the children of God. Help us to seek God and live in His love that we may enjoy true peace.

Ask your Son Jesus, Who gives us the peace that is not of this world and Who has washed away our hatred with His blood, to banish the violence and evil of sin and keep us safe from weapons of hate. Help us to overcome war and violence, and to establish God's law of love and justice.

May those who are at peace with one another keep the goodwill that unites them; may those who are enemies forget their hatred and be healed through the Blood of Your Son.

Mary, Queen of Peace, bring peace to the world.

Our Lady of Fatima, Queen of Peace, may we always profit by your prayers, for you bring us life and salvation through Jesus Christ your Son. Hear our prayer and give us peace in our time that we may rejoice in God's mercy and praise Him without end.

Prayer to Our Lady of Fatima

OUR Lady of the Rosary, ask your Son Jesus to have mercy on us and to give us His peace. Help us to heed your warning at Fatima that we amend our lives and stop hurting God, Who is already so deeply offended by our sins.

Our Lady of Fatima, Queen of the Holy Rosary, pray for us.

The
Our Father
and the
Hail Mary

By
Rev. Lawrence G. Lovasik, S.V.D.
Divine Word Missionary

Catholic Book Publishing Corp., New Jersey

The OUR FATHER

ONE day the Apostles said to Jesus: "Lord, teach us how to pray, as John taught his disciples." Jesus told them: "When you pray, say as follows:

"Our Father, Who art in heaven,
hallowed be Thy Name.
Thy Kingdom come.
Thy will be done on earth
as it is in heaven.
Give us this day our daily bread;
and forgive us our trespasses
as we forgive those who trespass
　　against us.
And lead us not into temptation,
but deliver us from evil."

2

NIHIL OBSTAT; Daniel V. Flynn, J.C.D., *Censor Librorum*
IMPRIMATUR: ✠ Joseph T. O'Keefe, D.D., *Vicar General, Archdiocese of New York*
© 1985 by *Catholic Book Publishing Corp., N.Y.* – Printed in Hong Kong   ISBN 978-0-89942-389-0

Jesus teaches the Apostles the "Our Father."

THE Our Father is also called the Lord's Prayer because Jesus Himself taught it to the Apostles.

There is no better or holier prayer. It fits the needs of everybody. It contains all that we, as children of God, can and should ask God for, to help us in soul and body.

We do not only ask God for what is good for us, but we also put the most important thing first. We ask first for God's glory, and then for help in our needs.

Our Father, Who Art in Heaven

MY God in heaven, I call You my Father,
    because You created me;
because Your Son became our Brother
when He was made man,
and we are all brothers and sisters;
and because at Baptism
the Holy Spirit made me Your child
and came to live in my soul.

I want to call You "Father"
    because the word fills my soul
    with love and trust in You.

Though You are everywhere,
    Your throne is in heaven,
    and only there do the Angels and Saints
    see You as You are.

Give me childlike love and trust in You,
    that I may always be with You by Your grace
    and see You face to face in heaven.

Before the "Our Father" in the Mass, the priest says:
**"Through Jesus, with Him, and in Him,
in the unity of the Holy Spirit,
all glory and honor is Yours, almighty Father, forever!"**

6

Hallowed Be Thy Name

HEAVENLY Father, You glorified Your Name when You created Angels, people, and the world.

You glorified Your name again
    when You redeemed the human race
    through the death and resurrection of Your
      Son.

On the night before He died to save the world,
    Jesus prayed to You: "Father, glorify Your
      Name."

You answered from heaven:
    "I have both glorified it and will glorify it
      again."

Father in heaven,
    may Your Name be honored by all people!

May I honor Your name all my life
    by doing all things for Your honor
    and for love of You.

Thy Kingdom Come!

HEAVENLY Father, may Your Kingdom come on earth!

I pray that You may be known and loved and served on earth.

I pray that the Catholic Church may spread throughout the world, especially in pagan countries.

I pray that through sanctifying grace,
your Holy Trinity—Father, Son and Holy Spirit—
may live in more Christian souls as in a temple,
for Jesus said: "The Kingdom of God is within you."

Jesus Christ, my Savior,
may Your Kingdom come for us,
the Kingdom promised us by the Father.

Jesus, reign over us as our King
in the Holy Sacrament of the Altar,
and in our hearts.

"Sacred Heart of Jesus, Your Kingdom come!"   9

Thy Will Be Done on Earth As It Is in Heaven

HEAVENLY Father, I ask for the grace
to do Your will on earth
as the Angels and Saints do it in heaven.

Let me do Your will
by obeying Your Ten Commandments
and the Laws of Your Church;
by accepting everything that happens to me
because I know that You allowed it to happen.

You are my Father,
and You know what is best for me.
You love me with a love that has no limit.
I honor You when I do Your will.

In all my prayers,
and especially in all my sufferings,
I always want to say: "Thy will be done!"

Jesus said: "If a man wishes to come after Me, he must deny his very self, take up his cross, and follow in My footsteps" (Mk 8, 34).

Give Us This Day Our Daily Bread

MY heavenly Father, Jesus taught me to
pray to You,
because You are my Father.
You love Your children and want them to be
happy in this world and in heaven.

Jesus said: "Your Father in heaven
knows you have need of all these things. . . .
Whatever you ask the Father in My Name
He will give you.
Ask and you shall receive."

I ask You, Father,
for all that I need for life here on earth,
such as food, clothing, work, health, and true
happiness.

I also ask for the daily Bread
of Holy Communion.
For Jesus said: "I am the Bread of Life."

May that Bread give me eternal life with You
as Jesus promised.

Jesus said, "I myself am the living bread come down from heaven. If anyone eats this bread he shall live forever" (Jn 6, 51).

13

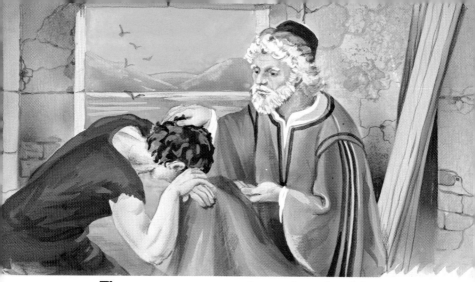

**The younger son returned and said,
"Father, I have sinned!"**

And Forgive Us Our Trespasses

HEAVENLY Father, I believe
that sin is the greatest evil in the world
because a serious sin makes me fail
in my love for You,
and turns me away from doing Your will.

But I also believe
that You are merciful and will pardon me
if I am truly sorry for my sins
because they offend You,
my loving Father and Highest Good.

God gives us his forgiveness in the Sacrament of Penance.

As We Forgive Those Who Trespass Against Us

I BELIEVE that in the Sacrament of Penance
  Jesus comes to forgive my sins
and brings peace with You, my God,
and with the Church, which is hurt by my
    sins.

Heavenly Father, on the Cross Jesus prayed:
  "Father, forgive them for they do not know
  what they are doing."

As Jesus forgave those who put Him to death,
  help me to forgive those who hurt me.
Only then can I expect You to forgive me.

Jesus said to the devil: "Away with you, Satan!"

And Lead Us Not into Temptation

HEAVENLY Father, Jesus, Your Son,
was tempted in the desert.
His prayer gave Him strength to overcome
the devil who tried to make Him do
what was against Your holy will.

I also ask You to help me
when the devil tempts me to do bad things.
Keep me from the persons, places, and things
that lead me into sin.

God gave me a Guardian Angel to protect me.

But Deliver Us from Evil

HEAVENLY Father, I ask You to protect me
   from evil—
from everything that may be harmful
such as sickness, accidents, and poverty.
Keep me in Your loving care,
and send Your Angels to protect me.

But I ask You to protect me
   from the greatest evil in the world—sin!
Help me to be sorry for my past sins
and to resist temptation in the future.

The "Our Father" in The Mass

HEAVENLY Father, I believe that the "Our Father"—the prayer Jesus taught us,—is never more powerful than when it is said with Jesus at Holy Mass.

In the Mass Jesus is our Best Gift to the Father, and our Best Gift from the Father in Holy Communion.

I believe that the sacrifice of Calvary
   is offered again in an unbloody way
   on our altar at Mass.

Through the offering of Jesus
   we have hope of obtaining Your forgiveness
   and the graces we need to save our souls.

In the Consecration we give You
   the best Gift we could offer—your own Son:
   to adore and thank You,
   to ask Your pardon, and to beg for Your help.

And in Holy Communion You give us
   your best Gift—Your own Son as the Bread
      of Life.
   Before going to the Holy Table
   to receive this Food for our souls,
   we pray: "Father, give us this day our Daily
      Bread."

Jesus is our Daily Bread in Holy Communion.

THE
HAIL MARY

The words of the Angel Gabriel:

**Hail Mary, full of grace!
The Lord is with thee.**

The words of Saint Elizabeth:

**Blessed art thou among women,
and blessed is the fruit
of thy womb, Jesus.**

The words of the Church:

**Holy Mary, Mother of God.
pray for us sinners,
now and at the hour of our death.
Amen.**

The Blessed Virgin has a special love for children. 21

Hail Mary, Full of Grace!

MARY, my Mother, the Angel Gabriel said to you:

"Hail, full of grace! The Lord is with you."

You are called "full of grace" because God poured His richest graces upon you.

The Angel Gabriel says to Mary: "Hail, full of grace! The Lord is with you."

The Lord Is with Thee

MARY, my Mother, the Angel Gabriel also said, "The Lord is with you."

The Lord was with you in a wonderful way,
 not only by His grace and power,
 but as your Son.

When you answered the angel with the words:
 "I am the servant of the Lord.
 Let it be done to me as you say,"
 the Son of God became man in your womb.
 The Lord was with you for nine months as
  your Child.
 resting under your heart.

Each time I say the Hail Mary,
 I remind you of this most wonderful honor
 of being the Mother of God,
 and I thank God with you for all He has done
  for you.

24   **Mary visits Elizabeth who greets her with joy.**

Blessed Art Thou
Among Women

MARY, my Mother, when the Angel had gone away,
you at once made a journey to visit your cousin Elizabeth.

When Elizabeth heard your greeting,
she was filled with the Holy Spirit and cried out:
"Blest are you among women
and blest is the fruit of your womb.
But who am I that the mother of my Lord should come to me?"

Mary, you knew that you were great and holy only because of God's love for you.
You knew that you owed everything to His mercy.

And Blessed Is the Fruit of Thy Womb, Jesus

MARY, my Mother, how wonderful
was your visit to your cousin Elizabeth!

The Holy Spirit let Elizabeth know
that the Son of God was already under your
heart.
The "Fruit" of your womb was Jesus, the Son
of God,
worthy of the praises of human beings
and Angels for all eternity.

Mary, your Son is the Way, the Truth, and the
Life—the Redeemer of the world.
The name of Jesus means "Savior."

Your Son saved His people from their sins
by shedding His Blood on the Cross.
Through the name of Jesus we are saved,
and we have hope of eternal life with God.

In saying the Hail Mary,
I want to join you, Mary, in thanking God
for all He has done for you,
and through you, for all human beings.

Holy Mary, Mother of God

MARY, my Mother, I honor you as the Mother of God.
I believe that Jesus Christ is God.
Since you gave birth to Jesus,
you are truly the Mother of God.

With Joseph, Mary adores her new-born Son Jesus. 27

Pray for Us Sinners

MARY, my Mother,
from the Cross Jesus gave to your care
the souls He was redeeming.
He said to you, "Woman, there is your son."
Then He said to the disciple John,
who took our place beneath the Cross:
"There is your mother."

We have sinned against God,
and Jesus died to take away our sins
and to open heaven for all of us sinners.
You wanted to do His Last Will,
especially by being a Mother to all of us.
You are the Mother of us sinners.

Mary, you are called
"The Refuge of Sinners,"
because you are the Mother of the Good
Shepherd
who laid down His life for His sheep.
Pray for us sinners, your children.

From the Cross Jesus gives us His Mother.

Now and at the Hour of Our Death. Amen.

MARY, my Mother, we need your help
above all at the hour of our death,
the hour of our greatest need,
because on your help depends an eternity of
joy.

When God called Joseph to heaven,
Jesus and you were at his side.
He loved and served you so faithfully.
Now he died happily in your arms.

Mary, stand at my bedside when I am dying.
Help me in my last moments.
Protect me from the enemy,
and obtain for me a happy death,
and the glory of heaven.

You are my most powerful friend
before Jesus, the Just Judge,
to whom you can pray for me
with the unfailing prayers of a mother.

Pray that I may prepare for death
by living a holy life on earth with your help.

JESUS, Mary, Joseph,
I give you my heart and my soul.

Jesus, Mary, Joseph,
help me in my last agony.

Jesus, Mary, Joseph,
may I die in peace with you.

Joseph dies in the care of Jesus and Mary.   31

The "GLORY BE TO THE FATHER"

The Holy Trinity

AFTER the *Our Father* and the *Hail Mary* there is perhaps no more important prayer for every Catholic to say than the prayer of praise to the Blessed Trinity, the *Glory be to the Father.* This prayer reminds us that there are three Persons in one God, that each Person has showed His love for us, and therefore deserves praise forever. Many times a day, say:

> Glory be to the Father,
> and to the Son
> and to the Holy Spirit.

> As it was in the beginning,
> is now, and ever shall be,
> world without end. Amen.

Padre Pio

REV. JUDE WINKLER, OFM Conv.

Imprimi Potest: Michael Kolodziej, OFM Conv., Minister Provincial of St. Anthony of Padua Province (USA)
Nihil Obstat: Rev. James M. Cafone, M.A., S.T.D., Censor Librorum
Imprimatur: ✠ **Most Rev. John J. Myers, D.D., J.C.D.**, Archbishop of Newark

The Nihil Obstat and Imprimatur are official declarations that a book or pamphlet is free of doctrinal or moral error. No implication is contained therein that those who have granted the Nihil Obstat and Imprimatur agree with the contents, opinions or
statements expressed.

© 2004 by CATHOLIC BOOK PUBLISHING CORP., Totowa, N.J.

Printed in Hong Kong   ISBN 978-0-89942-531-3

Padre Pio as a Boy

PADRE Pio was born on May 25, 1887, in the small village of Pietrelcina in the south of Italy. His parents, Grazio and Giuseppa Forgione, were poor and honest farmers. They owned a few pieces of land on which they raised grapes, wheat, corn, olives, figs and plums, almost all of the food that their family needed to survive.

Grazio and Giuseppa named their son Francesco (which in English is Francis). He was not known as Pio until he became a Franciscan.

Francesco was a good little boy. He loved to pray in church, especially when he could be there alone. He also hated to hear swearing, which was very common in the area where he was growing up. Whenever he heard someone swearing, either he would make a Sign of the Cross and say his prayers or he would rush away.

One day he saw a Capuchin Franciscan, Friar Camillo, passing by. The Capuchins are followers of St. Francis of Assisi, and they dedicate themselves in a special way to poverty and prayer. Friar Camillo was gathering the offerings of the people to help support the friars. Little Francesco decided that he wanted to join the "friars with a beard" (for in those days all Capuchins wore beards).

Francesco Grows Up

FRANCESCO would not have an opportunity to enter the Capuchins for several years. In the meantime he would have to learn his lessons. The family wondered where they would find the money to pay his tutors. They had enough to eat, but very little cash. So Grazio, Francesco's father, traveled first to Brazil and then to the United States to earn money for his son's education.

The boy was not a great student, but he learned enough to keep progressing. His greatest difficulty was his delicate health, something from which he suffered most of his life. There were times, in fact, when his family despaired for his life, but he would eventually recover.

Then, when Francesco was fifteen years old, he entered the novitiate of the Capuchins. This is the first year of religious life in which one learns the traditions and the spirit of one's order. It is a time of prayer and discernment (figuring out whether God has called one to this type of life).

Upon entering the novitiate, Francesco received the name he would use for the rest of his life, Pio (which is Pius in English).

Friar Pio Grows in Holiness

IN his early years in the order, Friar Pio traveled from friary to friary, learning the lessons he needed to be a Capuchin friar and eventually a priest. Those who knew him in these early days spoke of how pleasant it was to live with him. He was an example of obedience and humility. They missed him whenever he was away, and that was quite often. His illness continued to bother him terribly in those days.

It was during his early days in the order that the friars began to notice his extraordinary spiritual gifts. He would have periods of time when he saw and spoke with Jesus, the Angels and the Saints. This is called an ecstasy.

It was around this time that he is also said to have received the gift of bilocation (the ability to be in two places at one time). While he was in his friary, he appeared to a man who was dying very far away. The man was an enemy of the Faith, and Friar Pio convinced him to seek God's forgiveness. That very night the man's wife gave birth to a daughter to whom Padre Pio became a spiritual advisor years later. Padre Pio knew her even before they had been introduced (for he was present when she was born).

Padre Pio as a Young Priest

ON August 10, 1910, Friar Pio was ordained a priest. From then on he would be known as Padre Pio. On the holy card that was printed for that day, he wrote that he wanted to be "a holy priest, a perfect victim." From his earliest days as a friar and a priest, he offered himself up to God as a victim. He wanted to suffer for his own sins and the sins of others so that they might turn to God.

At first Padre Pio's suffering involved physical illnesses. For a number of years, he would enter one of the order's friaries and immediately become so ill that he would have to be sent home. It was at this time that he first received the stigmata, the wounds in his hands, feet and side that Jesus had on the Cross. The stigmata was not yet permanent, for it would appear and then fade away.

In 1915 Italy entered the fighting of World War I. The government drafted priests and friars into the army, where they often served in the medical corps. Padre Pio was called to his medical exam, which he failed, but the government drafted him anyway. Yet, almost as soon as he arrived in his barracks, he became so violently ill that he was sent home to recover.

Padre Pio as Spiritual Guide

BEFORE and after he was drafted, Padre Pio lived in a town called San Giovanni Rotondo. He would live there for the rest of his life.

He quickly acquired a reputation for holiness among the people in that region. Many people went to him for spiritual advice. He would often know more about them than they were willing to tell him. He received this knowledge directly from God.

Padre Pio would give direction only to those about whom God had given him information. He did not want to direct them on his own, for he felt that this would be an act of pride. He wanted to obey God in all things.

There were five rules that Padre Pio suggested for spiritual growth. He told people that they should go to confession once a week. They should receive Holy Communion every day. They should read spiritual books on a regular basis. They should meditate upon God and the truths of our Faith. Finally, they should examine their consciences daily so that they could become aware of the ways in which they were growing and find those areas in which they still needed work.

It was around this time that he began the first prayer groups that eventually spread worldwide.

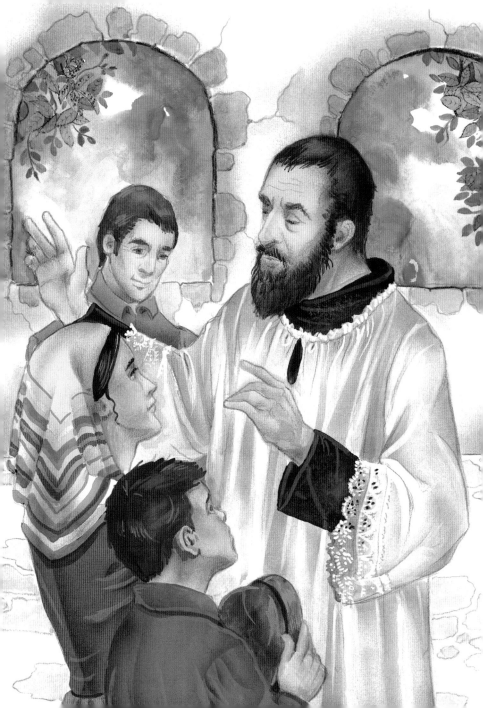

Padre Pio Receives the Stigmata

ON August 5, 1918, Padre Pio received the gift of the stigmata. He was to carry these wounds for the next fifty years.

Many Church officials and doctors examined his wounds. Some of them thought that he might be faking his wounds, but, after examining him, almost all were convinced that his stigmata was truly from God.

Padre Pio would especially suffer while he was celebrating the Holy Mass each day. It was as if he were experiencing just what Jesus did on the Cross. Like Jesus, he would lose much blood from his wounds. He always offered up these sufferings for the salvation of the world.

Word of Padre Pio's stigmata spread throughout the town and the region. Many people had become terribly discouraged by the war, and they needed the consolation of knowing that God was still working in their midst. Many people confessed their sins to him, firmly believing that this was an encounter with God's mercy.

Every once in a while there was a rumor that Padre Pio was going to be transferred from San Giovanni. The people of that village would hold meetings and march to his convent to make sure that no one would take their beloved friar from them.

Padre Pio Obeys
His Church Superiors

AROUND this time some Church officials began to question whether Padre Pio was truly saintly or not. Part of the problem was that there were people who seemed to have been jealous of him. They even made up lies, saying that he was not faithful to his vows.

Another part of the problem was that people who were loyal to Padre Pio were not always nice and gentle. They would push and shove to get a better spot in the chapel where he celebrated Mass and listened to confessions. There were even people selling clothes that were covered with blood from animals that they claimed were relics of Padre Pio.

For these and other reasons, the Church placed some rules upon how Padre Pio could do his ministry. Twice he was ordered to do things that would limit his contacts with people outside of the friary. For example, he was to say Mass at a different time every day so that the people would not know when to expect him.

It was during these periods that Padre Pio proved his holiness most. He humbly obeyed whatever orders he was given, even if some of these things made him sad. He always wanted to fulfill God's will as expressed through his superiors.

Padre Pio's Fame Grows

AS word of Padre Pio's stigmata and holiness spread throughout the region and all Italy, and then eventually over the whole world, he received more and more requests for prayers. It took a number of friars to answer these letters and to promise those requesting prayers that Padre Pio would remember them in his own prayers.

In those days, there was a young American woman from New Jersey named Mary Pyle who became a disciple of Padre Pio. She was quite rich, and she built a large house in San Giovanni. There she could host visitors to Padre Pio. She helped his ministry in whatever way she could until the day she died.

Padre Pio heard the confessions of many people. Those who were sincere found him to be understanding and gentle. But Padre Pio was harsh with those who just wanted to go to confession to a famous priest. He often sent them away until they were truly sorry for their sins. Then he would welcome them warmly, for he knew that they were ready to change their lives.

There were even a number of people who either belonged to other religions or did not believe in God at all who became Catholics as a result of meeting Padre Pio. They could sense that God was working through him.

Padre Pio, Example of a Humble Life of Service

MANY people began to make offerings of money to Padre Pio. At first, these were most welcome, for his friary was very poor and could use the money just to buy food and clothes for the friars. But as more and more money arrived, Padre Pio began to use it to help poor families. Some of them had visited or written to him, asking for his help; others did not even have to contact him. He had been informed by God that this or that family was in need, and he would send money to help them.

There was never a question of Padre Pio using the money for his own comfort. Everyone agrees that he lived a humble, simple lifestyle.

Padre Pio ate very little. He would join the other friars whenever they had meals, but he would hardly touch his food. No one could understand how he could survive. It was as if God was nourishing him with His love.

It also seemed as if he hardly ever slept. He would sleep only around three hours each night. His other time during the day was spent in prayer and meditation and serving God's people, especially by listening to their confessions and offering spiritual advice.

Padre Pio Battles the Evil One

IT is said that the holier one becomes, the more the devil bothers you. Padre Pio was bothered by terrible temptation, even by visits from the devil, for most of his life. The devil would try to trick him and make him do things that would not have pleased God.

Padre Pio was truly courageous in this battle. He would always make sure that his messages came from God by asking those who appeared to him to praise God and glorify Jesus. If they refused, Padre Pio would know that the messenger did not come from God.

He would also rely upon the protection of his Guardian Angel and the other Angels. He often told people who visited him in San Giovanni that they should go to a shrine not far from there that was dedicated to St. Michael. He is the Archangel who forced Satan out of heaven. Padre Pio told his visitors that St. Michael would protect them from the action of the devil.

But Padre Pio's greatest weapon against the devil was to dedicate himself to God's love more and more. Later in his life, he told people that he did not believe that there could be many people in hell because God was so merciful and loving.

World War II Arrives

IN 1939 World War II began in Europe. Italy became an ally of Germany and was fighting in Europe and Africa. At first the battles went well for Italy, but that did not fool Padre Pio. He predicted that it would go very badly for Italy and that she and her allies would lose the war. He felt that the leader of Germany, Adolf Hitler, was a very evil man and that Italy should never have become his friend.

In 1943 the war had gone so badly for Italy that many Italian cities were being bombed by American and English airplanes. San Giovanni was not a very large city, but it was still almost bombed a number of times.

Something very unusual happened whenever the bombers approached San Giovanni. The pilots spoke of seeing a bearded friar dressed in a brown robe, who stood in front of their planes. Sometimes the friar was normal in size, but other times he was enormous. Later, when these airmen visited San Giovanni, they would recognize the friar as Padre Pio.

Once the Americans landed in southern Italy, they began to make trips to San Giovanni to visit Padre Pio. Many of the soldiers who had been lazy and disobedient before their visit turned their lives around after their meeting with Padre Pio.

The House to Relieve Suffering

EVEN though Padre Pio suffered from illnesses all throughout his life, he did not like to see others suffer. This is why he had a small hospital built that was named St. Francis Hospital.

In 1938 the hospital was destroyed in an earthquake. Padre Pio decided that he would replace the hospital with a much larger building that would be called the "House to Relieve Suffering." Padre Pio provided the first donation, a coin that was worth only a few pennies. The coin had been given by a very poor woman who gave Padre Pio all that she had so that he might rebuild the damaged hospital.

Because of World War II and all the problems that it created, it took many years for Padre Pio and his helpers to collect the money needed to finish this project. The house finally opened in May of 1956.

Padre Pio hoped that the house would be a place where those recovering could receive both physical and spiritual assistance. He had been in hospitals during World War I, where staff took care of only the body but never showed the patients the love and prayer that they truly needed. This is why Padre Pio insisted that the House to Relieve Suffering not be called a hospital; it was to be so much more than that.

"God Will Provide"

A S Padre Pio began his project, he chose the doctor who would organize the construction of the House to Relieve Suffering. The doctor had not really believed in God when he first met Padre Pio. His whole life turned around when he met him and he became a good Christian.

Padre Pio told the doctor that he would have to be in charge of the project. The doctor answered that he could not do it because he had to earn a living for his family, a difficult task to do in San Giovanni. But Padre Pio told the doctor, "God will provide."

Upon returning to his home city of Florence, the doctor won the lottery. He was able to sell everything he had in Florence and move to San Giovanni, where he first designed and then supervised the construction of the House to Relieve Suffering.

In 1949 an even greater miracle was bestowed on a man named Giovanni Savino. On February 12, Padre Pio told him to be courageous because he would not die from what was about to happen. Then, three days later, he was seriously injured by an explosion on the job. He lost his right eye completely. But several days later the man said that Padre Pio had visited him. When the man's bandages were removed, the doctors discovered that his right eye had grown back.

Padre Pio Grows Old

BY the end of the 1950s and the beginning of the 1960s, Padre Pio had grown quite old. He had the normal aches and pains that one develops as one grows older, but he also suffered from the serious illnesses that plagued him all of his life.

In May of 1958, he grew sicker and sicker. He was so ill that he was not even able to listen to confessions or celebrate Mass. Some doctors even thought that he might be dying of cancer, but it was simply a problem with his breathing that had grown worse.

That August a statue of the Blessed Mother was brought to San Giovanni from Fatima, the city in Portugal where Mary had appeared to three young children in 1917. Padre Pio had always loved Mary in a special way, so he had himself carried to the church where the statue was on display. After he finished praying in front of the statue, he had himself carried home.

Then, the day that the statue was being taken back to Portugal, he told the Blessed Virgin Mary that as long as she (her statue) had been in Italy, he had been ill. He asked that his illness might be carried away when she left. The very minute that the statue was taken away, Padre Pio jumped up out of bed and proclaimed that he had been healed.

Padre Pio Dies on the Fiftieth Anniversary of Receiving the Stigmata

BY 1968 many of Padre Pio's friends and disciples had died. He himself had grown quite weak, and one of the friars kept watch on him day and night in case he needed someone's help. He had difficulty sleeping and could barely walk. He often asked Padre Carmelo, his guardian, for permission to die.

Then, on September 20, 1968, the community and people from all over the world gathered in San Giovanni to celebrate the fiftieth anniversary of Padre Pio's reception of the stigmata. This was also the First International Convention of Padre Pio Prayer Groups.

Padre Pio celebrated Mass that morning, and he was able to be present when the people recited the Rosary and prayed in front of the Blessed Sacrament.

But by the next morning, he was so weak again that he could neither listen to confessions nor celebrate Mass. On September 22 he did celebrate Mass once again, but he was clearly quite ill. Late that night his condition grew worse, and he asked one of the friars to listen to his confession. He gave his last blessing to his spiritual disciples and uttered his last words: "Jesus and Mary." At 2:30 that morning Padre Pio died peacefully.

Padre Pio Is Beatified and Canonized

SO many people believed that Padre Pio was a Saint that by the next year the Capuchin friars had asked the Church to consider making him a Saint. Over the next several years all of his writings and actions were examined, and by 1983 the official process for his beatification had begun.

He was named Blessed on May 2, 1999. Then, on June 16, 2002, Pope John Paul II declared Padre Pio to be a Saint. His feast day is celebrated on September 23, and to this day many people pray for his intercession and speak of the favors they have received from God through him.

MY FIRST CATECHISM

Rev. Lawrence G. Lovasik, S.V.D.
Divine Word Missionary

CATHOLIC BOOK
PUBLISHING CORP.
New Jersey

NIHIL OBSTAT: Daniel V. Flynn, J.C.D., *Censor Librorum*
IMPRIMATUR: ✠ Joseph T. O'Keefe, *Vicar General, Archdiocese of New York*
© 1983 by Catholic Book Publishing Corp., N.J.—Printed in Hong Kong   ISBN 978-0-89942-382-1

1. WHY I AM IN THE WORLD

1. **Who made you?**
God made me.

2. **Why did God make you?**
God made me because He is good
and He wants me to be happy
with Him in heaven.

Jesus speaks to us
through His Church

3. **What do you have to do to be happy with God in heaven?**
To be happy with God in heaven,
I must know about God,
I must love God,
and I must do what God wants me to do.

The Holy Family
teaches us
how to love
and serve God.

4. **How do you know what God wants you to do?**
Jesus tells me what God wants me to do
through the Catholic Church.

5. **How do you show your love for God?**
I show my love for God when I pray
and go to Holy Mass,
when I obey God,
and when I love everyone for the love of God.

People give God the highest worship at Holy Mass

6. **How do you serve God?**
I serve God when I keep God's commandments
and the laws of the Catholic Church,
and when I help others.

Jesus helps His
foster-father
Joseph

3

2. GOD

7. Who is God?

God is the highest Being because He made
everything.

God made all things from nothing. He also made man.

8. What does the Catholic Church teach you about God?

The Catholic Church teaches me
that God is the highest Good.
He always was and always will be.
He knows all things.
He can do all things.
He is everywhere.
He sees me and cares for me.

9. Since God is the highest Good what should you do?

Since God is the highest Good
I should love Him with all my heart,
above anything else in the world,
and I should worship Him.

10. How do you worship God?

I worship God by going to Mass on Sunday and by saying prayers.

3. THE BLESSED TRINITY

11. What must you believe about God?

I must believe that there is only one God, and that there are three Persons in God.

The three Persons in God are: the Father, the Son, and the Holy Spirit.

12. Who are the three Persons in God?
The three Persons in God are:
the Father, the Son, and the Holy Spirit.

13. What is the Blessed Trinity?
The Blessed Trinity is one God
in three Divine Persons.

14. Who told us about the Blessed Trinity?
Jesus, the Son of God, told us about the
Blessed Trinity.

15. How do you show your faith in the Blessed Trinity?
I show my faith in the Blessed Trinity
when I make the Sign of the Cross.

16. What do you say when you make the Sign of the Cross?
When I make the Sign of the Cross I say:
In the name of the Father, and of the Son,
and of the Holy Spirit. Amen.

4. CREATION

17. Why do we call God the Creator?
We call God the Creator
because He made all things from nothing.

God made the earth, the sky and the sea.

18. Who made the angels?
God made the angels.

19. What is an angel?
An angel is a spirit, without a body.

20. Who are the good angels?

The good angels obeyed God
and are now happy with him in heaven.

21. How do the good angels help us?

The good angels help us by praying for us
and by taking care of us.

God made the angels to honor Him and protect us.

22. Who is your Guardian Angel?

My Guardian Angel is the good angel
that God gave me to take care of me
and to help me to be good.

23. Who are the devils?

The devils are the bad angels
who did not want to obey God,
so God punished them in hell.

24. Who made man?
God made man.

25. Who is man?
Man is a creature of God with a body and a
soul.

26. Who were the first man and woman?
Adam and Eve, our first parents,
were the first man and woman.

God made Adam and Eve, our first parents.

27. How did Adam and Eve sin?
Adam and Eve sinned
by eating of the fruit of a certain tree
that grew in the Garden of Paradise.

28. **What happened when Adam and Eve sinned?**
When Adam and Eve sinned
they lost God's grace
and the right to heaven.

29. **How did God punish Adam and Eve?**
God punished Adam and Eve
by sending them from the Garden of Paradise
to work, suffer, and die on earth.

An angel sent Adam and Eve from Paradise.

30. **What happened to us on account of Adam's sin?**
On account of Adam's sin
we come into the world without grace.

31. **What did God promise Adam and Eve?**
God promised Adam and Eve to send into the
world a Savior.

5. GOD THE SON

32. Who is the Savior of all people?
Jesus Christ is the Savior of all people.

33. What does the Catholic Church teach about Jesus Christ?
The Catholic Church teaches
that Jesus Christ is God made man.

34. Is Jesus Christ only one Person?
Jesus Christ is only one Person —
the second Person of the Blessed Trinity.

35. When did the Son of God become man?
The Son of God became man
after the Blessed Virgin Mary said "yes" to
    God
when He asked her to be the Mother of His Son.

The Angel Gabriel asks Mary to be the Mother of God.

36. How did the Son of God become man?

The Son of God became man of the Virgin Mary
by the power of the Holy Spirit.

37. When was Jesus Christ born?

Jesus Christ was born of the Virgin Mary
on Christmas Day,
more than nineteen hundred years ago.

Jesus is born in Bethlehem.

38. Why is Jesus Christ both God and man?

Jesus Christ is both God and man
because He is the Son of God
and the Son of the Virgin Mary.

Children should pray to the Infant Jesus.

13

39. Why is Jesus Christ our Redeemer?
Jesus Christ is our Redeemer
because He offered His sufferings to God
to make up for our sins,
to bring us God's grace,
and to buy heaven back for us.

Jesus died
on the cross
to save us
from sin
and the devil.

40. What made Jesus suffer and die for us?
Jesus suffered and died for us
because He loved His heavenly Father
and because He loved us.

41. What does the Resurrection of Jesus mean?
The Resurrection of Jesus means that Jesus
came back to life again on Easter Sunday,
the third day after His death.

Jesus rose from the dead
that we may live forever.

42. **Why did Jesus rise from the dead?**
Jesus rose from the dead
to show that He is true God,
and that we also will rise again.

43. **When did Jesus go back to heaven?**
Jesus went back to heaven on Ascension Day,
forty days after His Resurrection.

44. **When will Jesus come again?**
Jesus will come again to judge everyone
on the last day.

6. GOD THE HOLY SPIRIT

45. Who is the Holy Spirit?
The Holy Spirit is God,
the Third Person of the Blessed Trinity.

46. When did Jesus and His Father send the Holy Spirit?
Jesus and His Father sent the Holy Spirit
to the Church on Pentecost—
fifty days after Jesus rose from the dead.

The Holy Spirit came upon the Blessed Virgin Mary and the apostles.

47. What does the Holy Spirit do for you?
The Holy Spirit makes my soul holy
through the gift of His grace.

48. What is grace?

Grace is a gift of God
that makes my soul holy and pleasing to God,
and helps me to live as a child of God.

49. How does grace make you holy and pleasing to God

Grace makes me holy and pleasing to God
because it helps me to believe in God,
to hope in God, and to love God.

50. How does God's grace help you to live as a child of God?

God's grace helps me to live as a child of God
because it gives light to my mind
and strength to my will
to do good and to avoid evil.

Jesus lives in our soul by giving us His grace.

51. How does the Holy Spirit give you grace?

The Holy Spirit gives me grace when I receive
the Sacraments
and when I pray and do kind things.

7. THE CATHOLIC CHURCH

52. What is the Catholic Church?

The Catholic Church is the union
of all baptized persons
under the Holy Father, the Pope.

53. What do the people in the Catholic Church have?

The people in the Catholic Church have
the same true faith,
the same Sacrifice of the Mass,
and the same Sacraments.

54. Why did Jesus start the Church?

Jesus started the Church to lead all people to
heaven.

55. How did Jesus start the Church?

Jesus started the Church by picking twelve
Apostles
who were always with Him.

Jesus sent His apostles
to spread His Church
in the whole world

56. What power did Jesus give His Apostles?

Jesus gave His Apostles the power to teach, to make people holy, and to guide them to God.

57. To whom did Jesus give special power?

Jesus gave special power to St. Peter by making him the head of the Apostles and the chief teacher and ruler of the Church.

58. Who takes the place of St. Peter today?

The Holy Father, the Bishop of Rome, takes the place of St. Peter today.

The Holy Father in Rome takes the place of Jesus and St. Peter.

59. Who takes the place of the Apostles today?

The bishops of the Church take the place of the Apostles today.

60. Who helps the bishops take care of God's People?

The priests help the bishops to take care of God's People.

61. What did Jesus give His Church?

Jesus gave His Church the truths of faith and the seven Sacraments.

8. THE SEVEN SACRAMENTS

62. What is a Sacrament?

A Sacrament is a holy sign
by which Jesus gives us His grace.

63. What are the seven Sacraments?

The seven Sacraments are: Baptism, Confirmation, Holy Eucharist, Penance, Anointing of the Sick, Holy Orders, and Matrimony

64. Why did Jesus give the Sacraments to the Catholic Church?

Jesus gave the Sacraments to the Catholic Church
to give us grace.

Jesus lives in the People of God through the grace of the Sacraments.

65. **What does grace do for us?**
Grace makes our soul holy and pleasing to God.

66. **How does grace help us lead a good life?**
Grace helps us to lead a good life
because it gives light to our mind
and strength to our will
to do good and to avoid evil.

67. **What is Baptism?**
Baptism is a new birth as a child of God,
the beginning of a new life
of God's grace in us.

We become children of God in baptism.

We receive the Holy Spirit
in confirmation.

68. What is Confirmation?

Confirmation is the sacrament
by which those born again in baptism
receive now the Holy Spirit,
the gift of the Father and the Son.

69. What does Jesus do for you in confirmation?

In confirmation Jesus sends the Holy Spirit
to me again
and gives me new strength
to live a Christian life.

70. What is the Holy Eucharist?

The Holy Eucharist is Jesus Christ
after the bread and wine have been changed
into His Body and Blood at Mass.

This is My Body...
This is My Blood

Jesus becomes present
in the bread and wine at Mass.

71. What does Jesus do in the Mass?

In the Mass Jesus gives Himself to His Father
as He did on the cross,
but He does not suffer anymore.

72. What does Jesus give you in Holy Communion?

In Holy Communion Jesus gives me Himself
as food for my soul.

Jesus comes to us
as our food
in Holy Communion.

73. What does Jesus do for you in the Sacrament of Penance?

In the Sacrament of Penance Jesus forgives my sins
and gives me grace to be a better Catholic.

Jesus takes away our sins in the Sacrament of Penance.

74. What does Jesus do in the Anointing of the Sick?

In the Anointing of the Sick Jesus gives His grace to the sick and to old people.

75. What does Jesus do in Holy Orders?

In Holy Orders Jesus gives us priests
to teach us, to offer Holy Mass
and to take away our sins.

76. What does Jesus do in Matrimony?

In Matrimony Jesus comes to a man and woman
to make them one in holy marriage
and to bless them.

9. PRAYER

77. What do you do when you pray?

When I pray I talk to God and He talks to me.

78. What do you tell God when you pray?

When I pray I tell God that I adore Him as my
  God,
that I thank Him for all He does for me,
that I beg Him to forgive all my sins,
and that I ask Him to help me and other
  people.

79. For whom should you pray?

I should pray for my mother and father
for my brothers and sisters and friends,
for my priests and teachers,
and the Catholic Church,
and for those who have died.

We should
pray often
every day.

80. When should you pray?

I should pray in the morning and at night,
before and after meals, when I need God's help,
at Holy Mass and anytime I want to think of
  God.

81. Do you pray to anyone else besides God?

I pray to the Blessed Virgin Mary
because she is the Mother of God and my
  Mother.
I pray to the Saints and to my Guardian Angel.

God gave Moses the Ten Commandments on Mount Sinai.

10. THE TEN COMMANDMENTS

82. What are the Ten Commandments?

The Ten Commandments are:
1. I, the Lord, am your God,
    you shall not have other gods besides Me.
2. You shall not take the name of the Lord,
    your God, in vain.
3. Remember to keep holy the sabbath day.
4. Honor your father and your mother.
5. You shall not kill.
6. You shall not commit adultery.
7. You shall not steal.
8. You shall not bear false witness against
    your neighbor.
9. You shall not covet your neighbor's wife.
10. You shall not covet anything that belongs
    to your neighbor.

83. What are the duties of Catholics?

The duties of Catholics are:

1. To go to Mass every Sunday and Holy day of obligation.
2. To receive the Sacrament of the Eucharist and Penance.
3. To study the Catholic religion.
4. To keep the marriage laws of the Church.
5. To help the Catholic Church.
6. To help the missions.

Catholics all over the world have the same duties.

11. SIN

Jesus teaches us through His Church
to keep the commandments and to avoid sin.

84. When do you commit a sin?

I commit a sin when I disobey God.

85. How do you know what God wants you to do?

I know what God wants me to do
in the Ten Commandments He gave us.

86. What does God tell you in the Ten Commandments?

In the Ten Commandments God tells me
to love Him with all my heart
and to love people for His sake.

87. Will God forgive all your sins?

God will forgive all my sins
if I am really sorry for them.

88. What do I say in the Act of Contrition?

In the Act of Contrition I tell God
that I am very sorry that I have offended Him
because I love Him,
and that I hate all my sins
and promise to try never to sin again.

89. Why should you be really sorry for your sins?

I should be really sorry for my sins
because they displease God, who is all-good,
and because they made Jesus suffer on the
cross.

We should be sorry for our sins because
they made Jesus suffer on the cross.

PRAYERS TO REMEMBER

OUR FATHER

OUR Father, who art in heaven,
hallowed be Thy name;
Thy kingdom come;
Thy will be done on earth as it is in heaven.
Give us this day our daily bread;
and forgive us our trespasses
as we forgive those
who trespass against us;
and lead us not into temptation,
but deliver us from evil. Amen.

HAIL MARY

HAIL Mary, full of grace
the Lord is with thee;
blessed art thou among women,
and blessed is the fruit of thy womb, Jesus,

Holy Mary, Mother of God,
pray for us sinners,
now and at the hour of our death. Amen.

PRAISE TO GOD

GLORY be to the Father, and to the Son,
and to the Holy Spirit,
as it was in the beginning,
is now, and ever shall be,
world without end. Amen.

THE APOSTLES' CREED

I BELIEVE in God the Father Almighty,
  Creator of heaven and earth;
And in Jesus Christ, His only Son, our Lord;
  who was conceived by the Holy Spirit,
  born of the Virgin Mary;
  suffered under Pontius Pilate,
  was crucified, died, and was buried;
  he descended to the dead;
  the third day he rose again from the dead;
  he ascended into heaven,
  and sits at the right hand of God
  the Father Almighty;
  from thence he shall come to judge
  the living and the dead.
I believe in the Holy Spirit;
  the holy Catholic Church;
  the Communion of Saints;
  the forgiveness of sins;
  the resurrection of the body;
  and life everlasting. Amen.

FAITH, HOPE, AND LOVE

I BELIEVE in You, my God,
  because You are the eternal Truth.

I HOPE in You, my God,
because You are merciful, faithful and powerful.

I LOVE You, my God,
because You are all-good and loving,
and I love all people for love of You.

ACT OF CONTRITION

O MY God, I am heartily sorry
for having offended You,
and I detest all my sins,
because of Your just punishments,
but most of all because they offend You,
my God,
who are all good
and deserving of all my love.
I firmly resolve,
with the help of Your grace,
to sin no more and to avoid
the near occasions of sin.

TO THE HOLY FAMILY

JESUS, Mary and Joseph, I give you my heart and
my soul.
Jesus, Mary and Joseph, help me in my last agony.
Jesus, Mary and Joseph, may I breathe forth my soul
in peace with you.

TO MY GUARDIAN ANGEL

ANGEL of God, my Guardian dear,
God's love for me has sent you here;
ever this day be at my side,
to light and guard, to rule and guide. Amen.

Praying to My
Guardian Angel

By
REV. LAWRENCE G. LOVASIK, S.V.D.
Divine Word Missionary

NIHIL OBSTAT: Rev. James M. Cafone, M.A., S.T.D., Censor Librorum
IMPRIMATUR: ✠ Most Rev. John J. Myers, D.D., J.C.D., Archbishop of Newark

The Nihil Obstat and Imprimatur are official declarations that a book or pamphlet is free of doctrinal or moral error. No implication is contained therein that those who have granted the Nihil Obstat and Imprimatur agree with the contents, opinions or statements expressed.

2

PRAYER TO MY MESSENGER FROM GOD

D EAR Guardian Angel,
God made you with no body.
That makes you a spirit.

Although I have never seen you,
I know that you are always with me.

You stand alongside me,
protecting me from harm,
and showing me how to be
faithful to God.

Thank you for being my
own messenger from God.

PRAYER TO
MY EVERLASTING FRIEND

DEAR Guardian Angel,
Jesus knew how important
you would be in my life,
and in the lives of all children.

He even told His Apostles
to become like little children
and never to harm little ones like me.

Jesus knew that children's
Angels in heaven
always see the face of God,
our Father.

Thank you for protecting me
as you watch from heaven above.

5

6

PRAYER TO MY CONSTANT COMPANION

DEAR Guardian Angel,
when I was born,
God sent you to watch over me
all the days of my life.

You truly are my protector,
my special helper,
my constant companion,
my everlasting friend.

Thank you for always being
so many things to me,
even if I may not always think of you
or if I take you for granted.

PRAYER TO MY
SPECIAL HELPER

D EAR Guardian Angel,
you know the great joy
of loving and serving God.

I, too, want to love God
and serve Him every day.

With your help,
I will please God
with my thoughts,
with my speech,
and with my actions.

Thank you for showing me the way.

9

PRAYER TO
MY PROTECTOR

D EAR Guardian Angel,
there are many ways
that harm can find its way to me.

I know that danger can sometimes
appear out of nowhere.

But I feel safe and embraced
by your protection.

I know that you watch over both
my body and my soul.

Thank you for your watchful care,
and for taking seriously
your responsibility to guard me.

PRAYER OF APPRECIATION

D EAR Guardian Angel,
you help me appreciate
all that God has made.

You help me smell
the sweetness of the flowers.

You help me feel
the warmth of the sunshine.

You help me to be happy
when I hear the birds chirping.

Thank you for making my senses
more aware of all around me.

13

14

PRAYER FOR
FAMILY LOVE

D EAR Guardian Angel,
you help me to know
that God loves me
and wants me to be happy.

You help me to share that love
with my parents and my siblings.

When I talk back to my mom or dad
or am mean to my brother or sister,
remind me of my special love for them.

Thank you for helping me
to love my family each day.

PRAYER FOR KINDNESS

DEAR Guardian Angel,
you help me realize
that I make Jesus happy
when I am kind to others.

I hear your whispers in my heart,
reminding me to be kind—
to my schoolmates,
to my friends,
even to people I may not like.

Thank you for showing me
how important it is
to be kind always.

17

18

PRAYER FOR SHARING

DEAR Guardian Angel,
you know how many blessings
God has given me.

Besides my family,
I have a home, warm clothes,
good food, and toys.

Some children may have more,
but many have far less.

Thank you for helping me
not to take for granted what I have
and encouraging me
to share with others
whenever possible.

PRAYER FOR
THOUGHTS OF GOD

DEAR Guardian Angel,
how lucky you are to be
in God's presence always.

He is ever in your thoughts
because you are there with Him.

I often am busy with all kinds of activities—
school, sports, practices,
television, video games, computers.

With all there is to do,
sometimes I forget about God.

Thank you for reminding me
to stop and think about God
and all He means to me.

21

22

PRAYER TO
OPEN MY HEART

DEAR Guardian Angel,
you do so much for me.
One of the best things is
that you pray for me.

And, even more,
you help me to pray.

With each day,
help me to pray better.
Help me not always to ask for something,
but to thank God and praise Him instead.

Thank you for this special help
to show God how much I love Him.

PRAYER FOR OBEDIENCE

DEAR Guardian Angel,
you help me realize how much
my mom and dad love me,
and how they want only
what is good for me.

By obeying them,
I keep the Fourth Commandment.

I honor them,
and I show them my love.

Thank you for encouraging me
to obey them in all things—
big and small.

PRAYER FOR
LOVE OF JESUS

DEAR Guardian Angel,
I know that Jesus loves me,
but I may not always show
my love for Him.

With your help,
I will work to be more grateful,
to be kinder to others,
to share myself and my gifts,
to pray better each day,
and to be more obedient.

Thank you for standing by me as I try
in all these ways to show Jesus my love.

PRAYER FOR PEACEFUL SLEEP

DEAR Guardian Angel,
when my busy day is over,
you are still beside me.

Although I am tired,
you remain ever watchful,
even as I sleep.

You make me feel safe,
and I have no fears or worries.

Thank you for all your days with me
and for all nights that are peaceful
because you are with me.

29

30

PRAYER OF LOVE

DEAR Guardian Angel, please help me to remember how special you are to me.

You help me to face each day with faith in God.

You help me to face each day with hope in what I can be.

You help me face each day with love for others.

I thank you and I love you for all your gifts each day.

PRAYER TO
MY GUARDIAN ANGEL

ANGEL of God,
my Guardian dear,
God's love for me
has sent you here.

Ever this day
be at my side,
to light and guard,
to rule and guide.

My First Catholic
Picture
Dictionary

A handy guide to explain the meaning of words used in the Catholic Church

By REV. LAWRENCE G. LOVASIK, S.V.D.

Divine Word Missionary

NIHIL OBSTAT: Daniel V. Flynn, J.C.D., *Censor Librorum*
IMPRIMATUR: ✠ James P. Mahoney, D.D., *Vicar General, Archdiocese of New York*

ADVENT

The four weeks before Christmas. **Advent** is a time of prayer in preparation for the birthday of Jesus Christ.

ALLELUIA

A Hebrew word of joy meaning "Praise God!" **Alleluia** is said or sung before the reading of the Gospel at Mass.

ALL SAINTS DAY

A solemn feastday on which we honor all the Saints. **All Saints Day** is celebrated on November 1.

ALTAR

The table in front of the church on which the Sacrifice of the Mass is offered. The **altar** reminds us of Christ and the table of the Last Supper.

AMEN

A word that means "So be it" or "I believe." **Amen** means that we agree with what the speaker says, or believe the prayer we have just said.

ANGEL

A created spirit with no body. Each **angel** is a person with a mind and will.

ANOINTING OF THE SICK

The Sacrament for the seriously ill, infirm, and aged. The priest gives the **Anointing of the Sick** to ask God to help the sick in body and soul.

APOSTLES

The twelve men that Jesus chose to spread His teaching to the whole world and to whom He gave the power to offer Holy Mass and to forgive sins. The **Apostles** are: Peter, James (the Greater), John, Andrew, Matthew, Philip, Bartholomew, Thomas, James (the Less), Simon, Jude, and Judas who betrayed Jesus and was replaced by Matthias.

"I WILL MAKE YOU FISHERS OF MEN"

APOSTLES' CREED

A short prayer of belief in twelve truths which contain the most important doctrines of the Christian Faith. The **Apostles' Creed** is said to have been given to us by the Apostles.

I believe in God the Father Almighty... and in Jesus Christ, His only Son, our Lord... I believe in the Holy Spirit....

3

ASCENSION

The day on which Jesus returned to heaven and was raised in the presence of His Mother and the disciples. The solemn feast of the **Ascension** is celebrated forty days after Easter.

ASH WEDNESDAY

The day when Lent begins. On **Ash Wednesday** we receive ashes to remind us of our death and to show that we should be sorry for our sins.

ASSUMPTION

The day on which the Blessed Virgin Mary was taken to heaven, body and soul, after her death. The feast of the **Assumption** is on August 15.

B

BAPTISM

A new birth as a child of God, the beginning of a new life of God's grace in us. The grace of **Baptism** helps us to become more like Jesus.

BIBLE

The written story of God's actions in the world and the teachings of Jesus, His Son, and of His apostles. The **Bible** is the Word of God.

4

BISHOPS

They take the place of the Apostles today as shepherds of the Church. The **bishops** are the heads of dioceses that include many parishes.

BLESSED SACRAMENT

The Sacrament in which Christ Himself, true God and true Man, is really present, under the appearances of bread and wine. The **Blessed Sacrament** is Holy Mass, Holy Communion, and the Real Presence of Jesus in the consecrated host and wine.

BLESSED VIRGIN

The Mother of Jesus Christ and the greatest of the Christian Saints. The **Blessed Virgin Mary** is the Mother of God and our Mother.

CANDLE

A sacramental used at Holy Mass and religious devotions. A **candle** is a symbol of faith and of Jesus.

CATHOLIC

A member of the Church founded by Jesus, known as the Roman Catholic Church. **Catholic** means it exists for all races, nations, and classes of people.

CHALICE

The cup used at Mass to contain the Precious Blood of Christ. The **chalice** is usually made of or covered with gold.

CHRIST

The official title given to the Son of God Who became Man to save us. **Christ** means "the Anointed One" or "the Messiah."

CHRISTMAS

The day on which Christ was born in Bethlehem. We celebrate the feast of **Christmas** on December 25.

CHURCH

The building in which we worship God. **Church** also means the People of God who believe in Jesus Christ and who follow Him.

COMMANDMENT

A law of God or the Church. God gave us the **Ten Commandments** in the Old Testament to guide us on our way through this life by teaching us to love Him and our neighbor.

6

COMMUNION

A holy meal in which we receive the Body and Blood of Jesus to nourish our soul. In **Communion** we receive Jesus and share in His Divine life.

CONFESSION

The telling of our sins to a priest in the Sacrament of Penance or of Reconciliation. In **confession** we express sorrow for sin and receive God's forgiveness.

CONFIRMATION

In **Confirmation** Jesus sends the Holy Spirit to us again and gives us new strength to live a Christian life. The bishop is the usual minister of the Sacrament of **Confirmation.**

CONSECRATION

That part of the Mass in which bread and wine are changed into the Body and Blood of Christ. At the **Consecration** we think of the Last Supper when Jesus gave us this Sacrament.

CONTRITION

Sorrow for sin because we have offended God Who is so good. We should always try to have true **contrition.**

CREATOR

God is called the **Creator** because He made all things in heaven and earth from nothing. We usually call God the Father, the **Creator.**

CROSS

Two pieces of wood placed over each other. Jesus was nailed to the **Cross** and died and redeemed the world after three hours of suffering.

DEACON

A man specially ordained to the service of the Church's ministry. The **deacon** receives the first grade of Holy Orders and helps the priest serve God's people.

"BEGONE, SATAN!"

DEVIL

A fallen angel or evil spirit who disobeyed God. The **devil** wants us to disobey God by tempting us to sin.

DISCIPLE

One who follows the teaching of Jesus Christ. The Apostles were sometimes called **disciples.**

"COME, FOLLOW ME!"

EASTER

The day on which we remember Christ's Resurrection from the dead. On **Easter** we celebrate Christ's victory over sin and death—the greatest of all Christian feasts.

EPIPHANY

The feast on which we remember Christ's making Himself known to the Gentiles in the person of the Magi. **Epiphany** comes from a Greek word meaning "manifestation."

EPISTLE

One of the letters in the New Testament of the Bible written by St. Paul, St. John, St. Peter, St. James, and St. Jude, to the first Christians. The **epistle** is also a Reading at Mass.

EUCHARIST

The true Body and Blood of Jesus Christ, Who is really present under the appearances of bread and wine, in order to offer Himself in the sacrifice of the Mass and to be received as spiritual food in Holy Communion. **Eucharist** means "thanksgiving." When Jesus instituted the **Eucharist** He "gave thanks."

EUCHARISTIC PRAYER

The central part of the Mass. During the **Eucharistic Prayer** Jesus becomes present on the altar.

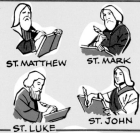

ST. MATTHEW ST. MARK

ST. LUKE ST. JOHN

EVANGELISTS

The writers of the four Gospels that tell us about the life and teaching of Jesus. The four **Evangelists** are: Matthew, Mark, Luke, and John.

F

FAITH

Faith is a gift of God by which the Holy Spirit helps us to accept God's word and to give ourselves to the heavenly Father. We have **faith** in Jesus as the Son of God.

FEAST

A day set apart by the Church for giving special honor to God, the Savior, Angels, Saints, and holy Mysteries and Events of our Lord's life. The greatest **Feast** is Easter.

FORGIVENESS

Pardon or remission of an offense. We receive God's **forgiveness** through the priest in the Sacrament of Penance or of Reconciliation.

GENUFLECTION

Bending the knee as an act of reverence to God. We **genuflect** before Jesus in the Blessed Sacrament.

GLORY

The praise and honor we give to God. In heaven we shall share His **glory**.

GOD

The infinitely perfect spirit Who is the Creator of all. **God** alone must be; all other beings exist only because of Him.

GOOD FRIDAY

Friday in Holy Week, anniversary of Christ's Death on the Cross. On **Good Friday** Catholics fast and abstain from meat.

GOSPEL

The Good News of salvation brought to the world by Jesus. At Mass Jesus teaches us in the **Gospel** reading.

GRACE

Sanctifying grace is a gift of God by which our soul shares in the very life of God. **Actual grace** gives light to our mind and strength to our will.

GUARDIAN ANGEL

The good Angel God gave us to take care of us and to lead us to heaven. We show our love for our **Guardian Angel** by praying to him and listening to him when he tells us to be good.

HAIL MARY

The most important prayer we say to the Blessed Virgin Mary. The **Hail Mary** contains the greeting of the angel Gabriel to Mary, and Elizabeth's greeting to Mary at the Visitation.

HEAVEN

The place where we shall live with God forever if we do good on earth. In **heaven** we shall see God face to face.

HELL

The place of punishment for those who do evil and are never sorry for their sins. **Hell** is the loss of God forever.

HOLY

A person who is close to God. God makes us **holy** by His grace.

HOLYDAY

Feast day to be observed by attendance at Mass and rest from unnecessary hard work. There are six **holydays** of obligation in the United States.

HOLY EUCHARIST

The Sacrament in which Christ Himself, true God and true Man, is really present, offered, and received under the appearances of bread and wine. The **Eucharist** is Mass, Communion, and the Real Presence of Jesus.

HOLY ORDERS

The Sacrament by which Jesus shares the work of His priesthood with the bishops, priests, and deacons of the Church. **Holy Orders** of priests gives power to offer Mass and forgive sins.

PRIEST   BISHOP   DEACON

HOLY SPIRIT

God, the third Person of the Holy Trinity, equal to the Father and the Son. The **Holy Spirit** makes us holy by giving us His grace.

HOLY WATER

Water blessed by the priest. By using **holy water** we ask for God's protection.

13

HOPE

A gift of God which helps us to know that God loves us and cares for us, and that we can trust in Him. We have **hope** in God for the grace we need to reach heaven because of His promises.

HOSANNA

A Hebrew exclamation of joy which means "save us, we pray!" We say or sing **Hosanna** at every Mass.

HOST

The bread that is changed into Christ's Body and Blood at the Consecration at Mass. We receive Jesus when we receive the consecrated **host** in Communion.

HUMAN BEING

Every person on earth who is made up of body and soul. We are **human beings** and God is a Divine Being.

IMMACULATE CONCEPTION

A title of the Blessed Virgin as sinless and full of grace from the first moment of her existence. The feast of the **Immaculate Conception** is on December 8.

14

INCARNATION

The taking of human nature by God the Son when He was made man by the power of the Holy Spirit at the consent of Mary. The **Incarnation** is the Mystery of God made Man.

INFALLIBILITY

Freedom from error. Christ promised **infallibility** to the Pope and to all the bishops in union with the Pope in a general council, when they teach in matters of faith or morals.

INSPIRATION

The Holy Spirit gave light to the writers of the Bible so that God Himself became the author of the books they wrote. **Inspiration** made them express God's word.

JESUS

The name of our Lord which means "The Lord is salvation." It was given by God to the Son of the Virgin Mary, Who was truly man but truly God as the Second Person of the Blessed Trinity. We should always honor the Name of **Jesus.**

JEWS

God's chosen people before the coming of Christ. The **Jews** are also called the Israelites or the Hebrews.

JOSEPH

The husband of Mary and the foster father of Jesus. **Joseph** was a carpenter and was known as a just man.

JUDGMENT

The judgment which will be passed on each one of us after death is called the **particular judgment.** At the **last judgment** all of us will stand before the judgment seat of Christ, so that each one may receive what we deserve, according to what we have done on earth, good or evil.

JUSTICE

What agrees with God's laws about the rights of God and human beings. We practice **justice** when we give everyone his or her rightful due.

KNEELING

Resting on bent knees as a sign of reverence. We **kneel** when we pray to God and Jesus in the Eucharist.

LAITY

The faithful who are not in Holy Orders and do not belong to a religious state approved by the Church. The **laity** must bear witness to Christ in the world.

LAST SUPPER

The last meal taken by Christ with His Apostles, the night before His Passion. At the **Last Supper** He instituted the Holy Eucharist and the priesthood, and gave the Apostles a long instruction on the Holy Trinity and Christian charity.

LENT

The season of prayer and penance, forty days from Ash Wednesday to Easter. During **Lent** we prepare for the feast of the Resurrection.

LITURGICAL YEAR

Each year the Church honors the Mysteries of Christ, the Blessed Virgin, Angels, and Saints. The Church reminds us of these Mysteries of the **Liturgical Year** especially in the Mass, the Divine Office, and other devotions.

OUR FATHER, WHO ART IN HEAVEN, HALLOWED BE THY NAME, THY KINGDOM COME; THY WILL BE DONE ON EARTH AS IT IS IN HEAVEN...

LORD'S PRAYER

The prayer which Jesus taught us. The **Lord's Prayer** is called the "Our Father," the most important prayer of Christian worship.

GOD   NEIGHBOR

LOVE

Love is a gift of God which helps us to love God, and to love all people for the love of God because they too belong to Him. **Love** of God and neighbor is called the Great Commandment.

MAGI

The Wise Men who came from the East to visit the Infant Jesus. The **Magi** adored Jesus and gave Him gifts.

MARTYR

A person who dies rather than give up his or her faith in Jesus. St. Stephen was the first **martyr.**

MARY

We honor the Blessed Virgin Mary by showing her our love and devotion as the Mother of Jesus, and the Mother of the Church, for she is our spiritual Mother. We pray that **Mary,** Mother of God, will ask her Son to help us.

18

MASS

In the Mass Jesus gives Himself to His heavenly Father, as He did on the cross, but now in an unbloody manner in this Sacrament, for He cannot suffer anymore. The **Mass** is a living Memorial of the Passion, Death, Resurrection and Ascension of Jesus Christ, as well as a holy Banquet in which we receive Jesus and offer ourselves to the Father with Him.

MATRIMONY

A Sacrament in which Jesus Christ makes marriage a lifelong, sacred union of husband and wife, by which they give themselves to each other and to him. In **Matrimony** God gives them His grace to do their duties toward each other and their children.

MEDAL

A piece of metal with an image of Jesus, Mary or a Saint on it. A **medal** inspires devotion to God and to the Saints.

MERCY

Showing forgiveness and loving help to others out of love for God. God has **mercy** on all who come to Him in faith and love and sorrow for sin.

THIS IS MY BELOVED SON

MESSIAH

Jesus Christ is the long-awaited Redeemer Who came to deliver us from sin. **Messiah** is a Hebrew word for "Anointed One" foretold by the Prophets.

MIRACLE

An event that takes place because God wills it and human beings alone could not do. Jesus worked **miracles** to prove that He was the Son of God.

MISSAL

The book containing the prayers re-cited by the priest at the altar during Mass. The **Missal** now contains the Sacramentary (prayers of the Mass) and the Lectionary (readings from the Bible used at Mass).

MYSTERY

A religious truth which we believe but cannot understand. **Mystery** also re-fers to events in the life of Jesus.

NATIVITY

Christmas, the birthday of Jesus Christ. The feast of the **Nativity** is celebrated on December 25.

NATURE

All that makes a person what he or she is. Each of us has a human **nature,** but Jesus has two natures—the nature of God and the nature of man, a Divine and a human nature.

NAZARETH

The town where Jesus lived and grew up. **Nazareth** is located in Galilee.

NEIGHBOR

Every person in the world, not only those who live near us. God commanded us to love our **neighbor** as ourselves, and Jesus wants us to love our neighbor as He loved us.

NEW TESTAMENT

The part of the Bible which tells us all that Jesus said and did while He was on earth. The Gospels are found in the **New Testament,** and also the writings of St. Paul, St. Peter, St. James, St. John, St. Jude, and St. Luke.

NUN

A woman who gives her life to serve God and to help people. A **nun** is also called "Sister."

OBEDIENCE **O**

A virtue that helps us to do the will of another who has the right to command. **Obedience** is pleasing to God because it means the sacrifice of our will out of love for God.

OLD TESTAMENT

The part of the Bible that tells us about God and His People before Jesus came. The whole **Old Testament** points to Jesus Christ, Who came to fulfill its prophecies.

ORIGINAL SIN

The sin which all people have who come into the world because of the sin of disobedience of Adam and Eve, our first parents. **Original sin** is the first sin and Baptism takes it away.

OUR LADY

A title given to the Blessed Virgin Mary to show that she is our Queen and our Mother. She is honored by many feasts that begin with the word **Our Lady.**

OUR LORD

A shortened form of our Lord Jesus Christ, the Second Person of the Blessed Trinity made Man. **Our Lord** spent the last three years of His life preaching the word of God and preparing the Apostles to continue His work.

PALM SUNDAY **P**

Sunday before Easter. On **Palm Sunday** we remember how Jesus came into the city of Jerusalem riding on a donkey while people welcomed Him.

PARABLE

A way of teaching by using a story. Jesus gave us many **parables** such as those of the Prodigal Son, the Good Shepherd, and the Treasure.

PARISH

A part of a diocese with a priest at its head as pastor. Our **parish** takes care of our spiritual needs.

PASSION

The Suffering and Death of Jesus Christ. The **Passion** shows how much Jesus loved His Father and us—enough to die to save us.

PASTOR

The priest who is in charge of a parish. The **pastor** cares for the spiritual life of his people.

PENANCE

The Sacrament which brings us God's forgiveness for sins committed after Baptism. **Penance** also means what the priest asks us to do after Confession.

PENTECOST

The day on which the Holy Spirit came down on the Apostles. The feast of **Pentecost** comes fifty days after Easter and is called the birthday of the Church.

POPE

The head of the Church who lives in Rome, and takes the place of Jesus on earth. Jesus gave special power in His Church to St. Peter, the first Pope, by making him the head of the Apostles. The **Pope** is the successor of St. Peter.

PRAYER

Turning our thoughts to God and talking with Him. We say **prayers** from a prayerbook or use our own words.

PRIEST

A man who has the power to offer Mass, to forgive sins, to give the other Sacraments, and to teach God's word. The **priest** receives his power from Christ in Holy Orders, and Christ acts through him.

PURGATORY

The place where souls are made completely pure after death before entering heaven. We help the souls in **purgatory** by offering Holy Mass and by praying for them.

SOULS ARE PURIFIED

QUEEN

A woman who rules. We call Mary **"Queen** of Heaven"** because she is the Mother of our King, Jesus Christ.

REDEEMER

Jesus is called our Redeemer because He paid our debt for sin and bought heaven back for us by His Suffering and Death, and by His Resurrection from the dead. Since Jesus is our **Redeemer** we belong entirely to Him and we must love and serve Him.

RELIC

An object connected with a saint, such as a part of the body or clothes. A **relic** is holy.

RELIGIOUS

A man or woman dedicated to the service of God. **Religious** Brothers and Sisters take vows of poverty, chastity, an obedience.

RESURRECTION

By the **Resurrection of Jesus** we mean that He came back to life on Easter, three days after He was buried, to show that He is God and to teach us that we, too, shall rise again. The **resurrection of the body** means that after the Last Judgment those who have done good will rise to live an eternal life with God and will receive the reward of seeing Him in unending joy, and those who have done evil will rise to be punished in hell forever.

REVELATION

What God has made known of Himself and His will to the human race through people whom He enlightened. **Revelation** is contained in the Bible and Tradition (God's Word was passed down through the centuries).

26

ROSARY

A prayer honoring the Blessed Mother of God. The **Rosary** recalls the important events in the lives of Jesus and Mary.

SACRAMENT

A sign that we can see, made by Christ to give grace. The seven **sacraments** are actions of Christ that make us holy.

SACRAMENTALS

Objects or actions that the Church uses to obtain graces for us. **Sacramentals** include blessings of homes and religious articles.

SACRED HEART

Jesus, God and Man, showing us His Heart as a symbol of His love. June and the first Friday of each month are dedicated to the **Sacred Heart.**

SACRIFICE

An offering to God our Creator to adore, thank, and praise Him and to ask for His forgiveness and help. The greatest **Sacrifice** we can offer to God is Christ Himself in the Mass.

SACRISTY

A room attached to a church, where the clergy vest or where sacred vessels and vestments are kept. We should visit the **sacristy** sometime.

SAINTS

Saints are those who were very close to God on earth and practiced virtue and who are now in heaven. The Church honors the **Saints** because they help us by their prayers and by the good example of their lives.

SCRIPTURE

The Holy Bible is often called Holy Scripture. **Scripture** is God's written word to us, which is the Old and New Testament of the Bible.

STEALING IS WRONG

SIN

Mortal sin is a serious offense against the law of God, and it is called mortal because it takes away sanctifying grace, God's life in our soul. **Venial sin** is a less serious offense against the law of God and displeases God, weakens our love for God, and shows that we do not love Him as we should.

SOUL

The soul gives life to the body and will live forever. The **soul** does not die when the body dies, but it goes to God.

SPIRIT

A being with a mind and free will, but no body. An **angel** is a spirit.

TABERNACLE

The place in church where the Blessed Sacrament is reserved. We adore Jesus present in the **tabernacle.**

TEMPLE

The building in which people worshiped God by offering prayers and sacrifices. As a boy Jesus visited the **Temple** in Jerusalem.

TEMPTATION

A strong desire to do something against God's law. God gives us grace to fight **temptation** if we ask for it and avoid places and things that lead us to sin.

TRINITY

The Mystery of the Holy Trinity is the one true God in three Persons—the Father, the Son, and the Holy Spirit. We should adore the Blessed **Trinity** when we pray to God—the Father, the Son, and the Holy Spirit—Who lives in our soul by grace.

"I AM THE WAY, THE TRUTH, AND THE LIFE"

TRUTH

Something that is really the way a person says it is. Jesus, by His words and actions, made known the deepest **truths** about God, which are now taught by the Catholic Church.

UNITE

To join together. All who belong to the Church **unite** themselves in worship of the one true God at Mass.

UNIVERSAL

Everywhere in the world and including all people. The Church is Catholic, or **universal,** because it exists for all.

VATICAN

A group of buildings and St. Peter's Basilica around the home of the Pope in Rome. The Pope directs Christ's Church from the **Vatican** State.

30

VENERATION

The honor given to the Mother of God and the Saints. We give **veneration** to the Saints but adoration to God.

VESTMENTS

Special garments worn by the clergy at the celebration of the Mass and the Sacraments. The use of **vestments** goes back to the garb of the priesthood of Aaron in the Old Testament.

VIRTUE

A good habit that helps a person to act according to the will of God. The greatest **virtue** is love of God and our neighbor.

LOVE THY NEIGHBOR

"MY WORD WILL NOT PASS AWAY"

WORD OF GOD

After speaking through the Prophets, God sent His Son Who told us the "Good New" of salvation. The Bible is God's letter to us, and we should listen carefully to **God's Word** during Holy Mass and read it often.

1

WORSHIP

We worship God by doing all that He wants us to do; by praying to Him; by offering ourselves to Him through Jesus in the Mass. We **worship** God especially in Holy Mass because in Holy Mass Jesus offers Himself to His Father, as He did on the Cross. He gives God the highest honor.

PATRON OF THE MISSIONS

XAVIER

The last name of a great Saint in the Church. Saint Francis **Xavier** is known as the "Apostle of the Indies."

YEAR

A period of twelve months. The Church **Year** begins with the Season of Advent when we prepare for the coming of Jesus.

ZEAL

Strong desire to obtain a goal. The virtue of **zeal** helps us to spread God's Kingdom on earth.

THE MIRACLES
OF JESUS

By REV. LAWRENCE G. LOVASIK, S.V.D.
Divine Word Missionary

CATHOLIC BOOK PUBLISHING CO.
NEW JERSEY

NIHIL OBSTAT: Daniel V. Flynn, J.C.D., *Censor Librorum*
IMPRIMATUR: ✠ James P. Mahoney, D.D., *Vicar General, Archdiocese of New York*

THE MARRIAGE OF CANA

JESUS was invited to a wedding feast at Cana, and His mother Mary was there.

When all the wine had been used, the mother of Jesus told Him, "They have no more wine." She knew that Jesus would do what she asked, so she said to those waiting on the table, "Do whatever He tells you."

There were at hand six stone water jars, each one holding more than fifteen gallons.

"Fill those jars with water," Jesus ordered. The servants filled the six large stone jars to the top. Then Jesus told them to pour out some of the water, and they saw that it had been turned into wine. When the waiter in charge tasted it, he called the groom over and said to him, "You have kept the good wine until now."

This was the first miracle of Jesus. A miracle is something only God can do. The disciples were full of wonder, and they believed that Jesus was God.

THE CURE AT THE POOL OF BETHZATHA

JESUS went up to Jerusalem to celebrate a Jewish festival. At the Sheep Pool in Jerusalem there was a building, called Bethzatha, which had five porticos under which crowds of sick people waited for the water to move. At certain times the angel of the Lord came down into the pool, and the water was disturbed. The first person to enter the water after it moved was cured.

One man there had an illness which had lasted thirty-eight years. Jesus asked him, "Do you want to be well again?"

"Sir," replied the sick man, "I have no one to put me into the pool when the water is disturbed; and while I am still on the way, someone else gets there before me."

Jesus said, "Get up, pick up your sleeping-mat and walk."

At once the man was cured. He picked up his mat and walked away.

Later, Jesus found the man in the temple and said: "Give up your sins so that something worse may not happen to you."

5

THE GREAT CATCH OF FISH

ONE day Jesus sat in a boat and talked to the people from it as they sat on the beach. After He had finished speaking, He said to Peter, "Row out into deep water, and lower your nets for a catch."

Peter told Jesus that they had been out on the lake all night and had caught nothing. "But," he said, "if You say so, I will lower the nets."

They caught so many fish that the nets were breaking. They called James and John, the two brothers, who were in the other boat, to help them. They came and filled the two boats until they nearly sank.

When Peter saw this, he fell at the knees of Jesus saying, "Leave me, Lord. I am a sinful man."

"Do not be afraid," said Jesus, "from now on you will be catching men."

Jesus said to Peter and the others, "Follow Me." They left everything and became His followers.

A PARALYZED MAN IS CURED

JESUS was preaching in a house. There were so many people that some had to stay outside. Four men came carrying a paralyzed man. They could not reach Jesus through the crowd. So they lifted the man up to the top of the house and opened the roof. Then they lowered the sick man into the house, right at the feet of Jesus.

Jesus said to the sick man, "My friend, your sins are forgiven you."

Some asked, "Who can forgive sins, but God alone?" Jesus knew their thoughts and told the sick man, "I say to you, get up. Take your mat with you and return to your house."

At once the paralyzed man stood up and walked out through the crowd, praising God.

Jesus worked this miracle to show that He could forgive sins because He was God.

9

THE WIDOW'S SON

WHEN Jesus came near to the gate of the town of Naim, He met a crowd of people who were carrying out the body of a dead man to be buried. He was a young man, and the only son of a widow. Jesus felt sorry for her and said, "Do not cry."

Going up to the stretcher, Jesus said, "Young man, I bid you get up."

At once the dead man sat up and began to speak. Jesus gave him back to his mother.

The crowd praised God and said, "A great prophet has risen among us and God has visited His people."

THE OFFICER'S SERVANT

A S JESUS came to Capernaum, He was met by an officer of the Roman Army. This officer had a young servant boy whom he loved very much. The boy was very sick and near death. The officer begged Jesus to cure him. Jesus said, "I will come and cure him."

But the officer replied, "Sir, I am not worthy to have You under my roof; just give an order and my boy will get better."

Jesus was surprised to see the great faith of the officer and said, "I have never found this much faith in Israel." Turning to the officer He said, "Go your way. It shall be done because you trusted." That very moment the boy got better.

JESUS CALMS THE GREAT STORM

ONE day Jesus got into a boat
with His disciples and said to
them, "Let us cross over to the far
side of the lake."

So they began to row across the lake. Jesus fell asleep. When they were halfway across, a great wind blew down from between the hills that were around the lake.

The storm drove great waves of water into the boat, so that it was in danger of sinking. The apostles were afraid. They came to awaken Jesus, saying, "Master, Master, we are lost."

Jesus stood up and looked out upon the sea. Then He said to the waves, "Quiet! Be still!"

At once the wind stopped blowing, the waves were quiet, and there was a great calm.

Jesus said to His disciples, "Why are you afraid? Where is your faith?"

The disciples wondered at what they had seen and said to each other, "Who can this be that the wind and sea obey Him?"

Jesus wanted to teach His apostles and us that we should trust in Him and pray in every trouble. He is our only hope. His word and power will bring peace into our lives.

JESUS CURES THE DAUGHTER OF JAIRUS

A MAN named Jairus fell down at the feet of Jesus and begged Him to come and heal his daughter who was dying. A little while later someone came to him and said, "Your daughter is dead."

But Jesus said to him, "Do not be afraid, only believe, and she will still live."

Jesus went into the house with three of His disciples, and the father and mother of the child. On the bed was lying the dead body of a girl, twelve years old. Jesus took her by the hand and spoke to her, "Little girl, rise up!" And life returned to the little girl. She opened her eyes and sat up.

Jesus then gave the little girl to her happy parents.

JESUS CURES THE TWO BLIND MEN

TWO blind men, who sat by the road when they heard Jesus was passing by, shouted, "Lord, Son of David, have pity on us!"

The crowd wanted to hear what Jesus was saying to them and told the blind men to be quiet. But they shouted all the louder, "Lord, Son of David, have pity on us!"

Then Jesus stopped and called to them, "What do you want Me to do for you?"

"Lord," they said to Him, "open our eyes."

Jesus felt sorry for them. He touched their eyes and at once they could see. The two men got up and followed Jesus as He went about teaching and working miracles.

When our faith is weak, Jesus will give light to our mind that we may understand His teaching. But we must pray for the gift of faith.

21

THE LOAVES AND FISH

A GREAT crowd, over five thousand men, besides women and children, was listening to Jesus. Toward evening, some of the disciples asked Jesus to send the crowd away, for it was near their supper time.

But Jesus said, "You give them something to eat." Knowing that they had enough food only for themselves, Andrew said, "A boy here has five loaves of bread and two fish. But what are they among so many people?"

Jesus had the people sit down on the grass. Then He took into His hands the five loaves and two fish. Looking up to heaven, Jesus thanked His Father and blessed the food. He then broke it and had the apostles give to everyone as much as they needed. After they had all eaten enough, twelve baskets were gathered of what remained.

At Holy Mass, through His priest, Jesus feeds our souls with the Bread of Life—His Body and Blood, in Holy Communion.

23

JESUS WALKS OVER THE SEA

JESUS went up into the mountain to pray. The apostles were far out to sea. A little after midnight, a great storm arose upon the sea. The apostles were working hard with their oars against the waves. Jesus came toward them, walking over the sea. The men cried out with fear, for they thought it was a spirit. But Jesus said, "It is I, do not be afraid."

Peter cried out to Jesus, "Lord, if it is really You, tell me to come to You across the water."

Jesus said to Peter, "Come!"

So Peter got out of the boat and began to walk on the water toward Jesus. But when he saw the high waves and felt the strong wind, he became afraid. As he began to sink, he cried out, "Lord, save me!"

Jesus at once reached out His hand and caught hold of him and lifted him up, saying, "How little faith you have. Why did you doubt My word?"

When Jesus got in the boat with Peter, at once the wind stopped and the sea became calm. The men in the boat fell down before Jesus and said, "You are indeed the Son of God."

25

JESUS CURES THE TEN LEPERS

JESUS was about to enter a village when ten lepers came His way. He was surprised because the Law did not allow them to come near other people. When they saw Jesus, they cried, "Jesus, Master, have pity on us!"

Jesus turned to them and said, "Go, show yourselves to the priests." On their way there they were cured.

One of them, seeing that he was cured, turned back, loudly praising God. He threw himself on his face at the feet of Jesus and thanked Him.

Jesus asked, "Were not all ten made whole? Where are the other nine? Was there no one to return and give thanks to God except this foreigner?"

Jesus then said to him, "Stand up and go your way. Your faith has cured you."

Jesus, our Savior, makes us clean by taking away our sins in the sacrament of Penance.

27

THE RAISING OF LAZARUS

MARTHA and Mary were friends of Jesus. When their brother Lazarus died, they sent for Jesus. As He came near, Martha ran out to meet Him and said, "Lord, if You had been here, my brother would never have died."

Jesus said, "Your brother will rise again. I am the resurrection and the life; whoever believes in Me will come to life."

Mary came and bowed in sorrow at the feet of Jesus. And seeing her tears and the sadness of her friends who stood nearby, Jesus wept.

As He came to the tomb, the men moved away the stone from the entrance of the cave. And Jesus turned to God in prayer. Then He called with a loud voice, "Lazarus, come out!" And he who had been dead came out. Many of the Jews then believed in Jesus.

JESUS CURES THE LEPER

L EPROSY was a terrible disease which no man could cure. While Jesus was on His journey of preaching, a leper came to Him and cried, "Lord, if You will to do so, You can cure me."

Jesus was full of pity. He reached out His hand and touched him and said, "I do will it. Be cured."

And in a moment all the scales of leprosy fell away, his skin became clean, and the leper stood up a well man. Jesus said to him, "Tell no one, but go and show yourself to the priest. Offer for your healing a gift to thank God, and let them see you have been cured."

This leper who had been healed was so happy that he told everybody he knew that Jesus, the great Prophet, had taken away his leprosy.

We should pray as the leper did, "Lord, if You will to do so, You can help me," leaving all to God's will.

31

PRAYER TO JESUS

JESUS, I love You;
  make me love You more.

I am weak;
please help me.

I have sinned against You;
forgive me.

You are kind;
be patient with me.

I want to know You better;
teach me.

I do not know what to do;
guide me.

My best Friend,
never leave me,
but take me to heaven with
    You when I die.

Going to Confession

HOW TO MAKE A GOOD CONFESSION

By
Rev. Lawrence G. Lovasik, S.V.D.
Divine Word Missionary

NIHIL OBSTAT; Daniel V. Flynn, J.C.D., *Censor Librorum*
IMPRIMATUR: Joseph T. O'Keefe, *Vicar General, Archodiocese of New York*
© 1986 by *Catholic Book Publishing Corp., N.J.* – Printed in Hong Kong
ISBN 978-0-89942-392-0

THE SACRAMENT OF PENANCE

IN the Sacrament of Penance
Jesus comes to forgive your sins
and brings peace with God
and with the Church,
which is hurt by your sins.

Jesus loves children.
He makes them happy
by keeping them close to Himself
through the Sacrament of Penance.

2

TO RECEIVE THE SACRAMENT OF PENANCE

To receive the Sacrament of Penance you must:

1. Find out your sins.
2. Be sorry for your sins.
3. Make up your mind not to sin again.
4. Tell your sins to the priest.
5. Do the penance the priest gives you.

1. EXAMINATION OF CONSCIENCE

Before going to confession,
quietly examine your conscience
so that you can find out
the sins you may have committed
since your last good confession.

Your conscience will remind you
if you have offended God
by committing any sins.

Ask the Holy Spirit to help you.

"Come Holy Spirit
and help me
to find out my sins
and to be really sorry for them."

Finding Out Your Sins

You find out your sins
by remembering the Commandments of God,
and asking yourself
how you have disobeyed God.

By going to confession often
children learn to know how they offend God by
   sin,
and find peace and joy by seeking God's forgiveness.

Questions You Ask Yourself

About God

THE TEN COMMANDMENTS

GOD SPEAKS:

1. "I, the Lord, am your God, you shall not have other gods besides Me."

- Did I miss saying my morning or night prayers?

- Did I miss saying a prayer during other times of the day?

You honor and worship God by being faithful in saying your daily prayers.

About the Holy Name of God

2. "You shall not take the name of the Lord, your God, in vain."

- Did I use holy names, like "Jesus," and "God" when I should not have used them?

When children get angry and fight they may easily use the name of God and Jesus. This is sinful.

About Sunday

3. "Remember to keep holy the sabbath day."

- Did I miss Mass through my own fault on Sunday or a Holy Day?

- Did I misbehave during Mass?

You keep Sunday holy by going to Holy Mass. It is a serious sin to miss Mass through your own fault.

About parents

4. "Honor your father and your mother."

- Did I disobey my parents or teachers?
- Was I mean to them?
- Did I answer back?
- Did I make fun of my parents or old people?

You honor your father and mother
by obeying them.

9

About being kind

5. "You shall not kill."

- Did I hate anyone?
- Did I do anything mean to anyone?
- Did I let myself get angry?
- Did I quarrel and fight?
- Did I wish anything bad to anyone?
- Did I make anyone sin?

Jesus said that if we forgive others, God will forgive us. Confession helps us to forgive others.

About being pure

GOD SPEAKS:

6. **"You shall not commit adultery."**
9. **"You shall not covet your neighbor's wife."**

- Did I do anything that was really impure?
- Was it alone or with others?
- Did I willingly keep impure thoughts in my mind?
- Did I sin by using impure words?
- Did I sin by looking at or reading anything impure?
- Did I sin by talking about or listening to anything impure?

Jesus said,
"Blessed are the pure of heart,
for they shall see God."

To be pure means to be without sin.
The Sacrament of Penance takes away your sins
and helps you to avoid evil.
If you are in God's grace—free from sin—
you will be truly happy.

About being honest

> 7. "You shall not steal."
> 10. "You shall not covet anything that belongs to your neighbor."

- Did I steal anything?
- Did I keep anything that did not belong to me?
- Did I damage what belongs to someone else?

Bobby stole some of Susie's lunch and made her very unhappy. He offended God by being selfish.

About being truthful

8. "You shall not bear false witness against your neighbor."

- Did I tell any lies?
- Did I tell mean things about anyone?
- Did I like to listen to unkind talk about others?

When you study your Catholic religion you will learn to tell the truth and to love all people in your words.

2. BEING SORRY FOR SIN

Before your sins can be for-
    given,
you must be sorry for them,
because by your sins
you have offended God, your
    Father,
and because Jesus suffered on
    the cross for your sins.

In confession you thank Jesus for having
died on the cross so that your sins may be
forgiven.

3. DESIRE NOT TO SIN AGAIN
An Act of Contrition

MY God,
I am sorry for my sins
with all my heart.

In choosing to do wrong
and failing to do good,
I have sinned against You
whom I should love above all things

I firmly intend, with your help,
to do penance,
to sin no more,
and to avoid whatever leads me
to sin.

Our Savior Jesus Christ
suffered and died for us.
In His name, my God, have mercy.
Amen.

O my God,
  I am heartily sorry
for having offended You,
and I detest all my sins,
because of Your just punishments,
but most of all,
because they offend You, my God,
who are all-good
and deserving of all my love.

I firmly resolve,
  with the help of Your grace
to sin no more
and to avoid the near occasions
of sin. Amen.

Father, Forgive Me

OUR Father in heaven;
 please forgive me
for the things
I have done wrong;

for being greedy
and wanting the best for myself;

for angry words and bad temper;

for making other people unhappy.

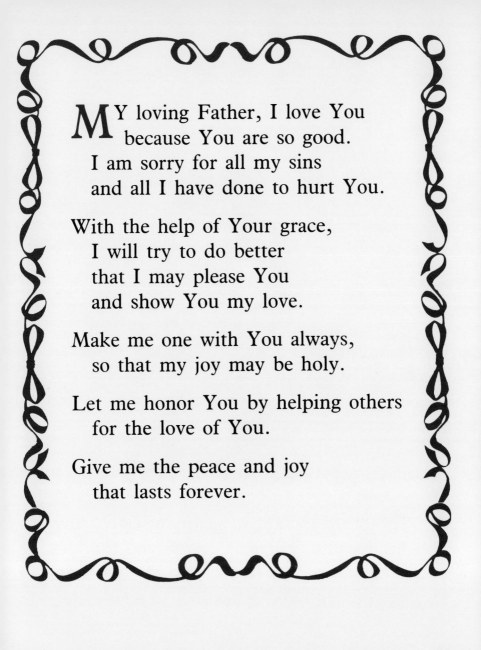

MY loving Father, I love You
because You are so good.
I am sorry for all my sins
and all I have done to hurt You.

With the help of Your grace,
I will try to do better
that I may please You
and show You my love.

Make me one with You always,
so that my joy may be holy.

Let me honor You by helping others
for the love of You.

Give me the peace and joy
that lasts forever.

The priest is sent to give you God's love and forgiveness, but it is Jesus who forgives your sins and sends His Holy Spirit once more to your soul with new grace to lead a holy life.

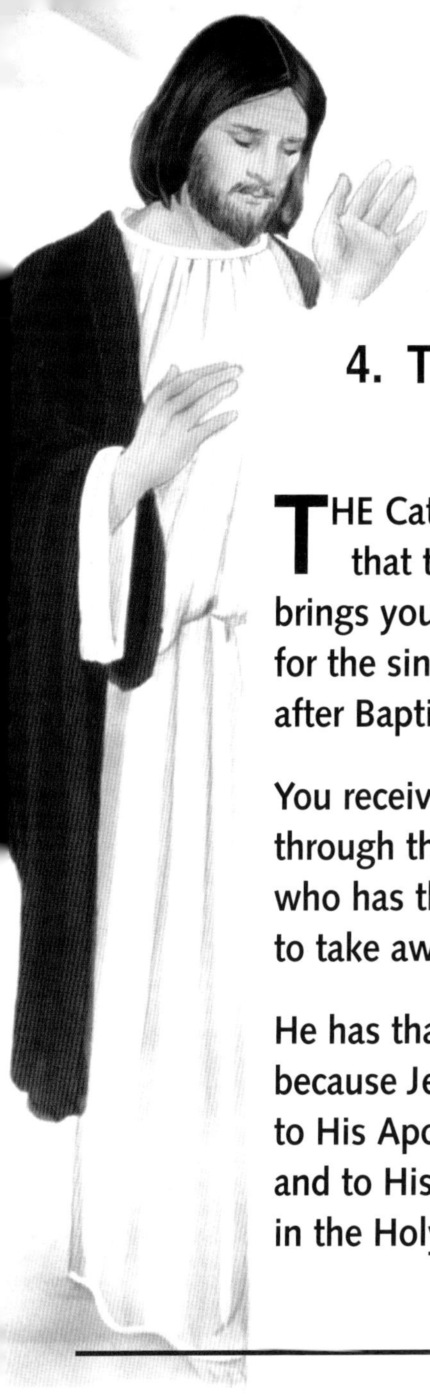

4. TELLING YOUR SINS TO THE PRIEST

THE Catholic Church teaches,
that the Sacrament of Penance
brings you God's forgiveness
for the sins you committed
after Baptism.

You receive God's forgiveness
through the priest
who has the power
to take away your sins.

He has that power
because Jesus gave that power
to His Apostles
and to His Church
in the Holy Priesthood.

How To Make Your Confession

1. Make the sign of the cross.
2. Tell the priest when you made your last confession.
3. Confess your sins.
4. Listen to what the priest tells you.
5. Say the Act of Contrition.
6. Thank the priest.

Jesus said that the angels in heaven are happy when a sinner repents of his sins.

In confession Jesus comes to forgive your sins and sends his Spirit to your soul with grace and strength.

5. WHAT TO DO AFTER CONFESSION

After confession:

1. Say the penance the priest has given you.
2. Thank God for forgiving your sins.
3. Ask God for the help you need to keep from offending God.

Thank God for the graces of His Sacrament and ask for His help to lead a good life.

Father, Thank You for Peace

HEAVENLY Father,
by dying on the Cross for love of us
Your dear Son Jesus
brought peace to the world
by taking away our sins
and giving us your forgiveness.

As a Catholic child I receive
this peace and forgiveness
in the Sacrament of Penance.

I thank You for your mercy to me
and to all who are truly sorry
for having offended You.

Help me to use this sacrament often.

May the power of Your love
given to me in this sacrament
guide me in all I do
to please You in all things.

Father, thank You for Your peace.

WHAT JESUS DOES FOR YOU IN THE SACRAMENT OF PENANCE

When you go to confession you receive a sacrament which Jesus Himself gave us the evening of His resurrection on Easter.

1. Jesus gives you more sanctifying grace, which makes your soul more holy and beautiful. It is God's own life and presence in your soul.

2. Jesus gives you more sacramental graces—actual graces—which give you the light to see and the strength to do what is good and to avoid evil.

3. Jesus helps you to love God, and people for the love of God, because this is His Great Commandment.

4. Jesus helps you to make up for your sins in this life that you may die in His grace and be united with Him in heaven forever.

Through frequent confession Jesus gives you His own peace and joy.

IN the Sacrament of Penance
Jesus helps you to be holy
because He sends His Holy Spirit
to your soul
with grace and strength
to live a better Christian life
and to keep away from sin.

True sorrow for sin
brings back the grace of God
if you have lost it by a serious
or mortal sin.

If you have committed a serious sin
you must receive the Sacrament of
    Penance
before receiving Holy Communion.

Through frequent confession Jesus unites you with Himself and also with the Father and the Holy Spirit, and helps you to be holy.

THANK YOU, MOTHER MARY

MARY, Virgin Mother of Jesus,
you are my dear Mother, too.

I thank you for leading me to Jesus
that He might take away my sins
in the Sacrament of Penance.

Keep me from all sin
that I may love Jesus with a pure heart
as you always did.

I give myself to you
that you may protect me
and lead me to Jesus, your Son,
in Holy Communion.

May I always enjoy
the help of your prayers,
for you bring us life and salvation
through Jesus Christ your Son.

Through frequent confession the Blessed Virgin Mary helps you to be more pleasing to Jesus in Holy Communion.

HOW OFTEN SHOULD YOU GO TO CONFESSION?

YOU should go to confession as often as you can—even every month—if you really love God and want to get the grace to keep away from sin and live a holy life.

The
WORKS
OF MERCY

By Rev. LAWRENCE G. LOVASIK, S.V.D.

The CORPORAL Works of Mercy

1. To Feed the Hungry 5
2. To Give Drink to the Thirsty 7
3. To Clothe the Naked 9
4. To Visit Those Who Are in Prison 11
5. To Shelter the Homeless 13
6. To Visit the Sick 15
7. To Bury the Dead 17

The SPIRITUAL Works of Mercy

1. To Admonish the Sinner 19
2. To Instruct the Ignorant 21
3. To Counsel the Doubtful 23
4. To Comfort the Sorrowful 25
5. To Bear Wrongs Patiently 27
6. To Forgive Injuries 29
7. To Pray for the Living and the Dead 31

CATHOLIC BOOK PUBLISHING CORP., New Jersey

NIHIL OBSTAT: Daniel V. Flynn, J.C.D., *Censor Librorum*
IMPRIMATUR: ✠ James P. Mahoney, D.D., *Vicar General, Archdiocese of New York*

Jesus Teaches about the Works of Mercy

Jesus speaks:

"WHEN the Son of Man comes in His glory, with all the angels of heaven, He will sit upon His royal throne, and all the nations will be assembled before Him.

© 1982 by *Catholic Book Publishing Corp.*, N.J.—Printed in Hong Kong 978-0-89942-305-0

"The king will say to those on His right: 'Come. You have My Father's blessing! Inherit the Kingdom prepared for you from the creation of the world. For I was hungry and you gave Me food, I was thirsty and you gave Me drink. I was a stranger and you welcomed Me; naked and you clothed Me. I was ill and you comforted Me, in prison and you came to visit Me.'

"Then the just will ask Him: 'Lord, when did we see You hungry and feed You or see You thirsty and give You drink? When did we welcome You away from home or clothe You in Your nakedness? When did we visit You when You were ill or in prison?'

"The King will answer them: 'I assure you, as often as you did it for one of My least brothers, you did it for Me.'

"The just will go off to eternal life."

(Matthew 25:31-40)

Michael collects money to help
feed the starving people of the world.

4

The 7 Corporal Works of Mercy

1st CORPORAL WORK OF MERCY

To Feed the Hungry

Jesus speaks:

"I was hungry and you gave Me food."

(Matthew 25:35)

THERE are many millions of people to-day who are very hungry because they are poor. Some children can get less than one meal a day. Our country sends them food and clothing. Many die of starvation.

Naturally, you feel sorry for them and try to help them by praying for them. But you can also collect money for them which can be sent to some missionaries or to the Bishop of the diocese.

This is one way by which you can show God that you love your neighbor and that you are thankful of the good food your parents give you every day. Food is a gift of God and you must thank Him for it.

Billy and Marie share their lunch at school
with Timmy whose family is poor.

6

2nd CORPORAL WORK OF MERCY

To Give Drink to the Thirsty

Jesus speaks:

"I was thirsty and you gave Me drink."

(Matthew 25:35)

JESUS once said: "I promise that whoever gives a cup of cold water to the
least of My followers because that person
is My follower will certainly receive a reward." (Matthew 10:42).

By these words Jesus taught us to be
kind to people when they are in need.
Giving a thirsty person a drink of water is
a kind deed and Jesus will reward it.

You can do many favors for people
who need your help. There are many children in the world who are hungry and
thirsty. Pray for them.

Be kind to your playmates, too. Be
willing to share your food and drink with
them. This is a work of mercy if you do
these things for the love of Jesus as He
asked You to do.

Helen and John are bringing their used clothes to the Sisters at the Orphanage to help poor children.

8

3rd CORPORAL WORK OF MERCY

To Clothe the Naked

Jesus speaks:

"I was naked and you clothed Me."

(Matthew 25:35)

THERE are many poor people who need clothing. Your mother and father buy such beautiful clothes for you to wear. Do you ever think of the many children who have to wear old and torn clothes, even rags?

Why don't you ask your mother to collect all your clothes which you hardly ever wear or which are too small for you so that you can give them to some poor child who needs them?

You can always bring used clothes to the St. Vincent de Paul Society collection box in your parish. Your parish priest or your teacher will tell you what to do with them. Each year before Thanksgiving Day, parishes have clothes collection drives for the poor. Do your part to help them.

Jerry visits his friend Andy who was sent to a
Reform School. He brings him a rosary and
prayerbook and asks him to pray to God and
the Blessed Virgin for help.

10

4th CORPORAL WORK OF MERCY

To Visit Those Who Are in Prison

Jesus speaks:

"I was in prison and you came to visit Me."

(Matthew 25:36)

THERE are many children who are in Reform Schools. Why don't you and some of your friends visit them sometime? This will show them that you really care about them.

But there are many men and women in prisons all over our country. You cannot visit them, but you can pray for them that they may try to live a good life by turning to God in prayer. God alone can help them to be good.

Thank God for having given you good parents and teachers to lead you on the right path. God has commanded you to be obedient to them in His Fourth Commandment: "Honor your father and mother."

12 **Donna welcomes a poor family to her home for dinner.**

5th CORPORAL WORK OF MERCY

To Shelter the Homeless

Jesus speaks:

"I was a stranger and you welcomed Me."

(Matthew 25:36)

THERE are many poor people in the world who do not have a beautiful home like you have. How thankful you should be to God for all that your mother and father have done to make you happy! How good it is to have a nice warm home in winter!

Never be ashamed to bring poor children to your home. Since you have been so blessed by God, you should at least pray for those who do not have a home like yours.

Even though you cannot share your home with others, you can be kind to people everyday by helping them in small ways and trying to make them happy. If you do this for others, you do it for Jesus. He will reward you for being generous.

Joseph and his sister Elizabeth bring some food
to two old people in the neighborhood.

14

6th CORPORAL WORK OF MERCY

To Visit the Sick

Jesus speaks:

"I was ill and you comforted Me."

(Matthew 25:36)

THERE are many sick people in your neighborhood whom you can visit. You can make them very happy just by coming to talk to them for a while. They are often very lonely.

Old people also like company because they are often left alone. You can ask your mother to give you some food for them. She will be happy to see that you care for others.

In this way you can be like Jesus Who spent so much time healing the sick. Visit the sick and old people for the love of Jesus.

Someday you will be sick and grow old, and you will be pleased when someone comes to visit you and cheer you up. Be a friend of those who are sick and lonely, and you will be a friend of Jesus,

Raymond and his sister Rose like to take care
of the grave of their grandmother.

7th CORPORAL WORK OF MERCY
To Bury the Dead

Jesus speaks:

"I am the Resurrection and the Life. Whoever believes in Me, though he should die, will come to life." (Jn 11:25-26)

AFTER Martha and Mary, the sisters of Lazarus, had buried their brother, Jesus consoled them by telling them that He Himself is the Resurrection and the Life. Even though their brother died, Jesus raised him to life again.

Jesus will also console us when our loved ones die. We all shall live forever because of our faith in Jesus. But we must pray for our dead, attend their funeral when we can, and visit their grave to show that we really love them even though they are no more with us.

The Church remembers the dead by offering Holy Mass for them. She remembers the Poor Souls in Purgatory especially in the month of November and on All Souls Day.

Bob tells Fred that it is wrong to fight.

The 7 Spiritual Works of Mercy

1st SPIRITUAL WORK OF MERCY

To Admonish the Sinner

Jesus speaks:

"There will be joy among the angels of God over one repentant sinner." (Luke 15:10)

JESUS Christ came into the world as God made man, to be its Savior and Redeemer. God so loved sinners that He gave His Son to make peace between God and all people by His death on the Cross. Jesus often spoke to sinners to help them give up their evil ways.

If Jesus loved sinners so much, you should try to help them by your prayers and sacrifices. You can also speak kindly to other children when you see they are doing wrong.

Fred hit Bob with a bat. Bob was not angry, but he told Fred that it was wrong to fight. Susan, Bob's sister, wiped her brother's bleeding head and also told Fred not to fight anymore.

Karen tells Pat that it is a serious sin to miss
Mass on Sunday through his own fault.

To Instruct the Ignorant

Jesus speaks:

"Your light must shine before men so that they may see goodness in your acts and give praise to your heavenly Father."

(Matthew 5:16)

JESUS teaches us that the best way to instruct the ignorant is to give them a good example. A good deed is like light which shines in the minds of people and makes them want to do good and stay away from evil.

Karen stopped her friend Pat when she saw him riding his bicycle instead of going to Mass on Sunday. Karen told him that it was a great sin against God not to go to church on Sunday or Saturday evening.

Pat did not think it was too bad to miss Mass. He remembered Karen's words and never missed Mass again. The light of Karen's good example helped Pat to do what was right.

Billy asks Betty whether it is wrong to mow the lawn on Sunday. She tells him it is all right if he does it to get some exercise.

22

To Counsel the Doubtful

Jesus speaks:

"If you wish to enter into life, keep the Commandments." (Matthew 19:17)

A MAN once came up to Jesus and said: "Teacher, what good must I do to possess everlasting life." Jesus told him to obey the Commandments of God: to love God and his neighbor. The man was not sure what he had to do till Jesus showed him the right way to reach heaven.

It was Sunday. Billy's parents were out of town visiting friends. He asked his sister, Betty, whether it would be wrong for him to mow the lawn to get some exercise instead of playing ball with his friends.

Betty told him that it would be all right. Billy was then able to get his exercise with a clear conscience.

Kathy tries to cheer her sister up when she dropped her ice cream cone.

To Comfort the Sorrowful

Jesus speaks:

"Come to Me, all you who are weary and find life burdensome, and I will refresh you." (Matthew 11:28)

JESUS tells us that He will comfort us when we are sorrowful if only we come to Him asking for His help in prayer. Many things can happen in your life that can make you sad. Go to Jesus, your best Friend, and He will give you peace and joy. He will help you to be patient when you have something to suffer.

Be like Jesus. Try to cheer your friends up when they are sad.

Kathy tried to comfort her sister when she dropped her ice cream cone. Kathy even offered Mary her own cone. Mary stopped crying and was glad to share the cone with Kathy.

Ann tried to love Frank even though
he smashed her baby buggy.

To Bear Wrongs Patiently

Jesus speaks:

"My command to you is: 'love your enemies, pray for your persecutors.' "

(Matthew 5:44)

JESUS teaches us to be patient when others hurt us, and even to pray for them. We cannot always like our enemies, but we must love them for the love of God.

One day Frank was so angry that he smashed Ann's baby buggy. Ann was hurt, but she did not get angry at Frank. She did not fight back to get even with him. She told him that they would still be friends and that her Daddy would fix the broken buggy.

Ann did not like Frank for what he did, but she tried to love him because she knew that this is what Jesus wanted her to do. She bore this wrong patiently. Try to do the same when someone hurts you.

Jesus said: "Treat others the way you would have them treat you."

Steve asks Mike and Joe to stop fighting and to forgive each other.

6th SPIRITUAL WORK OF MERCY

To Forgive Injuries

Jesus speaks:

"If you forgive the faults of others, your Heavenly Father will forgive you yours. If you do not forgive others, neither will your Father forgive you." (Matthew 6:14)

JESUS taught us to pray: "Forgive us our trespasses as we forgive those who trespass against us." You say this prayer every day when you say the "Our Father."

How can you expect the Heavenly Father to forgive your sins if you do not want to forgive others when they hurt you?

Mike and Joe got into a fight and were calling each other bad names because they were very angry at each other. Steve separated them and told them to shake hands and make up. They did. They became friends because they were willing to forgive each other.

The best way to help people, living and dead, is to offer Holy Mass for them. Holy Mass is the Greatest Prayer because it is the Sacrifice of Jesus.

7th SPIRITUAL WORK OF MERCY

To Pray for the Living and the Dead

Jesus speaks:

"Ask, and you will receive. Seek, and you will find. Knock, and it will be opened to you. For the one who asks, receives. The one who seeks, finds. The one who knocks, enters. (Matthew 7:7)

GOD is Our Heavenly Father. He loves us as His children and wants to give us everything we need for our soul and body. But He wants us to ask for it.

Pray for your mother and father, brothers and sisters, relatives and friends, and for all who are in need of God's help, that they may reach heaven someday.

Pray also for those who have died, especially for your family, relatives, and friends. If they are in Purgatory, your prayers will help them to see God in heaven. The best way to help them is by offering Holy Mass for them.

A PRAYER OF THANKS FOR ANIMALS

ETERNAL Father, in Your wisdom and love You created the whole world. You told Adam to be the master of all the animals You made. Help me to be kind not only to people, but also to animals. Thank You for all the living things You made, especially for our pets.